A Band of
Noble Women

Syracuse Studies on Peace and Conflict Resolution
Robert A. Rubinstein, *series editor*

A Band of
Noble Women

RACIAL POLITICS IN THE
WOMEN'S PEACE MOVEMENT

Melinda Plastas

SYRACUSE UNIVERSITY PRESS

Copyright © 2011 by Syracuse University Press
Syracuse, New York 13244-5290

All Rights Reserved

First Edition 2011

11   12   13   14   15   16   6   5   4   3   2   1

∞ The paper used in this publication meets the minimum requirements
of the American National Standard for Information Sciences—Permanence
of Paper for Printed Library Materials, ANSI Z39.48-1992.

For a listing of books published and distributed by Syracuse University Press,
visit our Web site at SyracuseUniversityPress.syr.edu.

ISBN: 978-0-8156-3257-3

Library of Congress Cataloging-in-Publication Data

Plastas, Melinda.
   A band of noble women : racial politics in the women's peace movement /
Melinda Plastas. — 1st ed.
        p. cm. — (Syracuse studies on peace and conflict resolution)
   Includes bibliographical references and index.
   ISBN 978–0-8156-3257-3 (cloth : alk. paper) 1. Women's International League
for Peace and Freedom—History.   2. Women and peace—United States—
History—20th century.   3. Peace movements—United States—History—20th century.
4. African American pacifists—History—20th century.   5. United States—Race
relations—History—20th century.   I. Title.
   JZ5578.P53 2011
   303.6'6092520973—dc23   2011020053

Manufactured in the United States of America

This book is dedicated to and in memory of my mother, Patricia Plastas.

MELINDA PLASTAS teaches in the Women and Gender Studies program at Bates College.

Contents

Illustrations

Preface

IN FEBRUARY OF 1926 an interracial group of five women and one man sailed from New York to Haiti to investigate the continued United States occupation of the island. After traveling for three weeks and talking with a vast array of Haitians, the team, under the auspices of the Women's International League for Peace and Freedom (WILPF), returned to the United States and wrote *Occupied Haiti*, a 250-page report that chronicled the deteriorating cultural, agricultural, economic, and political conditions Haitians faced as a result of US intervention. The report heavily criticized the use of paternalist racism by government officials as justification for the occupation and it recorded the prevalence of Jim Crow practices and attitudes among the marines stationed on the island.

Historians have noted that this WILPF mission accelerated anti-imperialists' criticism of US dollar diplomacy, deepened grassroots interest in opposing the occupation, and increased progressives' leverage with congressional officials.[1] But the mission also marked the deepening of interracial alliances among middle-class women interested in securing world peace and racial justice. When Emily Greene Balch and Addie Hunton, two nationally prominent social reformers, led the Haiti mission, they publicly united the political power of the primarily white women's peace movement and the black women's club movement. The very presence of the WILPF Haiti mission, in its racial diversity and female leadership, challenged US Jim Crow policies and paternalism. According to *Occupied Haiti*, Haitians in Port-au-Prince welcomed the WILPF team and were delighted that the interracial group of women was sharing "in most friendly fashion" the same sleeping quarters. Emily Greene Balch and Addie Hunton's joint mission to Haiti did more than protest US foreign policy; it personified the possibility of racial harmony and world peace in the form of women's interracial unity.[2] As *A Band of Noble Women* reveals, complex political, intellectual, and social relationships emerged among the women's peace movement, African American women's reform politics, and black internationalism more generally. And this race-conscious women's peace activism helped cultivate proto–civil rights consciousness, indicating the relevance of peace activism to the emergent civil rights movements of later decades.

This book examines how the WILPF responded to and shaped the prevailing currents of racial thought and politics that dominated the first four decades of the twentieth century. Assembling a multivalent history of the women's peace movement and the black women's club and social reform movements, this work provides a fresh perspective on an important story of race, gender, class, community, and consciousness building between the two wars. These "noble women" also coalesced around cosmopolitan ideals of internationalism, interdependency, and mutual humanity; and practicing interracial unity—from sponsoring investigative missions to Haiti to arranging interracial study groups on US foreign policy—allowed them to challenge nationalism, foster world-mindedness, and confront the tenets of Jim Crow.[3]

Arguably, activists like Emily Greene Balch and Addie Hunton would not have been able to achieve what they did without the WILPF, an organization founded in 1915 and dedicated to uniting women around the world to secure the conditions necessary for social justice and peace. *A Band of Noble Women* considers three intricate ways in which the WILPF negotiated and influenced the racial politics of the early twentieth century. First, it examines the WILPF's work to challenge the major racial ideologies of the period and to forge counter or dissident ideologies as a part of its campaigns against war and for peace and freedom. Second, it traces the leadership the WILPF provided on some of the central racial justice issues of the interwar period, namely, US foreign policy in Haiti and Liberia and efforts to pass antilynching legislation. Third, it takes up the WILPF's uneven and fraught attempts at racial integration within its own membership and leadership. In this way, this case study encourages us to attend to the contradictions that constituted the shifting ground of US racial politics during the interwar period.

I begin by offering a revised history of the founding years of the WILPF. The introduction resituates the WILPF within the context of early twentieth-century race relations and politics and the rise of the National Association for the Advancement of Colored People (NAACP), the black women's club movement, the New Negro movement, and Pan-Africanism. The book is then divided into two parts. The two chapters in the first part investigate the influence of World War I on the intellectual frameworks and political strategies of six prominent women—three of them African American and three of them Anglo-American. Chapter 1 features the political careers and literary contributions of three leading black reformers—Addie Hunton, Alice Dunbar-Nelson, and Jessie Fauset—whereas chapter 2 explores the influence of race on the social thought and political strategies of three influential white WILPF members: Rachel Davis Dubois, Emily Greene Balch, and Anna Melissa Graves.

The second part examines the work of women's interracial peace committees in four WILPF communities from 1927 to 1940. Chapter 3 considers the flagship Philadelphia interracial committee, whereas chapter 4 turns the focus to interracial activism in Cleveland, Washington, DC, and Baltimore. Finally, the conclusion explores the relevance of the WILPF's interwar era struggles with race and racism for today's movements for peace and racial justice.

A Band of Noble Women provides an opportunity to consider women's successes and failures as they addressed the manifold issues of militarization, racism, and women's freedom during the interwar years. As our world continues to seek models of political engagement and community building that rest on the principle of a common humanity and mutual dependence, as opposed to war profiteering and race profiling, we might be better able to fashion a more sustainable and just future with a deepened understanding of the antiracist peace efforts in which women engaged in the shadow of World War I.

Acknowledgments

I OWE GRATITUDE to many people who have made this book possible. But I first want to acknowledge the unending and often unnoticed work for social justice done by everyday people who struggle to provide for their families and communities and to live free from war.

At this project's earliest stage, the members of my dissertation committee provided me with invaluable direction, criticism, and unending support. I could not have asked for a better committee chair in Susan K. Cahn. Susan patiently guided me as I searched to turn my research interests into a viable project. Through her own scholarship and leadership in the field of women's history, she modeled for me an approach to women's history that could be grounded in both local studies and national developments and that paid attention to the intersecting issues of race and class. It was Elizabeth Lapovsky Kennedy who nudged me to enter the PhD program. Thanks, Liz. As a scholar, member of my committee, and a friend, she guided the development of this book in its nascent stage and remained a believer in this project and my ability to complete it. It was in a graduate seminar with Masani Alexis De Veaux that I first discovered the work of Addie Hunton, a woman who figures centrally to this book. Masani not only expanded my understanding of the field of African American women's literature, history, and activism, she reminded me to be fearless and to find enjoyment in my work. Likewise, Michael Frisch believed in my scholarship, supported me throughout the process, and offered a model of community-engaged research. Other people I had the good fortune of working with while a graduate student and who influenced my thinking and scholarship include Ruth Meyerowitz, Alice Echols, and Hester Eisenstein. I want to call particular attention to my good buddy and respected colleague, Robin Hicks, who died in December 2005. Robin's commitment to African American women's history and the politics of education inspired me. As well, her great humor and unwavering friendship were unmatched.

Members of my writing group, Lisa Botshon, Monica Chiu, Robin Hackett, Rebecca Herzig, Eve Raimon, and Siobhan Senier, gave of their time and offered unwavering support throughout this endeavor. Thanks to all of you for your keen reading of my work. I have gained so much not only from your comments and advice, but just as importantly I have been emboldened to persevere as I have watched you all bring your books to fruition. In the final stage of this work I made additional requests of Lisa, Eve, and Rebecca, who graciously did yet another set of readings of my work and answered my questions about the mechanics of turning my work into a book.

Over the many years and versions of this project, Wendy Chmielewski of the Swarthmore College Peace Collection offered her insight on the WILPF. Her professionalism and friendship helped this project along in many ways. I must also thank the rest of the staff at Swarthmore for their diligence and patience over the years. My colleagues at Bates College have provided friendship and encouragement and an overall warm working environment. The Dean of Faculty's office and Bates College Faculty Research Grants made possible numerous trips to archives and the general completion of this manuscript. At Syracuse University Press, I want to thank former acquisitions editor Annelise Finegan, Kay Steinmetz, Marcia Hough, and Lynn Hoppel for ushering me through the process of bringing this book to completion. The insightful comments of the Syracuse University Press reviewers, Frances Early and one anonymous reviewer, also helped give shape to this project.

For general encouragement, I want to thank my family and friends who remained by me as this project took on a life of its own and spanned many years. My mother-in-law, Carol Jane Gottfried, never failed to ask how the book was going and to remind me that she looked forward to reading it. Thanks also to my sister Andrea and her partner Joyce Lupack for remaining key members of my fan club. I also want to acknowledge Jim and Kay Plastas for their support. Special thanks go to Candace Kanes and Barbara Murphy for being there during an important moment in my life and for continuing to provide warmth, great food, and irreverence just when it was most needed. To the many friends who gave encouragement at different stages, I can't say enough. Thanks go to Marta Albert, Lisa Collins, Mary Dougherty, Junko Kanamura, Madeline McMahon, Jo Power, Susan Shacter, Mazz Whitaker, and Mary Zepernick. To my nieces and nephews, you brought joy and levity at all the right moments. And my deepest appreciation goes to my partner Laura Gottfried. Thanks for sticking by me and this project every step of the way and for always believing in me.

This book is dedicated to and in memory of my mother, Pat Plastas.

A Band of
Noble Women

Introduction

Race and the Politics of Peace and Freedom

ON AUGUST, 29, 1914, more than fifteen hundred white women marched in solemn silence through New York City protesting the war that had just begun in Europe. Although women had participated in antiwar and peace crusades before, most notably the abolition movement and protest of the Spanish-American War, the demonstration that took place in immediate response to what would become the Great War marked a new development. Initiated and led by white women who were active in the woman's rights and suffrage campaigns of the past decades, the march marked the emergence of what would become a vibrant, multifaceted, and international women's peace movement. Parade organizers and participants represented socialist feminists, labor union activists, descendents of the abolition movement, and initiators of the social settlement movement. Coalesced, women intended to keep the United States out of the war and to foster international conditions that would end the war swiftly. Irritated by the sexism of male-dominated peace associations, emboldened by the state-to-state successes of the suffrage fight, and well equipped by recent years of social reform work, the women marching through the streets of New York City brought a new feminist outlook to issues of war and peace and a determination that women's voices be heard in the fight for peace and freedom. Believing that war was the negation of progress and civilization, they took to the streets, to the halls of Congress, and to women around the world in hopes of fostering a new approach to conflict.[1]

Three summers after the women's peace march, another dramatic, silent march in New York City marked a turning point in African American resistance. On July 28, 1917, nearly ten thousand African Americans—women in white outfits, men in black suits—walked in procession down Fifth Avenue to protest the upsurge of racist violence in the United States. In particular, they decried the racist assault on black citizens of East St. Louis, which had started weeks earlier on July 2. Whites angry at the employment of black workers at a local factory had rampaged through the city. At the end of the days of white violence, close to forty African Americans and eight whites were dead and more than six thousand people, mostly African American, were left homeless. The East St. Louis riots along with an upsurge of lynchings in Tennessee and Texas were on the minds of African Americans as they marched in New York City. Many marchers responded to the racist violence by questioning the nation's claim that in the turmoil of World War I, the United States could offer the world the best model of harmony and progress. Carrying banners that asked "Mr. President, Why Not Make America Safe for Democracy?" the marchers sought to expose the hypocrisy of the nation. The protest signaled growing black frustration with the racial politics of the war. This disillusionment would soon transform into what would be known as the New Negro political consciousness. The New Negro embraced a more international political philosophy and was a more aggressive critic of the failure of American democracy to treat black citizens equally.

Although in the 1914 and 1917 marches white and African American women took to the streets of New York City separately, their participation in these public events represented a shared belief in the political and discursive power of "noble womanhood." Through their silent stoicism, African American and white women looked to capture the heart and will of the nation. These activists believed that women's wisdom, morality, and concern for the common good needed to prevail if there was any hope of directing the nation and the world away from the path of warmongering and racism. Both marches raised questions about the character of the United States and challenged the proposition that war was the way to achieve democracy in the world or bring an end to racial hatred.

By the winter of 1919, the Great War had come to an end and the details of the peace were being negotiated by the victors who convened at the Paris Peace Conference. In response, African Americans and white

American and European women organized two parallel international gatherings in order to analyze the peace proceedings. The Pan-African Congress convened in Paris in February and the International Congress of Women took place three months later in Zurich. Initiated by W. E. B. Du Bois and attended by fifty-seven delegates, the Pan-African Congress placed primary focus on the postwar future of African colonies. Seeking self-government for black nations, the Pan-African Congress linked the disempowerment of blacks in the United States to the mistreatment of colonized peoples worldwide. The more than two hundred women delegates who gathered in Zurich in May also protested the terms of the peace treaty. They believed that the isolation of Germany and the lack of rigorous and universal terms for disarmament did little to contain or control the forces of nationalism and militarism. They also called on the fledgling League of Nations to earnestly promote the rights of women and address the "odious wrongs for which women are the victims in times of war."[2] Although gender was not the only lens through which the women analyzed the war, they did believe that women must take leadership in postwar developments. These two congresses signaled the postwar expansion of international- and transnational-minded consciousness and politics. In the war's aftermath, activists asked questions about war's impact on women and people of color as they attempted to build new forms of community that could transcend the confines of the nation-state.

In addition to sharing a new vision for the postwar world, both meetings marginalized black women. White women prevailed at the 1919 Zurich women's peace congress and black women were underrepresented at the Paris Pan-African Congress. Through the participation of Addie Hunton and Mary Church Terrell, two women who would become leading forces in the WILPF, black women did have at least a minimal presence in Paris and Zurich. In their remarks, Hunton and Terrell brought together the threads of race and gender and war and demanded a place for black women in the international movements emerging from the war. Having recently completed work with the black US soldiers stationed in France, Hunton joined the Pan-African Congress delegates who were eager to critique the racism of the war and to launch New Negro and Pan-African principles. In her remarks to the congress, Hunton informed the overwhelmingly male audience that it would be the world's women who would lead the way away from war and towards peace.[3] Three months later in Zurich, Mary Church Terrell, a founder of the National Association of Colored Women (NACW), addressed the international audience of peace women as the sole African American representative. In her speech, Terrell reminded the white female audience that the end to war was dependent upon the end to racism. These early events revealed some of the central questions and fault lines that would vex the WILPF. One question the organization repeatedly attempted to answer concerned the role that race played in the promotion, prevention, and impact of war. Black women internationalists, situated at the intersection of these developments, asked how they could ensure their influence on these internationalist movements. White women pondered, often reluctantly, how their own organizational practices reflected or contested American racial attitudes.

As the 1914 and 1917 New York City marches and 1919 European conferences demonstrate, American women's peace efforts came of age into a world not only anxious about women's growing political power and changing gender norms, but also engaged in a deep and often deadly struggle over the position of people of color and the very meaning and function of race. World War I disrupted and challenged ideas about nation, race, gender, and citizenship; it set into motion new social movements, and altered and accelerated those already in existence. The war also helped stimulate a renewed interest in internationalism and appeals to the principles of a common world humanity. As historian Leila Rupp documents, the war helped escalate internationally organized "worlds of women." And others have shown how it invigorated interest in the building of a black diaspora.[4] But this idea of separate or opposing internationalisms or transnationalisms misses the important interaction that was at work. Indeed, for radical critics of the war, the meaning of the nation, nationalism, and national belonging was under scrutiny as new forms of community were being imagined and practiced. The internationalism of the women's peace movement developed in concert with the internationalism of early twentieth-century black leaders.

In this chapter, I offer different snapshots of early moments in the history of the US WILPF as a way to begin illustrating the varied ways in which race and racism contributed to the development of the organization. This chapter serves as a general introduction to the founding of the WILPF and the women's peace movement, but it departs from the standard histories of the movement that cast gender as the central organizing principle. Race mattered to the US women's peace movement. And to gain a greater appreciation of the complexity of Progressive Era reform movements, we need to consider the role the women's peace movement played in both contesting and conforming to the Jim Crow politics of the interwar era.

The Birth of the WILPF

Years of women's suffrage and social reform work made the August 1914 women's peace protest march possible. The parade committee included suffrage leaders Harriot Stanton Blatch and Carrie Chapman Catt, social settlement house leader Lillian Wald, labor activists Leonora O'Reilly and Rose Schneiderman, and feminist theorists and writers Charlotte Perkins Gilman and Mary Beard. The organizational resources and political savvy of this first generation of New Women helped transform the sentiments expressed through the march into an expansive, multi-organizational, and influential women's peace movement. Women's objections to the direction of the war coupled with their frustration with the bureaucratic style of male-led peace societies caused them to form separate women's peace societies.[5]

Speaking tours throughout the United States in 1914 by European suffragists Emmeline Pethick-Lawrence and Rosika Schwimmer contributed to the urgency American women felt about the need to respond swiftly and effectively to the war. In January of 1915, at the bequest of Jane Addams and Carrie Chapman Catt, three thousand women attended a conference in Washington, DC. Out of the conference the Woman's Peace Party (WPP) was formed. A few months later more than one thousand women gathered at The Hague to devise a peace strategy. Out of the April 28 to May 1 meeting they formed the International Committee of Women for a Permanent Peace (ICWPP). Jane Addams was selected the first president of this new international women's organization. At the end of the war in May of 1919, ICWPP women gathered in Zurich and out of this meeting formed the WILPF. In November of that same year the US WPP decided to become the US WILPF.[6]

According to historian Nancy Cott, women's peace and disarmament work represented a key "arena of [women's] voluntary participation" during the post-suffrage interwar years.[7] Women who had struggled to pass the suffrage amendment, establish settlement houses, or lobby for improved health and work standards for new immigrants now focused their skill and resources on international foreign policy and securing world peace. Those women who sought to participate in efforts to stop war and promote peace found many options open to them as the movement unfolding in the 1910s and 1920s represented a range of political perspectives and styles.

The development of the WILPF and three other women's peace societies documents the varied agendas and strong appeal of peace work to post-suffrage New Women. The Women's Peace Society (WPS) and the Women's Peace Union (WPU) gave feminists options as they considered how they wanted to work for peace. The membership of the WPS, a strictly pacifist and single-issue organization dedicated to achieving mandatory universal disarmament, never surpassed sixteen hundred. The WPU, another single-issue organization, sought to pass a US constitutional amendment that would outlaw war. The WPU used the outlawry of war campaign as a vehicle to talk about the effects of war on women with a particular focus on violence against women.[8] The National Committee on the Cause and Cure of War (NCCCW), founded in 1924 by former suffrage leader Carrie Chapman Catt, represented the last major and most moderate women's peace group of the interwar years. The NCCCW functioned as a "clearinghouse for the peace interests of other women's organizations."[9] Consisting of eleven major women's associations, including the League of Women Voters, the PTA, and the American Association of University Women (AAUW), by 1930 the NCCCW boasted that it represented at least "one out of every five women in the United States."[10] The WPU, WPS, and NCCCW contributed immensely to the nationwide pro-peace spirit of the 1920s and 1930s, but unlike the WILPF these women's peace societies could not weather the strain of World War II. The NCCCW folded in 1947, leaving the WILPF as the only women's peace society still functioning in the years following WWII.

As Frances Early and Kathleen Kennedy point out, World War I also produced serious concerns about civil liberties in the United States.[11] Many young antimilitarist feminists contributed to new organizations designed to challenge the government's crackdown on war resisters, labor activists, socialists, and immigrants. New York City members of the WPP encouraged fellow member Frances Witherspoon to devise a way to provide legal assistance to people being harassed for their political beliefs. With financial support from the WPP, Witherspoon created the Bureau of Legal Advice, which gave counsel to draft-age men and conscientious objectors. The Civil Liberties Bureau, the precursor to the American Civil Liberties Union, also took shape in response to the repression produced by the war. As Early documents, "civil liberties activism represented a new direction for women."[12] In the midst of the war, progressives, socialists, feminists, liberals, left-wing labor groups, and civil liberty activists all contributed in various ways to an emerging peace culture.

In comparison to other women's and mixed-gender peace organizations, the WILPF offered a more comprehensive political agenda; a more aggressive position on US economic imperialism; and a stronger commitment to building an international movement. By the mid-1920s, the US section supported paid staff in a national office in Washington, DC. International headquarters in Geneva functioned as a watchdog over the developments of the League of Nations and fostered the growth of international WILPF sections. The US WILPF's membership increased steadily until World War II, rapidly growing from an initial membership of about one hundred in 1919 to two thousand members in 1920. At its pre–World War II high, the US WILPF maintained more than fourteen thousand members. By 1925 the international WILPF consisted of more than twenty-five national sections.[13] World War II divided the leadership of the WILPF and led to a dramatic decline in membership. In the initial years of the war, the WILPF worked along with other peace organizations on the "Keep America Out of the War" neutrality campaigns. As information about the impact of Hitler's fascism on European Jews spread and the Japanese bombing of Pearl Harbor brought the war more directly into a US arena, WILPF women found it increasingly difficult to maintain organizational unity over a position of neutrality and complete pacifism. By the end of the war the WILPF's membership stood at 3,789 members, a decline of eleven thousand from its prewar high.[14]

After the passage of suffrage, the WILPF worked less directly on issues of particular concern to women. Instead the WILPF sought to educate and mobilize women on issues of direct importance to securing a sustainable peace. The WILPF's political program started in 1915 with the protest of military preparedness and the militarized US budget. The US WILPF's political agenda during the 1920s and early 1930s focused on legal efforts to limit the machinery of war and reverse US military and economic foreign policy in Latin America. Once World War I ended, the WILPF helped direct national and global campaigns to support the League of Nations and unsuccessful efforts to pass legislation outlawing war. These campaigns included international programs to pressure the government representatives attending the 1930 London Naval Talks to endorse complete universal disarmament and halt the production of naval warships. The WILPF also established numerous campaigns to investigate and denounce US intervention in places like Haiti, Nicaragua, and Panama.

Community Internationalism: 1915 Hague Congress

The proceedings of the 1915 International Congress of Women held at The Hague indicated the type of organization the WILPF would become. The 1915 meeting signaled the centrality of transnationalism to the WILPF, and it underscored women's commitment to devising implementable peace programs and policies. Although fifteen hundred women representing twenty-two countries and 150 organizations attended the congress, the leadership would be dominated by European women for the duration of the interwar years.[15] The women at The Hague believed in the ability of educated middle-class women to influence the thinking of governmental representatives and the moral direction of the world. The congress dispatched envoys of women to lobby dignitaries from the warring and neutral nations to stop fighting and start negotiating a peace. The Hague meeting also established the WILPF as an organization committed to denouncing the destructive powers of nationalism. As European suffragist Aletta Jacobs stated: "If we can bring women to feel that internationalism is higher than nationalism, then they won't stand by governments, they'll stand by humanity."[16]

The years surrounding World War I marked the "high tide of internationalism" as women deepened their belief that a strong international sisterhood was necessary to the expansion of women's rights and the curtailment of war.[17] The WILPF women gathered at The Hague represented this trend of growing international engagement and world-mindedness. For many women, including Jane Addams, the immediate roots of their community internationalism emerged from their experiences as workers in and inhabitants of urban social settlement houses. In her 1907 book, *Newer Ideals of Peace*, Addams credits the myriad immigrants living in the nation's burgeoning cities with showing her that coexistence and fellowship under difficult and trying circumstances was possible. Dislocated from their home countries and living in disheveled, underresourced, and unfamiliar cities, the country's new immigrants were, for Addams, the "humble harbingers of the newer ideals of peace."[18] In direct contrast to the individualistic and combative ethos of the Darwinian survival of the fittest ethic, Addams saw immigrant communities "develop the power of association which comes from daily contact with those who are unalike."[19] In other words, difference of origin, nationality, race, and ethnicity need not lead to conflict and violence. Community internationalism, based as it was on observations of and admiration for immigrants, not only served as a blueprint for women's ideals of peace, but it also served as a direct critique of the racist anti-immigrant sentiment that overtook much of American politics in the early twentieth century. Peace women's belief in the possibility of coexistence stemmed also from the practical work underway in the social settlement houses administered by them. In this work they experienced the "bread politics" of cosmopolitanism. From directing coal and kitchen cooperatives to practicing shared decision making, women applied these practical experiences of equanimity and sharing of resources to the problems of negotiating and sustaining peace.[20] As community internationalists they arrived at The Hague "thinking in terms of family, community, and the brotherhood of mankind."[21]

The 1915 Congress established three founding principles. First, suffrage for all women was necessary. Second, pacifism needed to supplant militarism. And third, transnationalism must replace nationalism. As future WILPF leader Emily Greene Balch observed, "what stands out most strongly among all my impressions of those thrilling and strained days at The Hague is the sense of the wonder of the beautiful spirit of the brave, self-controlled women who dared ridicule and every sort of difficulty to express a passionate human sympathy, not inconsistent with patriotism, but transcending it."[22] The "Principles of a Permanent Peace" that were adopted by the congress registered attendees' strong support for the advancement of women's rights. The plank about the Enfranchisement of Women underscored that women could only have an "effective influence when they have equal political rights with men." Resolutions also protested the "horrible violation of women which attends all war."[23]

Learning to Speak for Peace

The women of the new peace movement were suffragist-pacifist peace activists.[24] One of the first tasks they faced was convincing the public that women had something to contribute to the political efforts to curtail war. To do so they turned to the language of social motherhood to explain women's participation in issues of war and foreign policy. Social motherhood, though useful in explaining women's work on behalf of women and children in urban settings, did not easily convince men that women understood war. Jane Addams addressed this public resistance in her 1915 article "Women and Internationalism." Men, Addams wrote, "argue that a woman's municipal vote may be cast for the regulation of contagious disease, her state vote for the protection of working children," but that it is "preposterous" for women who "cannot fight" to find solutions to war.[25] Addams struggled to explain women's interest in war and peace without only relying upon the argument that women were naturally opposed to war. In the article she proposes that women's interests in war and peace originate both from their experiences of motherhood and from their shared common humanity with the entire world's people. Addams noted that: "The belief that a woman is against war simply because she is a woman and not a man cannot of course be substantiated. In every country there are women who believe that war is inevitable and righteous."[26] Yet Addams did believe that women's experience of motherhood produced for many women a unique and necessary standpoint on war. Women "who have brought men into the world and nurtured them" must "experience a peculiar revulsion when they see them destroyed."[27] Even though Addams located the legitimacy of some women's antiwar participation in their maternal qualities, she resisted claiming that women alone understood the true meaning of war or possessed the key to peace. She concluded that organized womanhood sought to be but "one more outstanding voice" in the urgent effort to stop the bloodshed of war.[28]

Although it can be difficult to gauge the exact influence of the WILPF and the women's peace movement on national politics and public ideology, it is clear that belief in peace flourished in the United States from the late 1920s until the eve of World War II. After World War I, public sentiment turned against war as the wartime promise of democracy failed and economic hardship increased. Mass media, best-selling fiction, and public outcry indicted World War I as senseless carnage, waged by innocent youth on the behalf of greedy industrialists. The peace movement capitalized on this growing critical public stance. By the late 1920s pro-peace activity had emerged in many corners of the nation with women, students, and clergy leading the way. One sign of the shifting public attitude could be gauged at Vassar College. In 1917 Vassar women marched in support of war, but in 1933 five hundred graduating seniors—led by the college president—marched down the main street of Poughkeepsie in caps and gowns protesting for peace.[29]

From its earliest days as the WPP, the WILPF gained the attention of members of Congress, of the US president, and of everyday citizens. In the early years of World War I, President Woodrow Wilson entertained numerous visits from women peace leaders who pleaded the case for maintaining US neutrality. From July to December of 1915 Jane Addams met with President Wilson six times to persuade him to maintain US neutrality and take leadership in negotiating a mediated end to the war. Emily Greene Balch and Aletta Jacobs also met with Wilson during the same months.[30]

Though Addams's, Balch's, and Jacobs's visits did not stop US entrance into the war, Wilson's attentiveness to the women indicated the power of the women's peace lobby. The US WILPF would maintain access to Capitol Hill for many decades. In part this access was a reflection of the skill and intellect of WILPF lobbyist, Dorothy Detzer, who many considered to be the most effective liberal lobbyist at work in the 1920s and 1930s. On the eve of the London Naval Conference in 1930, President Hoover called for a private meeting with Detzer. He wanted to explain why the United States was not advocating complete disarmament or standing behind a proposal to abolish the building of battleships and submarines. He also wanted to pressure her to curtail the disarmament lobby campaign waged by the WILPF. Detzer listened to Hoover's explanation for the weakened US position. When Hoover asked Detzer what she would do in his shoes, she advised him to be bold and "discard all ideas of 'parity' and 'reduction' . . . and offer a program so audacious . . . that the world would rise up and call me blessed."[31]

The WILPF reached people outside of the White House and its own membership. Peace marches, community events, petition campaigns, and savvy use of the media helped familiarize people with the organization. A 1916 War Against War art show drew more than five thousand people in Brooklyn during its opening days. The exhibit then traveled to Chicago and Massachusetts. In 1930, NBC offered the WILPF—for free—the primetime evening spot of 6:30 to 7:00 Saturday evenings during the London Naval Conference for a show entitled *Radio Peace Program*. In the era of radio popularity, the show could reach thirty to forty thousand people.[32]

Dealing with the Influence of Racism

If social anxiety over gender and the changing role of women influenced the founding of the WILPF, so too did social unrest over race and the role of people of color in the nation and world. The racial politics of the woman suffrage movement and social reform work clouded the question of the involvement of African American women in the founding years of the women's peace movement. Just one year before the 1914 women's peace march, an elaborate 1913 suffrage parade in Washington, DC, restricted black women from marching with white women. In planning for the suffrage parade and the heated battle for the vote, many white women forthrightly embraced segregation in order to gain the support of Southern states. White women eased Southern fears over the potential enfranchisement of black women by pledging that as white women they would vote on behalf of white interests.[33] Likewise, during the Spanish-American War the Women's Christian Temperance Union (WCTU) embraced racism as their reason for opposing the war. The WCTU feared the potential acquisition of Cuba and the Philippines because they believed that these island nations would lead to the demise of white power and hasten national moral decay.[34]

The effect of race on the US WILPF was complex. Unlike the WCTU's position on the Spanish-American War, at the turn of the century Jane Addams opposed the war in part out of a clear antiracist position. Yet, like many white women's organizations, the WILPF functioned within the shadow of the segregation policies and practices of the women's club and suffrage movements and the Jim Crow atmosphere of the nation at large.[35] World War I had a large effect on the direction and meaning of interracial politics in the United States. Out of the urgency of the war, some African American and white women pushed against traditions of racial segregation. Through their work with War Work Councils of the YWCA that were established to meet the needs of women in the war industries and enlisted soldiers, some white women questioned the efficiency of racially segregated women's committees. Women's wartime work also increased the frequency of women's cross-racial interactions. As historians have documented, the idea and practice of formalized "interracial cooperation" gained appeal in the context of the war. Yet, if the call by whites for cooperation was intended to improve race relations, it was not necessarily a call for racial integration. For instance, the founding in 1920 of the Southern Commission on Interracial Cooperation (CIC) sought to temper the extreme white racial violence that flared in 1919. The women's committee of the CIC became a significant avenue through which Southern African American and white women attempted interracial organizing. Although the CIC worked to foster working alliances with moderate black leaders, it did not call for political racial equality.[36] Starting as early as 1907 the

YWCA looked to formalize its relationship with middle-class African American women, although the YWCA would not formally desegregate its branches until 1947. World War I also gave shape to the race relation politics of women's peace associations. In order to most effectively agitate for peace, many white women in the WILPF believed it was necessary to enhance their relationship with middle-class black women. For reasons of expediency and political philosophy, the WILPF engaged in coalition building with African American leaders, sought the participation of African American women in the organization, and became a central figure in a number of domestic and international campaigns that criticized the racism of the US government and championed the freedom of people of color. Yet, as Joyce Blackwell and others have noted, the WILPF's efforts to work with African American women in the peace movement suffered often from the same attitudes witnessed in the YWCA and other women's associations.[37]

The Jim Crow climate of the first two decades of the twentieth century and the postwar rise in racial violence influenced developments in the US WILPF. From the end of Radical Reconstruction in 1877 through the rise of the postwar New Negro, black Americans experienced what historians have called the nadir of the postbellum period. In 1896, the United States Supreme Court sanctioned racial segregation with the *Plessy v. Ferguson* ruling that legalized the separate but equal doctrine. Throughout the South, public facilities including transportation (railroads, steamboats, taxis, and trolleys), parks, theaters, workplaces, restaurants, and hotels implemented what came to be known as Jim Crow policies, relegating black citizens to separate and lesser accommodations. Jim Crow restrictions were one part of a multifaceted system that sought to strip blacks, particularly in the South, of any vestiges of political power and to instill a climate of second-class citizenship, fear, and instability. Jim Crow left its imprint on the North as well. Although segregation was less severe in the North, black Americans still frequently found their access to public facilities like restaurants, nightclubs, and educational institutions limited or prohibited.

Racist violence swept the country in the first few decades of the century as whites attacked blacks who attempted to forge economic, political, and social freedom. The renewal of the Ku Klux Klan in the early part of the twentieth century, the resurgence of lynching, and a wave of race riots in 1919 marked a revitalization of white aggression. The pinnacle of this violence took shape during what James Weldon Johnson coined the Red Summer of 1919. The participation of black troops in World War I coupled with black migration from the South to Midwestern and Northern cities in search of jobs in wartime industries escalated antiblack vigilantism in the country. During the last six months of 1919, twenty-five race riots tore through the country. Whites rioted for five days in Chicago and Washington, DC. In Elaine, Arkansas, an attack by whites against the political organizing of black sharecroppers resulted in the murder of at least two hundred black residents.[38]

This racial violence touched the lives of women and men who would become associated with the WILPF. It forced some black women to leave their homes in search of safety in the North and inspired some white women to lend their voice and expertise to new organizations, like the NAACP. In the fall of 1906, up to ten thousand whites rioted in Atlanta, resulting in the death of twenty-five to one hundred black Atlanta residents. Armed with pitchforks, knives, and guns, the vigilante mob swept through the Five Points neighborhood, killing black residents and destroying the once vibrant black middle-class business and entertainment district. The Atlanta riots caused Addie Hunton and her husband to flee their home. With a sick child in tow, they relocated permanently to New York City.[39] Only thirteen years old at the time, Walter White also witnessed the racist violence that overtook the city, including the beating death of a black youth. White, who went on to become the executive director of the NAACP and a strong supporter of the WILPF, remembered the Atlanta atrocities as one of the defining moments of his life.

In response to this upsurge in violence and the mistreatment of black soldiers, a new and diverse wave of political protest and consciousness took shape. The New Negro movement adopted a defiant, outspoken, and international political consciousness. Out of the "revolutionary crucible" of 1919, a range of political voices took hold of the country and promised to make the demand for justice a public and constant cry.[40] From sharecroppers to domestic workers to middle-class clubwomen, the postwar years opened the doors to more defiant forms of black resistance politics.[41]

Established in 1909, the NAACP responded to postwar developments with increased condemnation of the US race record and with the
embrace of a more fervent internationalism. An interracial organization
formed in response to the 1908 Springfield, Illinois, race riots, the NAACP
represented the liberal wing of race politics during the interwar years.
It engaged in legislative and educational projects to push for an end to
discrimination in housing, education, employment, voting, and transportation. It also was at the forefront of the campaigns to stop lynching.
Through its magazine, the *Crisis*, the NAACP took the lead during the
1920s and 1930s in promoting the literary and cultural accomplishments
of the flourishing Harlem Renaissance.

The first executive committee of the NAACP included future WILPF
International President Jane Addams and Mary Church Terrell. The general committee of the newly formed NAACP included other members
who would become associated with the WILPF: Anna Garlin Spencer,
founding member of the WPP and the first president of the US WILPF;
women's labor activist Leonora O'Reilly; and Leslie Pinckney Hill, member of the American Friends Service Committee (AFSC) and president of
Cheyney College, a black school located outside of Philadelphia, Pennsylvania. Hill would later help establish the Philadelphia WILPF's interracial
extension committee.[42]

The NAACP appealed to many WILPF women because of its progressive liberalism. For Jane Addams, participation in the NAACP represented
a logical extension of the social justice ideals she promoted through the
Hull House settlement in Chicago and her already established relationships with W. E. B. Du Bois and Ida B. Wells. Through Addams's invitation, Du Bois spoke at Hull House, delivering an address on Abraham
Lincoln to a capacity crowd. Addams traveled to Atlanta University in
1908 to participate in a conference organized by Du Bois in advance of the
publication of his edited collection, *The Negro American Family: Report of a
Social Study* to which Addams had contributed.[43] Through their support of
the NAACP, white women like Jane Addams helped establish Progressive
Era support for interracial collaboration while building strong working
relationships and good faith with black liberals.

The National Association of Colored Women

Predating the NAACP and the rise of the New Negro movement, African American women established the National Association of Colored Women (NACW) in 1896. With the motto Lifting as We Climb, the NACW endeavored to protect the reputation of black women while working to provide for the day-to-day needs of black Americans. Clubwomen set up day care centers, provided job training and housing for women, and established literary societies. By the second decade of the twentieth century, the NACW had a membership of one hundred thousand. African American women created their own associations and clubs in order to meet the ongoing needs of black Americans who faced Jim Crow, and they created them because of their own exclusion from white women's clubs. As Anna Julia Cooper wrote in her 1892 book *A Voice from the South*, African American women occupied a "unique position" at the turn of the century. In the face of the post-Reconstruction backlash against African American advancement, middle-class black women believed they were especially qualified to lead the race and nation to a place of justice and equanimity.[44] As "race women," middle-class black women used their "unique position" to educate white women on the needs of black Americans and black men on the role of women in the uplifting of the race. Parallel with their white counterparts, middle-class African American women's lives expanded during the Progressive Era as women manipulated the discourse of maternalism to extend women's duties into new areas of social housekeeping— teaching, settlement and missionary work, and protesting for the political rights of women.[45]

Many of the women who joined and most influenced the WILPF were leaders in the NACW and members of the International Council of Women of the Darker Races (ICWDR). Mary Church Terrell, Addie Hunton, and Addie Dickerson, for instance, all played pivotal roles in one or both of these organizations. Even though the NACW, like many middle-class black Americans, initially supported World War I in hopes that black participation would result in black freedom, the racism of the war hastened the organization and its members to take up the cause of peace. The NACW established a peace department to educate its members on issues and campaigns related to disarmament and US foreign policy. In 1922, the ICWDR was formed to bring together clubwomen to study the history and conditions of people of color around the world, with a particular focus on women. Unfortunately, the ICWDR struggled as an organization due to its limited financial resources and the onerous existing responsibilities and affiliations of its members. For this and other reasons, the organization's first president, Margaret Washington, encouraged ICWDR members also to join select internationally minded white women's organizations, like the WILPF.[46]

Considering Class, Considering Race

Class and race early on influenced the membership of the WILFP. In theory, the WILPF was open to all men and women dedicated to peace, but questions about who was suitable for the organization emerged from the beginning. Even though the WILPF was philosophically opposed to divisions based on race, class, and nationality, these very categories often served as dividing lines within the movement and as points of concern among the WILPF's leadership. Jane Addams and Emily Greene Balch, for instance, often discussed with each other the obstacles the organization faced as it endeavored to appeal to a wider audience without sacrificing its radical politics. In a letter to Addams, Balch observed that the WILPF was "so bourgeois we are not acceptable to the working people and so to the left that we are not acceptable to the bourgeois groups."[47]

Class distinctions marred the landmark 1915 Hague Congress. Remarkable for its ability to bring women from warring and neutral nations together in one place, the congress could not transcend all political or social divisions, and debate ensued. For instance, the American feminist Lenora O'Reilly and the British feminist Emmeline Pethick-Lawrence held differing assessments of the level of unity achieved at the congress. Suffragist Pethick-Lawrence remembered the gathering affectionately. In particular she believed that the congress not only transcended nationalism, but produced a unifying womanly bond. As she observed:

A visitor who sat in the gallery was impressed by the similarity in personality and dress of the delegates who occupied the body of the hall. There was nothing in general appearance to distinguish one nationality from another, and looking into our own hearts we beheld as in a mirror the hearts of all those who were assembled with us, because deep in our own hearts lies the common heart of humanity. We realized that the fear and mistrust that had been fostered between the peoples of the nations was an illusion. We discovered that at the bottom peace was nothing more or less than communal love.[48]

Though supportive of the movement's radicalism and admiring of the transnational goodwill practiced by the women at The Hague, O'Reilly contested the conclusion that a common heart or communal love had been achieved. As a leading labor rights activist, O'Reilly found Pethick-Lawrence's treatment of class particularly troubling. In one of the daily notes O'Reilly penned to her mother apprising her of the congress proceedings, she shared her observations of Pethick-Lawrence's attitude:

To Mother Mine,
   Supper over some stories about lives of working women by Mrs. Pethick Lawrence . . . women such as Mrs. P. L. can talk of these human beings with tears in her voice but yet as if they were made of different matter.[49]

The differences in the observations offered by O'Reilly and Pethick-Lawrence are instructive. Not only do they raise questions about the classism of the congress, they also remind us of the immense stakes and potential adversity inherent in coalescing an international group of women in the shadow of the war. Congress participants pledged to demonstrate—through their ability to convene, peacefully, women from enemy nations—that peace was possible. Their espousal of a common good and a common heart stood in heroic and stark contrast to the deadly divisiveness of the war. Yet, women's claims of unity ran the risk of masking the fault lines of class, race, and nation that remained unresolved in most women's organizations—even those organizations that adopted the ideals of unity, antiracism, workers' rights, and transnationalism. So it is perhaps no surprise that a paradox emerged early on in the WILPF. Even though the WILPF worked stoically against racism's sway over world and US politics, it struggled when it came to identifying and abolishing racism within its own organization.

The difficulties that accompanied Mary Church Terrell when she joined the US WILPF's leadership in 1918 illustrate the paradox. On the one hand, it is because of Terrell's stewardship that the international WILPF went on record pledging to fight against racism around the world. On the other, Terrell's own participation in the organization would be disputed because she was an African American woman. In December of 1918, Terrell was notified that she had been selected to serve as a US delegate to the upcoming 1919 Zurich Women's Peace Congress. At the time of her notification, Terrell was working in the South with the War Camp Community Services. Through her work, Terrell helped recently decommissioned black soldiers resettle and she addressed the needs faced by their families. Terrell's work in the South hastened her desire to join the emergent peace movement and to make fighting racism a central tenet of her involvement. Honored to have been chosen to travel to Zurich, Terrell quickly arranged to be released from her duties in the South. Reflecting in her autobiography, Terrell remarked with admiration that she was given the opportunity to have a leadership role in the 1919 proceedings. As she noted, "There were many women who had been deeply interested in the peace movement, who had contributed liberally to the cause and were financially able to go. For that reason I felt a signal honor had been conferred upon me."[50]

The selection of Terrell acknowledged her long-standing leadership and power as a black clubwoman, her ongoing relationships with white feminists, and her preexisting international experience. In 1896 she helped to found the NACW and became its first president. In 1898 she addressed the National Woman's Suffrage Association in honor of the fiftieth anniversary of the Seneca Falls Women's Rights Convention. Her speech, "The Progress of Colored Women" conveyed to white suffragettes the issues faced by black women at the turn of the century. In 1904 she delivered a speech in German before the International Congress of Women convened in Berlin. As a suffragette, clubwoman, and charter member of the NAACP, she knew many of the women involved in the women's peace movement. Her selection as a delegate indicated white peace women's understanding of Terrell's stature and power. In 1919, Terrell traveled to the congress by ocean liner in the company of other prominent women, including Jane Addams, Alice Hamilton, Emily Greene Balch, and Jeannette Rankin. On board the ship the group of US delegates met regularly in Addams's stateroom to hammer out the resolutions and policies to be offered by the US women to the international body of women they would soon join. Once they arrived in Zurich, Terrell was awarded further honor when she was informed that she had been selected to deliver the US delegation's address. In her autobiography Terrell recalled that "on the third day of the Congress Miss Addams called me to her and told me that the American delegates had voted unanimously to have me represent them."[51] That next night, after a day of hurried preparation, Terrell delivered her speech in German to the hundreds of women gathered in the grand church—the first time a woman was allowed to speak from this particular church's pulpit. In her speech she addressed issues of racial equality and reminded the audience that to obtain peace, racism must simultaneously be eliminated.

Terrell's contributions to the Zurich Congress went beyond her speech. She took the lead in drafting and presenting a resolution to the congress that addressed the issues of racism and freedom. The resolution, entitled *Nationality, Race, and Color*, helped set the course for the international and US WILPF's official political position on race discrimination and it marked Terrell as a leader on race reform in the peace movement. The resolution stated:

> Holding that no human being on account of their nationality, race or color should be deprived of education, or of civil and political rights, prevented from earning a living, debarred from any legitimate pursuit he may wish to follow, or subjected to humiliation, this International Congress of Women resolves to work for the abrogation of laws and change of customs which lead to discrimination.[52]

Not only did Terrell help the congress devise a platform on race and racism, Terrell was the only nonwhite woman attending the congress. She noted in her autobiography that she was the "only delegate who gave any color to the delegation at all" and as such represented not only African American women, but all women of color from around the globe.[53]

In 1921 Terrell became the first African American woman to serve on the national board of the WILPF. Clearly, Terrell's Zurich participation assisted in her move into the leadership ranks of the organization. Her recruitment reflected the WILPF's understanding of Terrell's powerful standing within black political circles and the organization's expressed desire to expand its membership both in terms of numbers and racial diversity. During the June 1921 executive committee meeting, board members rejoiced in the report that the organization's membership had grown from 494 members to 1,460 members in the span of one year. The executive committee moved quickly to build on this new momentum and set new membership goals that focused on recruiting working women, African American women, foreign-born women, and women from farming communities. Terrell's election to the board and the allocation of 166 dollars to finance the travel of another African American woman to the upcoming 1922 WILPF International Congress in Vienna represented two early indicators of the WILPF's intentions to diversify its membership and leadership.[54]

Yet Terrell's tenure as a board member revealed the fraught nature of racial integration efforts in white women's organizations and the influence of the deep legacies of racism on the politics of women's community building and peace reform. In her brief two-year board service, Terrell confronted issues that caused her alarm. Moreover, during her tenure organizational leaders questioned Terrell's commitment to the WILPF's peace philosophy and scrutinized her leadership potential. Though no stranger to the complexities of interacting with predominately white associations, Terrell immediately found herself in a situation that required her to contest an action proposed by the WILPF. Almost as soon as she joined the board, Terrell was asked to sign a petition that called for the removal of black troops stationed in Germany because of their rumored sexual violation of white German women. According to Terrell, the board was looking for unanimous support for the petition. In a letter to Jane Addams, Terrell explained why she found the petition thoroughly objectionable and offered to resign from the board to which she had been recently elected.

I have been asked to sign a petition asking for the removal of the black troops from occupied German territory. The most terrible crimes are said to be committed by these black troops against the German women. I belong to a race whose women have been the victims of assaults committed upon them by white men and men of all other races. As a rule, these men have ruined and wrecked the women of my race with impunity. For that reason I sympathize deeply with the German women, if they are really the victims of the passions of black men. . . . However, I am certain that the black soldiers are committing no more assaults upon the German women than the German men committed upon French women or that any race of soldiers would probably commit upon women in occupied territory. Our own American solders treated the Haitian women brutally. . . . I can not sign the petition asking for the removal of the black troops, because I believe it is a direct appeal to race prejudice. . . . The propaganda against the black troops in this country is simply another violent and plausible [sic] appeal to race prejudice. . . . It is very painful to me not to do anything which you or the organization I love would like to have me do. Knowing you as well as I do, however, I feel sure you do not want me to be untrue to myself or to the race with which I am identified simply to please my friends.[55]

In the end, Terrell did not resign over the petition. In response to Terrell's stern protest, Addams intervened and successfully had the petition removed from the organization's agenda. Though the specific issue of the petition was resolved, the controversy and Terrell's letter to Addams revealed a number of dynamics that would influence the relationships between many African American and white women within the WILPF in the coming decades. As this incident illustrates, African American women's "unique position" was also a vexed position. Within the WILPF, African American women were specifically recruited because of their race, and yet their race made them suspect members. For instance, when Terrell was perceived as taking action as a "race woman"—in other words, when she spoke out against the racism-laden petition—some WILPF members concluded that her advocacy on behalf of black men and women hindered her ability to be fully committed to working for peace. The insistence by some of polarizing these two causes, the struggle against racism and the struggle against war, would remain unresolved for years and complicate African American women's participation in the organization.

In 1923, Mary Church Terrell was not reelected to the board. Although this disappointed Terrell, it also created a flurry of debate among WILPF leaders. Some leaders were "much distressed" to learn that Terrell had not been reelected. Amy Woods and Belle La Follette, for instance, expressed their concern and announced that they felt strongly that the WILPF "should have a representative of the Negro Race."[56] Others debated whether or not Terrell had been a significant contributing member to the board during her two years of service. Lucy Biddle Lewis, a Swarthmore College trustee who had "thought a good bit on the subject of a colored representative on the board," felt that Mary Church Terrell had been "rather futile."[57] Emily Greene Balch shared Biddle Lewis's assessment of Terrell's board participation. Yet board minutes record that Terrell attended at least five board meetings during her two-year membership and participated actively in the business at hand.[58] Biddle Lewis also believed that Terrell was ideologically ill equipped to be a board member. She remarked about Terrell that "at the bottom of her heart she has not the fundamental understanding of our ideals I am sure."[59] One specific criticism launched at Terrell was that in her public speeches, including her Zurich address, she glorified black soldiers' participation in the Civil War and World War I.[60] Indeed, in many of her talks, Terrell did draw upon black military service as a way to illustrate the dilemmas black Americans faced as they tried to secure their equality in the nation. Through her invocation of African American soldiers' contributions on the battlefield, Terrell intended to expose the hypocrisy and depth of American racism, not to endorse war itself. The questioning of Terrell's comprehension of the WILPF's "ideals" can be read, of course, not as an indication of her failure to comprehend but of the WILPF's inability to understand thoroughly how race, gender, and war intersected.

This brief examination of Mary Church Terrell's tenure in the WILPF offers us one snapshot of how race influenced the early development of the organization. Terrell's status in it as an African American woman was both exalted and assailed. Also, the WILPF went on record both committing itself to help end racism around the world and recognizing its difficulty in identifying it when it emerged within the organization. The following discussion of the 1924 WILPF international congress enhances our picture of the ways in which race mattered to the emerging movement. African American women and men, including Terrell, played consequential roles in the conference—a conference that confirmed the US and international WILPF's ambition to make central to its call for a New International Order the commitment to speak forthrightly about the dangers of racism-driven foreign policy.

Working Toward Racial Unity and a New International Order

In the spring of 1924 the international WILPF held its congress and International Summer School in the United States for the first time. With a theme that called for the development of a "New International Order," the seven-day-long WILPF meeting, held in Washington, DC, was attended by eminent women from twenty-two countries including Liberia, the Philippines, Guatemala, and Japan. Women and men attended workshops, heard plenary speeches, and partook in entertainment throughout the nation's capital. The call for a New International Order reflected the complexity of the WILPF's political agenda and its need to build a range of alliances with organizations outside of the traditional peace movement. Many concerns were rolled into the 1924 call for a radical transformation of world affairs. Activists were losing faith in the ability of the League of Nations to function as an effective international watchdog and arbiter. The WILPF fretted over the persistence of economic imperialism and the link between corporate interests and, for instance, US military involvement in Latin America. Congress participants wanted military conscription ended and war outlawed. In addition, the congress tallied the ways in which racism informed numerous aspects of US and world affairs. The International WILPF Congress signaled the growing popularity of the peace movement and the increasingly radical political agenda of the WILPF.

In the years prior to the 1924 Congress, the peace movement galvanized public sentiment against the merchants of war and encouraged parents and young people to think critically about the creation of army reserves and compulsory military training. In 1920, under pressure from the peace movement, the United States Congress allocated only half of the one million dollars requested by the War Department. The WILPF, in its own efforts to destabilize support for the War Department, implemented nationwide campaigns that targeted for defeat congressional office seekers who supported the War Department. Secretary of War John Weeks, unhappy with the popularity and tactics of the peace movement, devised a publicity campaign that would "counter the headway the peace groups were making in opposition to the War Department's national defense policy."[61]

The WILPF's ability to galvanize an international group of women to contest US domestic and foreign policy threatened the War Department. In an effort to smear the WILPF and scare women from the peace movement, in 1924 the War Department published the Spider Web Chart. The chart linked proponents of women's peace work with international socialism. This red-baiting campaign signaled the government's frustration with the appeal of the peace movement. To weaken the appeal, the chart directly accused organizations like the League of Women Voters and the National Congress of Parents and Teachers, organizations that had been associated with the women's peace movement, of socialism and national disloyalty. The Spider Web Chart threatened women by suggesting that their link to peace issues would jeopardize their ability to advance other women's issues, like labor legislation.[62] The government also feared the strengthening of the WILPF's relationships with leading black activists. In the early 1920s, the WILPF and its allies like Jessie Fauset, James Weldon Johnson, Mary McLeod Bethune, Walter White, and W. E. B. Du Bois shared criticism of the United States for its domestic racial politics, interventionist postures, and the links between the two. The organization's strong internationalism and deepening ties with black critics of US military policy, evident at the 1924 congress, worried the US government and indicated the WILPF's maturation.

On the first morning of the 1924 international congress, Jessie Fauset, literary editor of the NAACP's magazine, the *Crisis*, gave one of the welcoming addresses. Also a novelist and essayist, Fauset had extensive international experience and was in Europe when World War I broke out. As literary editor, she brought the literature of the Pan-African world, including Haiti and Liberia, to the magazine's readers and cultivated emerging Harlem Renaissance talent. In 1921, she attended and reported on the second postwar Pan-African Congress which was held in London, Paris, and Belgium. As part of her 1924 WILPF remarks, Fauset sent greetings from "women of the darker races" from around the world and in this way prompted the WILPF to expand the reach of the organization to include them. Sunday afternoon of the congress was dedicated to a Youth Mass Meeting that commenced with a performance by the Musical Quartet of Hampton Institute, a black land-grant college formed after the Civil War. The afternoon consisted of lectures by former soldiers and workshops informing students of the state of militarization and peace from the perspective of the United States, Europe, Japan, Mexico, and India. At the end of a day of speeches and workshops, the Hampton Institute Quartet led the students in a round of the peace song, "Ain't Gonna Study War No More."[63] Sunday evening featured a concert at Howard University by the Howard University Choral Society hosted by Mary Church Terrell.

In a show of the 1924 congress's support of black student activism, the antimilitarization protests of Howard University students received front-page coverage in the June issue of the *Pax Special,* a publication produced in honor of the International Congress. The article applauded the four hundred students who went on strike to denounce the militarization of their campus. Angry about compulsory military drills and the presence of Army Reserve officers and the Army Training Corps, students carried signs that read: "What is this going to be, an army or a university?" and "Before we will be slaves, we will be in our graves." They also demanded that the five antimilitarists dismissed by Howard's president be reinstated. The Howard student protest not only indicated general youth antiwar sentiment, but also the particular outrage black students felt because of the mistreatment of black soldiers during and after World War I.[64]

The NAACP's James Weldon Johnson continued with these themes in his speech to the 1924 summer school that followed the international congress. Held in Chicago, the summer school enabled delegates to engage in more extensive study of various topics. Johnson, the first black executive director of the NAACP, delivered a speech entitled "The Race Problem and Peace." Johnson began his lengthy talk stating that the cause of war was complex, not singular. Yet after offering a familiar litany of the motives behind war: "greed, gain—in a word, Money," Johnson shifted his focus to the role that racism played in softening the ground for colonialism and mass-scale warfare. In order for European colonizers of Africa to "justify acts of treachery and cruelty and metamorphose them into acts of benefi- cence and Christianity," they had to produce the idea that the "darker races" were innately less civilized and incapable of self-rule.[65] After an examination of the racial ideology embedded in European colonialism, Johnson turned his attention to the United States. He reviewed the race- tainted discourse of civilization and its use by the US government to justify the fact that it had "taken all the little Africas on this side of the ocean." Johnson asked if American measures of civilization were objec- tive and preferable as he questioned "who could judge with finality about civilization." Did convincing Haiti farmers to forgo bare feet for patent leather shoes or a straw hat for an "American derby" really produce a better Haiti and justify intervention by the United States? Johnson next turned to the practice of lynching and the fact that thousands of men, women, and children "gathered around to watch a human being baptized by gasoline and then set on fire." He emphasized that in order for the United States to proclaim superiority in the face of the practice of lynch- ing, whites in America must abide by the belief that African Americans, like Haitians, were not human.[66]

Johnson concluded his lecture with the proposition that "the surest safeguard against future wars is the abolishment of the idea of innate race inferiority." He directed women to debunk the conceit that European and American interventions were based on benevolence. He also encour- aged peace activists to spend less time debating the policies of the League of Nations, and more time educating the world away from modern rac- ism. Endorsing the cosmopolitanism of the WILPF, Johnson concluded his speech by observing that the "points of difference between people are not necessarily points of inferiority."[67] Johnson's words and sentiments aligned with Emily Greene Balch's observation in 1915 that "[i]f we would end war, let us enlarge our hearts and rejoice in the otherness of others."[68] Johnson's speech was so favorably received that in the fall of 1924 the WILPF executive committee voted to print ten thousand copies of "The Race Problem and Peace." The expense of the printing and distribution was shared with the NAACP.[69]

The issues foregrounded by Johnson, namely the role of racism in legitimizing international military conquest and domestic policies, had surfaced in earlier discussions by WILPF leaders and would continue to inform the politics of the organization. In 1915 Balch wrote a number of articles that pursued the concerns addressed by Johnson. In her March 6 article, "Racial Contacts and Cohesions," published in the *Survey*, Balch took the position that "racial or national arrogances, greed, fears, intolerances are in part at least to blame for war."[70] In fact, exploration of the relationship between war and racism frequently appeared in speeches presented at WILPF congresses and articles featured in WILPF publications during the interwar years. In 1923, Lewis Gannett, associate editor of *The Nation*, delivered the speech the "Modern Methods of Imperialism" to the US WILPF's Annual Meeting. In the speech he observed that in regard to Haiti, "We have even exported our race prejudices to this republic which was proud to be black. . . . Haitians today cannot be received in the dining rooms of the best hotels of Port-au-Prince because Southern white American officers will not permit it." Gannett's speech became the cover article in the May 1923 issue of the WILPF *Bulletin* and it was printed in Spanish and English.[71] In April of 1925, feminist historian Mary Beard delivered a talk entitled "The Japanese–American Crisis" at the US WILPF Annual Meeting. Her speech, published in the June 1925 WILPF *Bulletin*, attacked the role of racist saber rattling in fostering conditions that could produce US military involvement against Japan. In addition, Beard assailed the newly passed and sweeping anti-immigrant legislation that targeted, among others, the Japanese. In her remarks, Beard condemned the attitudes of white citizens and policy makers. As she observes, "There is a white menace. But where is the yellow peril? The handful of Japanese or Chinese on the Pacific coast?"[72]

The New International Order that the WILPF pursued necessitated an unearthing of and accounting for, among other things, the racial fissures woven through international and US postwar power politics. As the 1924 international WILPF congress and surrounding US WILPF annual meetings indicated, the US WILPF believed that its ability to construct and sustain a successful critique of global militarism required the organization to foster among its membership a sophisticated analysis of the links between war, capitalism, and racism. It needed leaders—white and black—within the organization who understood these connections and also strong alliances with the likes of the NAACP and the NACW if it was serious about its mission.

Disarmament and Race

The interwar era campaign for disarmament also emerged as an important venue through which the WILPF was challenged to strengthen its relationship with black leaders and to clarify its understanding of the links between race and war. From 1927 to 1933, the international peace community focused its energies on a series of disarmament conferences planned by the League of Nations. Under the slogan "War Is Renounced—Let Us Renounce Armaments," the US WILPF determined to collect signatures from one million Americans as a part of a global petition drive designed to influence government delegates attending the 1932 Geneva conference. The petition, translated into eighteen languages, started to circulate in May of 1930. By February of 1932 eight million signatures had been collected internationally, six million of them through the work of the WILPF. With its sights set on securing an arms reduction treaty, the US WILPF took to work expanding the role of black women in the organization. Likewise, many black leaders earnestly supported the campaign believing, as W. E. B. Du Bois wrote, that disarmament "should have the heartfelt sympathy and goodwill of every colored citizen of the world" because the "menace . . . lies in battleships, armaments, and the will to war."[73]

WILPF women generated excitement and public support for disarmament by appealing to churches, schools, and voluntary associations. The success of these campaigns rested in large part on the work of local groups of women throughout the country. In numerous WILPF branches interracial peace campaigns emerged as an avenue for increasing black support for the disarmament movement. In effect, the appeal of the call for disarmament produced new opportunities for racial cooperation. And for some women, the interwar era movement for world disarmament transformed into a movement for the end to societal racial segregation. In the best of cases, the interracial campaigns for disarmament set the stage for local WILPF women to assist in the postwar expansion of antiracist politics.

Black women's leadership and organizational resources contributed considerably to the popularity of the international disarmament movement. Starting in June of 1931, a WILPF transcontinental car caravan began a nine-thousand-mile journey through twenty-five states, stopping in communities across the country to drum up support for disarmament and collecting signatures. When the caravan reached Washington, DC, the following fall, a parade of more than seven hundred women, headed by Jane Addams, escorted the caravan and the half-million petitions down Pennsylvania Avenue. At the culmination of the parade, President Hoover met with Addams for the official presentation of the signed petitions.[74] As a symbol of their support of and involvement in the disarmament venture, Addie Hunton, Mary Church Terrell, and Terrell's daughter participated in the celebration. Julia West Hamilton, the secretary of the NACW, also joined Hunton and Terrell to greet the caravan and toast Jane Addams. Hamilton remarked with pride that the disarmament caravan was "quite the affair."[75]

The pride peace women took in their work was not shared by everyone. For their adversaries, WILPF women's tenacity and outspokenness on racism raised alarm. On August 18, 1930, the WILPF's powerful executive director Dorothy Detzer was, after much campaigning, granted a meeting with Gano Dunn, the president of the J. G. White Engineering Company. The previous June, the WILPF's international secretary, Mary Sheepshank, had been informed by a member of the British Anti-Slavery Society that Dunn's company was in negotiations with Ethiopia to build a dam on the Nile River using slave labor.[76] Upon receiving Sheepshank's report, Detzer went to the US State Department demanding clarification. She also requested a meeting with Dunn. It took two months of pressure and publicity before Dunn granted Detzer the meeting. The voracity of the publicity Detzer and the WILPF generated about Dunn's company unnerved Dunn and took him by surprise. Until the story exploded, Dunn had no idea who Detzer or the WILPF were.[77]

The one and a half hour meeting, during which Dunn refused to take phone calls or messages from his secretary, took place in his New York City office. Once inside Dunn's office, Detzer noted with amusement that on Dunn's desk was an "enormous pair of tusks," which Dunn, without reticence, informed her was a gift from Ethiopia's new emperor, Ras Tafari (Haile Selassie). On the wall behind Dunn's desk was a photograph of him with the Ethiopian leader. In describing the photograph to Emily Greene Balch, Detzer noted that Dunn and Tafari appeared to be "on quite cozy terms." The photograph and tusks supported Detzer's fear that Dunn's company was in alliance with the Ethiopian leader. At the time, control of the Nile River and industrial development along its shores interested many Western countries and developers. The British and the Italians all vied to lay claim to the Nile and were worried what the presence of a US corporation in Ethiopia meant for their own future presence along the river. Detzer's main concern was whether Dunn's negotiations with Tafari involved the use of slave labor and ascertaining if the State Department had any tacit involvement in arranging these developments. Dunn, on the other hand, spent the first half of his meeting with Detzer trying to figure out why the WILPF "was interested in slavery." Dunn shared with Detzer that he could not understand what the issue of slave labor "had to do with the Woman's Movement."[78]

Dunn's question, although seemingly thoughtless in retrospect, is nonetheless quite germane. Why was the WILPF engaged in the politics of race during the interwar years? In fact, interest in and concern about the WILPF's attention to race came from all quarters. For those like Dunn and the US government who came under the WILPF's scrutiny, the presence of an interwar-era women's organization that served as a critic of American racism was disconcerting. Some WILPF members believed that attention to racism distracted from the organization's main mission, peace. And still other members and allies looked cautiously upon the organization's unfolding interracial projects hoping that they were not an oblique form of segregation. Hence, frequent assessment by WILPF women like Addie Hunton and Dorothy Detzer was designed to encourage the WILPF to get it right, to bring into existence a multivalent internationally minded organization that promoted in deed and in word a form of political engagement that could, in the shadow of World War I and all its attendant issues, both challenge the prevalence and potency of American racism and reverse the legacy of racism that hindered US women's organizations.

Race, of course, has always shaped the intricate histories of women's politics and gender politics in the United States. As this book aims to show, for a comprehensive understanding of the interwar-era women's peace movement, we need to attend to the various and often contradictory influences of race on the movement. As the following chapters illustrate, the WILPF served as one of the venues through which early twentieth-century racism was both practiced and contested. With World War I, the political consciousness and activities of African American and white women interested in contesting war and injustice changed and sometimes merged.

1

African American Women and the Search for Peace and Freedom

Cano, I Sing

There's murder and hate in the Balkans;
    There's vengeance in far Cathay;
Injustice and tyranny threaten
    Where men and greed have their sway;
They're lynching my sisters in Texas,
    They're flogging my sons on the farm;
But I know the Omnipotence watches,
    That God has a far-flung arm.

—ALICE DUNBAR-NELSON, 1929

IN 1933 the NACW published, in their organizational magazine *National Notes,* an elegant quarter-page photograph of fifty-seven-year-old esteemed clubwoman and writer Alice Dunbar-Nelson with a large caption that read "Advocate of Peace."[1] This photograph and Alice Dunbar-Nelson's 1929 poem "Cano, I Sing" capture the rich and complicated history that surrounded many middle-class African American women's relationships to World War I, the women's peace movement, and African American internationalism. By linking the lynching of black women, the atrocities of the war-torn Balkans, and Asian unrest in her poem, Dunbar-Nelson consciously sought to place the black female body into the center of the narratives of war and peace and freedom that were unfolding during the first three decades of the century. Many African American women developed from their various experiences of the war—their work as propagandists, home front defense workers, and witnesses to racism—a particular

34

perspective on how to achieve peace. As Addie Hunton solidly believed, "there can be no world peace without right local and national relations."[2] This pragmatic perspective linked the local and the global through the terrain of black women's experiences. As they endeavored to bring together the middle-class movements for peace, Pan-Africanism, and racial uplift and justice, black women turned to their own history as reformers and experiences of oppression to devise strategies for change. By making the achievement of their own freedom the litmus test for peace, women like Addie Hunton, Alice Dunbar-Nelson, and Jessie Fauset connected the local conditions of their own lives to the global strife faced by so many.

The life and writings of Addie Hunton (1866–1943), Alice Dunbar-Nelson (1875–1935), and Jessie Fauset (1882–1961) capture the complexity of middle-class African American women's postwar ideology and activism. Their postwar politics as evidenced in speeches, committee reports, newspaper columns, novels, and essays revealed a double-edged story of brilliance and isolation. The contemporary liminality surrounding black women's contributions to the postwar restructuring and reimagining of the meanings of race, gender, nation, and citizenship replicates in many ways the very conditions of marginalization African American women navigated during the postwar era. The near erasure today of women like Hunton, Dunbar-Nelson, and Fauset from historical inquiry into postwar political and intellectual developments recreates the marginality African American women maneuvered during the interwar years.[3]

African American women's interwar era peace activity and ideology must be placed within the context of the complex developments and allegiances they negotiated. At the war's end, the fact that women had won the right to vote, that black women had participated in large numbers in the war effort, and that the racism of the war had reignited black resistance and internationalism caused black women to expand the reach of their political influence. Simultaneously, middle-class black women were still expected—through the arenas of social reform and racial uplift—to attend to the basic daily needs of the race.[4] In 1920, W. E. B. Du Bois acknowledged the magnitude of the responsibilities shouldered by black women in the immediate postwar moment. In his book *Darkwater: Voices from Within the Veil*, Du Bois pondered the advice black women had to offer: "What is today the message of these black women to America and to the world? The uplift of women is, next to the problem of the color line and the peace movement, our greatest modern cause. When, now, two of these movements—woman and color—combine in one, the combination has deep meaning."[5] Here he praised black women for their accomplishments and their ability to link the struggles for gender and racial equality. Yet he also went on to compare their achievements and message with what he deemed the "noisier and more spectacular advances of my brothers." Du Bois admired the robust political engagement of black men, yet he concluded that it was "the five million women of my race who really count."[6] Du Bois's comments were prescient in many ways. At the cusp of the interwar era, black women were indeed charging ahead into the peace movement—the other great modern cause Du Bois referenced. And they would contend with their changing status as race women as male leadership took on new importance. With the war just ended, black women also took anew to the international stage. Mary Church Terrell joined the 1919 WILPF Congress in Zurich where women analyzed the Versailles proposals and Addie Hunton spoke before the Pan-African Congress held that same year in France. In a few years, African American women would found their own organization, the ICWDR, charged with charting a course for black women's internationalism.

With World War I and its aftermath, African American women confronted what Alice Dunbar-Nelson believed was a Gordian knot. Their influence and expertise was needed more than ever—by the War Department and the movements for peace and racial justice—yet the race and gender politics of the time troubled their every move. The promising New Negro movement that developed in response to the racism of the war produced a highly masculinist black political culture.[7] From the war, black men emerged as the de facto leaders. Or as Joy James observes, the postwar landscape "masculinize(d) black agency" and "naturalize(d) the male intellectual."[8] Men's prominence—or, as Du Bois would state, their "spectacular advances"—sidelined and overshadowed the forty years of work middle-class women had given in the pursuit of racial progress. Additionally, black women faced the racial politics of the new women's peace movement, which, although not averse to the involvement of black women, held an image of the ideal female peace reformer as white. Challenged within these two important movements, black women spent much of the interwar era fashioning political strategies that opened up opportunities through which they could influence the political content and outcome of the increasingly merged struggles for racial freedom and peace.

African American women approached peace work from many avenues. They aligned with existing organizations like the WILPF, they established peace departments in their women's clubs, and they created new organizations. For instance, in addition to the ICWDR, middle-class women like Hunton and Fauset formed the Circle for Peace and Foreign Relations. Newspaper columns, like poet Idabelle Yesier's *Philadelphia Tribune* "Peace Corner," informed female readers about international disarmament campaigns, Cuba, and efforts to stop the manufacturing of children's war toys. Black women also helped initiate interracial peace campaigns in major cities like Washington, Detroit, Los Angeles, New York, Boston, and Baltimore. And artists like Laura Wheeler Waring and Meta Warrick Fuller created and donated paintings and sculptures to benefit the women's peace movement.[9] Dunbar-Nelson conjectured that black women possessed particular qualities that would enhance the efforts under way to make war obsolete and to secure racial democracy. Black women's outlook on war, honed from the daily challenges of living in the world as black women, Dunbar-Nelson believed, elevated their understanding about how power worked and hence bestowed upon them specific ideas about the necessary approaches to achieving freedom and peace.

World War I and the Politics of Black Masculinity

World War I symbolized an era marked by the twin forces of racial pride and racial discrimination, and the black soldier served as the central emblem of those forces. Starting with the Revolutionary War, the military service of black men sparked national debate. Many whites asked if black men were fit to fight and lead. And many worried how black service might change the landscape of race and masculinity in the nation. Black men who sought to serve in World War I hoped to prove once and for all that African Americans were as patriotic as whites and as fit to defend the nation. Yet, as in the past, black male service during World War I was riddled with contention. For instance, though a segregated officer's camp was established by the War Department in Des Moines, Iowa, only twelve hundred men out of the more than 350,000 black men mobilized were recruited for it. And only a few of them rose to the rank of officer. Of the black men who did make it to France, most served in the Service and Supply Sector, unloading ships, setting up camps, and maintaining the day-to-day operations of the mobilization.[10] Once in Europe, black soldiers faced segregated army facilities and mistreatment by US officials. They were frequently labeled cowardly, lazy, and unfit for the duties of a soldier. The ultimate insult came on Bastille Day, July 14, 1919, when the United States barred the black troops from marching in the military victory parade.[11] Near the war's end, black servicemen in the United States encountered relentless discrimination and violence. One of the many incidents that became symbolic not only of the depth of American racism but of the rising New Negro consciousness occurred at Camp Logan outside of Houston, Texas. Black servicemen in Houston had regularly experienced mistreatment and Jim Crow segregation while, for instance, riding the city's streetcars. In August of 1917, a black soldier confronted two white police officers he witnessed harassing a black woman. The police officers beat the solider. In response to the beating other black soldiers, who were "tired of being treated like dogs," took up arms. In the ensuing riot four blacks and twenty whites died. In retaliation against these acts of black self-defense, nineteen black soldiers were executed by hanging and another fifty soldiers received life sentences.[12]

In the end, World War I only reinforced the tenacity of American racism. And the racist mistreatment of black soldiers at home and in Europe became a key factor in igniting a new era of black resistance. Black Americans looked upon the soldiers' contributions to the war with pride and determined to bring the fight for democracy home. Although white Americans would rather forget the presence of black soldiers, black Americans feted the returning soldiers with gallant parades. To them the black soldier represented dignity, leadership, patriotism, and the model of real American manhood. The fact of his wartime service in the face of mistreatment became the spark for a new black political consciousness.

Black Americans would no longer fight for equality quietly, hesitantly, or politely. As W. E. B. Du Bois wrote in his May 1919 editorial "Returning Soldiers," "we are cowards and jackasses if, now that the war is over, we do not marshal every ounce of our brain and brawn to fight a sterner, longer, more unbending battle against the forces of hell in our own land."[13] The New Negro era had begun.

With the image of the mistreatment of the black soldier foremost in everyone's mind, it was commonly agreed that it was the black man's reputation that needed to be redeemed and that it was the black man's rights that were most directly and publicly trampled. Who better to lead the fight for the future of democracy for black Americans than the black men who had just risked their lives for world democracy? The prominence of the image of the black soldier stimulated an important new era in black resistance politics, but it also complicated black women's efforts to establish their role in this movement.

The New Negro era also accelerated Pan-African and world consciousness. Marcus Garvey's United Negro Improvement Association (UNIA) and Du Bois's Pan-African Congress movement represented the two most significant aspects of this idea. In general, Pan-African consciousness encouraged black Americans to establish personal and political allegiance with black nations and all racialized colonial subjects. Garvey espoused black separatism, economic self-sufficiency, and black pride through the development of strong African affiliations. Founded in 1914, UNIA was extremely popular with the working class. The organization peaked in the 1920s with more than eight hundred chapters in forty countries.[14] Du Bois's brand of Pan-Africanism was initially more intellectual and less confrontational, and maintained a hope for interracial existence. The Pan-African Congress movement sought to negotiate freedom for black colonial subjects and to develop "spiritual sympathy and intellectual understanding and cooperation" among all people of the darker races.[15]

Garvey and Du Bois's Pan-Africanism shared a masculinist political ethos. Though women numbered strongly in the Garvey movement, the philosophical underpinnings of UNIA's nationalism promoted the ideal of the black male patriarch and an idealized black womanhood. Du Bois's

Pan-African Congress movement imagined the new Pan-African consciousness as a development of black "brotherhood," leaving few doors open for women's participation and leadership. In the wake of these and other developments sparked by the war, women like Addie Hunton, Alice Dunbar-Nelson, and Jessie Fauset searched for doors through which they could enter into the changing world of political participation and consciousness.[16]

Addie Hunton: Crusader for Democracy

Hunton in France

Born in 1866 in Norfolk, Virginia, Addie Hunton attended Boston's Girls Latin School and Philadelphia's Spencerian College of Commerce where she was the only African American student. In 1893 she married William Alphaeus Hunton, who became the first black secretary of the international office of the YMCA. The Huntons lived in the South until 1906 when the Atlanta race riots forced them to move north to Brooklyn, New York. They lived in Brooklyn for the remainder of their lives. William's 1916 death from tuberculosis left Addie alone to raise their two children, Eunice and William Alphaeus. But the loss of her husband, her new role as a single parent, and her own compromised health did not cause Hunton to retreat from the increasing and changing political responsibilities brought on by the war.[17]

Before the war, Hunton played a leading role in the black women's club movement, attending the 1896 founding meeting of the NACW and serving as a field organizer for the association from 1906 to 1910. Hunton was also one of the first black women to work for the YWCA; starting in 1907 she helped the organization develop separate centers for black women. She also directed a study of the working conditions that black women endured in the factories and mills of Winston-Salem, North Carolina. As a YWCA representative, Hunton attended the landmark 1916 Amenia Conference along with other leading African American clubwomen, including Mary Church Terrell, Lucy Laney, and Nannie Burroughs. Hunton served as president of both New York State's Empire State

Federation of Women's Clubs and the ICWDR. Her stellar history of service work, her employment with the YWCA, and her husband's reputation with the international YMCA made her an obvious choice for the select role of administering to the needs of the black troops in France.[18]

In the summer of 1918 Hunton and former NAACP field organizer Kathryn Johnson sailed from New York City to the southern coast of France.[19] Under the auspices of the YMCA, they served as the first two African American women allowed to staff the canteen and hostess huts that served 150,000 black troops stationed in France. This trip changed fifty-three-year-old Hunton's life dramatically, launching her into an expanded career as an internationalist and a peace activist. Hunton and Johnson left for France on a bright sunny June day after having lunch on Fourteenth Street with family and friends. Seeing Hunton off were her two children and the close female friend who would look after them for what would be more than a year. Also joining the women on their trip were William Sloane, chair of the YMCA War Council Committee, and several other white and black Y workers. Hunton's and Johnson's treatment on board the ship presaged their experiences in France. Black women were required to sleep in bunks located a floor below those of the white women who had also been deployed to France. Though Hunton spoke fondly of the meals, entertainment, and movies provided on board, the dining rooms were segregated, with Dutch civilians serving as the barrier between white and black US passengers.[20]

In 1920 Hunton and Johnson published an account of their service in *Two Colored Women with the American Expeditionary Forces*. In their book they ardently recounted the racism experienced by the black soldiers and passionately championed the humanity and dedication of the soldiers under their care. They also claimed the war and its aftermath as rightful territory for black female analysis and activism. Through the publication of *Two Colored Women with the American Expeditionary Forces* they helped usher in a reconfigured black political consciousness and clarified the political responsibilities of black women. After the war, Hunton became a leading figure in the NAACP, the Pan-African Congress movement, and the women's peace movement. She capitalized on her more than twenty years of leadership in the club movement to enhance her work in these other organizations. Although the war raised the stature of black male leadership, Hunton's political record also illustrates that black women's political contributions never receded.

Although *Two Colored Women in the American Expeditionary Forces* was primarily concerned with the struggles of black men in France, Hunton and Johnson's account, of course, also documented how black women were treated. As they documented, black women were denied the opportunity to serve in ways that paralleled the status of white women. The Red Cross excluded black women from serving as battlefield nurses, yet Alice Dunbar-Nelson reported that three hundred black women served in this capacity by passing as white. Relief and government agencies also strictly limited the number of black women allowed to "spread their influence" in canteens.[21] Initially, only three black women—Hunton, Johnson, and Helen Curtis—received YMCA appointments as canteen workers. Eventually protests by black leaders resulted in an increase to eighteen women by the end of the war. The YMCA's circumscription of black women's involvement in war relief work reflected the YMCA's dismissal of the needs of black soldiers. It also severly limited black women's opportunities to display their civic fitness and patriotism.[22]

Female canteen workers provided important services to soldieries. Additionally they brought the symbol of American home life and stability to the war front. They also reassured Americans back home that their sons, brothers, fathers, and husbands were being cared for. These familiar and gendered images of idealized home life—women nurturing men through home-cooked meals and attending to their spiritual pain—helped improve public sentiment about the war. Denying black women equal opportunity to care for black soldiers not only limited the services the men received by the black troops, but it also served to thwart the symbolic power of black women's service.

Hunton and Johnson reported that because there were so few black female canteen workers, each woman did the work equivalent of six workers. They recounted that in Camp Lusitania in St. Nazaire—home to nine thousand black stevedores—there was only one female YMCA worker, and she was responsible for everything from shopping to literacy training to arranging social hours. This circumscription of black women's opportunity to attend to black soldiers recalled other histories of white intrusion into black community and family life. Slavery denied black women the ability to attend to the basic needs of their families. And the Jim Crow practices of the war promised to make it difficult for black Americans to attend to the basic needs of their soldiers. These limits mattered not only because they affected the health and well-being of the soldiers, but also because they limited black women's ability to fight for racial uplift. In the first two decades of the twentieth century, the successful performance of motherhood symbolized civic maturity. Hence, restricting black women's opportunities to "mother" the black troops made more difficult their efforts to capitalize on the symbolism associated with women's wartime service. This mattered because black Americans supported the war, in part, as a way to showcase their patriotism, which for women meant their care of the fighting forces. By preempting black women's work in Europe, the United States defied black women's determination to claim the mantle of motherhood, civic fitness, and equal citizenship as rightfully theirs.[23]

Hunton and Johnson also experienced little support from the white women with whom they served in France. Hunton and Johnson described feeling ignored by them, "not withstanding the fact that they were women, and Americans, just like the others."[24] Even after the initial YMCA regulations forbidding white women from providing services to black troops were liberalized, Hunton and Johnson reported disappointment with the women's behavior. Some of the white workers still refused to do anything on behalf of the black troops. Others resisted the more personal tasks like letter writing or mending the men's clothing. This behavior reminded Hunton of the importance of her presence in France. It also confirmed that she served in France not as a woman serving her country, but as a race woman serving her men. Additionally, because so few black women served in France and those who did often received a cold reception from white women, women like Hunton often found themselves with very few outlets for female friendship.

Even though their numbers were small, black women's presence in Europe at times troubled military officials. Not only did women like Hunton provide needed services, they were also witnesses to the mistreatment of black men. As Hunton and Johnson noted in *Two Colored Women with the American Expeditionary Forces,* white and black troops were treated differently. Black soldiers injured in the line of duty could wait three days to receive services at a military hospital while white soldiers were given priority care. YMCA huts that dispensed everything from ice cream to religious sermons also were often affixed with Whites Only or Blacks Only signs. Although Jim Crow policies were not necessarily unexpected, these restrictions served as a constant source of tension. This tension flared at Camp Romagne where black troops were assigned the physically and emotionally arduous task of reburying soldiers in an official military cemetery. In this already taxing climate, black soldiers rebelled when a "whites only" Knights of Columbus tent was erected at their camp. As Hunton described, the black men "raze[d] the tent to the ground." In response, the white soldiers turned a machine gun on the black soldiers. The black women at the camp were ordered removed to Paris so that they could not interfere with or serve as witnesses to the riot.[25]

Popular magazines, like the *Ladies Home Journal,* regularly featured (white) female canteen workers and depicted their service to the men stationed abroad as that of "little mothers of the battlefield."[26] These popular news stories fostered a patriotic resignification of motherhood. As peace historian Susan Zeiger documents, government and cultural forces sought to link American women with the war effort by shifting the appropriate role of mothers from that of antiwar agitators to supporters of "citizen" soldiers.[27] This resignification of motherhood took a different form for Hunton. Although Hunton used her "maternal touch" and "womanly comprehension" to ease men's experiences of the pain of war, she also used her "motherly" services to foster in the men a political consciousness that was critical of the nation.[28] Under Hunton's leadership, the canteens were a place in which men could gather to build racial pride and strengthen their racial consciousness. By providing the men with a warm and comforting "home," she assured the black soldiers that they were loved by their own race and especially by the women of the race, if not by the nation at large. As Hunton wrote, "Always, whether in the little corner set aside in the Y barracks for our reception room, or among the books they liked so well to read, whether by the side of the piano or over in the canteen, we were trying to love them as a mother or a dear one would into a fuller knowledge and appreciation of themselves."[29] The fuller appreciation Hunton helped the men achieve was a recognition of their black manhood as a politicized identity. In the canteens men heard lectures about the contributions of the leading men of the race and read the race literature made available by Hunton and Johnson. If the US military despised and maligned them, black women saw in these soldiers the future of the race. Hunton encouraged the men under her care to carve out a new role for themselves as the leaders of a new movement designed to seize equal rights for black Americans.

The championing of black male leadership marked a turning point in African American gender relations. Previous to the war, some African American women publicly criticized black men's efforts to lead the race. After the passage of the Fifteenth Amendment to the US Constitution extending voting privileges to black men, many black clubwomen expressed dismay at the way in which black men exercised their new political rights. Black women also spurned black male leaders who failed to defend black women from character assassination. In Hunton's 1904 article, "Negro Womanhood Defended," she chastised black men for publicly concurring with whites that the "moral weakness of black womanhood" was at the center of the "race problem." Describing in great flourish the pain and humiliation exacted on black women during slavery—"the burden of those soul-trying times when, to bring profit to the slave trade and to satisfy the base desires of a stronger hand, the Negro woman was the subject of compulsory immorality"—Hunton used her essay to acknowledge the strength and resilience of black womanhood. Hunton retorted in typical Woman's Era fashion that black women were the salvation, not the ruin, of the race. "The Negro woman," Hunton reminded her readers, "ha[d] been the motive power in whatever ha[d] been accomplished by the race." Through her thrift she had educated twenty-five thousand teachers and secured fourteen thousand dollars for black education. Within her "womanhood" resided the "moral and conservative qualities" of the race.[30] She, alone, would uplift the race.

World War I brought a change to this uplift discourse and set into motion a new racialized gender discourse. The postwar climate found women like Hunton using the maternal language of the Woman's Era not to trumpet their own move into public life, but to verify the strength of black manhood. The hearth-like atmosphere of wartime canteens functioned as transitional spaces—locales in which black men and women awakened to new individual and collective consciousness. Hunton's "heart-to-heart" talks with the men in her St. Nazaire YMCA canteen revealed black men's capacity to respect black womanhood and to lead the race:

> Over in the canteen in France we learned to know our own men as we had not known them before, and this knowledge makes large our faith in them. Because they talked first and talked last of their women back home, usually with a glow upon their faces, we learned to know that colored men loved their own women as they could love no other women in all the world . . . We learned to know that there was being developed in France a racial consciousness and racial strength that could not have been gained in a half century of normal living in America. Over in the canteen in France we learned to know that our young manhood was the natural and rightful guardian of our struggling race. Learning all this and more, we also learned to love our men better than ever before.[31]

Hunton's reflections illustrate that the racism embedded in the war encouraged a significant amelioration and transformation of the intraracial gender strife that many black women, like Hunton, had felt during the Woman's Era. Hunton's relationship with the men in her canteen revealed to her previously hidden aspects of black manhood. Reflected through the wartime double prism of black patriotism and white racism, Hunton realized that black men could indeed be strong leaders, protectors of black womanhood, and exemplars of American manhood. Her endorsement of the superiority of black manhood served the radical purpose of ushering in the New Negro movement through the mantel of masculinity. It also challenged the foundation of white American manhood. This reformulated narrative of racialized masculinity took shape through Hunton's encounters in the canteens and her observation of black men's work on the battlefields and in the labor battalions.

By sharing her observations, Hunton provided her readers with proof of black male exceptionalism. In her most poignant passages, Hunton explored the significance of the fact that it was black soldiers who were primarily responsible for consigning to graves the men killed in battle. Gazing out her canteen kitchen window, Hunton watched the grave diggers as they gathered and buried the US war dead. Through the "sweat of toil" ten thousand black troops searched 480 square miles of battlefield to retrieve the dead soldiers' bodies, a task deemed too dirty for white soldiers. Hunton trumpeted the black men for their "matchless patience and endurance." Hunton stood witness as the men, working at the "electric-lighted cemetery," performed the "heartbreaking task" of lowering boxes into the newly dug graves. The black soldiers placed white crosses on twenty-two thousand graves and hence "linked the place of sainted pilgrimage on the Western Front with [the] homes" of American families. Although at the time many argued that the dirty, disease-ridden task of handling the dead was given to black soldiers because they were deemed dispensable and disease ridden, Hunton saw a different significance in the assignment. She asserted that the black labor battalion was "rendering the American army and nation a sacred service," and that these black men were the "10,000 real Americans" of the war. Her decree helped to cultivate a new and more strident postwar black identity and politic.[32]

Similar to clubwoman and journalist Ida B. Wells's analysis of lynching and masculinity, Hunton used her observations of the war to challenge and rearrange the national discourse on manhood. At the turn of the century, Ida B. Wells traveled to Europe and used her international platform to call into question the foundation of US white bourgeois masculinity. Northern white men's refusal to speak out against the crime of lynching, Wells charged, weakened white men's moral character and fitness for leadership. Similarly, Addie Hunton concluded that white men's refusal to take on the symbolically important and physically taxing task of reburying the war dead signaled their moral and physical weakness as well. Black men, Hunton professed, emerged from the war more civically fit and prepared to lead the race and the nation into a new day.[33]

Like the black men she administered to, the conditions of war reshaped Hunton's racial and civic consciousness and radicalized her approach to political change. When Hunton told her readers that her fifteen months in France felt like living "close to the edge of a smoldering crater," they knew that the crater symbolized the racist misdeeds and failed promises of US politicians, as much as, if not more than, the general dangers of warfare.[34] Juggling the multiple tasks of taking care of the troops, navigating white attitudes, and representing black womanhood to the world—all within the arena of war—steeled Hunton for a new approach to the postwar world. She announced to her readers that she emerged from the war committed to "righteous and indignant protest" and hoped to instill the same sentiment in the hearts and minds of the clubwomen who awaited her return. Coupled with a new yearning for protest, Hunton still held out hope that sharing her experiences would also "make universal and eternal the practical application of the time-worn theory of the brotherhood of man."[35] Yet little could Hunton realize that through her own wartime promotion of black manhood, she would contribute to the formation of a black social and political climate that would befuddle black women's postwar search for political agency.

Even though Addie Hunton's wartime writings would contribute to the repositioning of black men as the leaders of the New Negro movement, she nevertheless expected to play a central role in the postwar pursuance of peace and racial equality. For although the war stimulated renewed appreciation of black manhood, it also created the desire among clubwomen to establish fresh meaning, consciousness, and expectation for their own political development and world outlook. Hunton's wartime work in France, combined with her attendance at the 1919 Paris Pan-African Congress, held simultaneously with the Versailles Peace Treaty Conference, signaled to many black women the increasingly global nature of the future direction of their own work.

A New Psychology

Addie Hunton returned from France to a nation that was determined to deny the humanity of black Americans. The postwar years ushered in the disenfranchisement of black women voters in the South, where three-fourths of black women lived. Though the passage of the Nineteenth Amendment in 1920 gave women the right to vote, property taxes, literacy tests, and overall harassment effectively denied most Southern black women the franchise.[36] The prospect of black female suffrage, the symbolism of the black soldier, and the growth in black urban centers threatened many whites. The Red Summer of 1919 convulsed with race riots in twenty-seven cities and the lynching of seventy-seven black Americans, including five women and eleven black men in uniform.[37] Faced with these national tensions and the need to repair the international destruction caused by the Great War, Hunton spent the rest of her life (until her death in 1943 from diabetes at the age of seventy-seven) working tirelessly to heal the wounds of war and racism.

Immediately after the war, articles and photographs appeared in the black press that recorded and championed black women's political influence abroad. Coupled with the publication in 1920 of *Two Colored Women with the American Expeditionary Forces*, these writings contributed to and captured the unfolding of a more internationalist and less conciliatory black female political ethos, one interested less in racial uplift and more in racial justice. The December 1919 issue of the *Crisis* featured a half-page photograph of Mary Church Terrell, honoring her for representing "American Negroes" as a delegate to the International Congress of Women for Permanent Peace in Zurich, Switzerland. One month later the *Crisis* ran a full-page photograph of a reception honoring Addie Hunton's return from the Western Front. Readers of the January issue gazed upon a gathering of forty stately dressed, middle-aged Brooklyn clubwomen who beamed with adulation for Addie Hunton, a woman they now saw as a central figure in the postwar expansion of black female political life. Hunton's wartime journey from her home in Brooklyn to France and back concretely coupled the talent, outlook, and experience of turn-of-the-century clubwomen to the propagation of a new consciousness and activity. This new outlook linked the daily life of African American women to the future health of the nation and the world.[38]

"Colored Women Are More than Colored Women Today"

In her 1922 address to the NAACP national convention held in Newark, New Jersey, Addie Hunton made clear to those gathered—men and women, black and white—that black women intended to fully participate in all struggles for democracy and international peace. Her speech was fueled in part by a recent protest with the National Woman's Party (NWP) and the founding of a women's antilynching crusade within the NAACP. Hunton declared to those gathered at the Fifth Avenue Presbyterian Church that "colored women are more than colored women today; they are American citizens" who are "tremendously interested in all that bespeaks the welfare of this country."[39] Hunton spoke truthfully, if not humbly, when she reported that black women were "a part of this great struggle . . . to make the whole world a fitter and better place."[40] Hunton outlined to her audience the unfolding trajectory of women's clubs, which had "changed radically in the past few years." The clubs, Hunton believed, had acquired a "new status" and a "new psychology" that resulted in "bigger thought" because women were "thinking in terms national and in terms international."[41] This understanding emerged from the combination of Woman's Era leadership, wartime internationalism, and New Negro militancy. For Addie Hunton, to be *more than colored women* also meant that not only did black women's trials and tribulations serve as indicators of the particularities of black women's lives, but also that their lives held universal significance. Written onto the contested space of the black female body were the webs of power that marred the postwar world. And so, to attend to and free black women was to attend to and free the world of all forms of violence and injustice.

Addie Hunton put black women's new postwar protest mentality to the test during her 1921 controversy with Alice Paul, the feisty president of the NWP. Founded by Paul in order to offer a militant voice in the fight for woman's suffrage, the NWP, after the winning of suffrage, hoped to transform the female electorate into an effective lobbying force. Yet, as was true during the fight for woman's suffrage, Paul and many others continued to turn their backs on the political needs of black women. When Paul refused in 1921 to place on the NWP national conference agenda a discussion of the recent violations of Southern black women's voting rights, an infuriated Hunton struck back. In ten days, Hunton organized sixty women from ten states to pressure Paul to change her mind. When Paul denied the protesters' request, Hunton turned up the heat and used other means to bring black women's concerns to the national convention. By distributing one thousand pamphlets to conference attendees that detailed the disenfranchisement of black women in the South, Hunton sought to "harass" Paul "very thoroughly" and "bring our issue to the floor."[42] In the end, a resolution requesting an investigation into Southern voting infringements reached the floor for a vote after it was introduced by a white delegate. The resolution was voted down.[43] Hunton turned this purported feminist gathering into an occasion to showcase the radicalized collective consciousness of black womanhood. She also linked the future of white womanhood to the civic status of black women. Hunton warned those who rebuffed her protest that "five million women in the United States can not be denied their rights without all the women of the United States feeling the effect of that denial. No women are free until all women are free."[44] Hunton's words and actions marked a stark difference from her prewar belief that idealism, Christianity, and the politics of respectability could win the battle for black female citizenship.[45]

In 1920 the NAACP commissioned Addie Hunton to strengthen existing branches and develop new ones. Hunton worked for the NAACP until 1924, traveling to places like Utica, New York; Lima, Ohio; and Kansas City, Missouri, in her efforts to vitalize the organization. In Columbus, Ohio, she "penetrated the Garvey ranks" and "won back" those who had been "carried away." In Atlantic City she tried to loosen the influence of the "conservative" elements of the YMCA on the branch. And in Raleigh, North Carolina, she struggled with the observation that "fear" and "timidity" constrained the work of members. These trips and meetings with folks throughout the country contributed to Hunton's growing indignation with the United States. In Virginia, the Carolinas, and Georgia she realized that "Truth could not have a hearing" because the terror imposed by racism limited the risks people were able to take. "Fear," Hunton reported, "lurks even in stately homes, beautiful schools and splendid business enterprises" where "nothing else matters if one answers to the description of a Negro."[46]

While her indignation grew, so too did Hunton's belief in the importance of the NAACP in the postwar world. In the fall of 1922, she traveled in Springfield, Illinois, where people were designing a campaign to end school segregation and "seem[ed] determined to fight" the Jim Crow schools "out of existence." Hunton spoke before an "immense crowd" where "standing room was at a premium." The interest in the evening's event was so overwhelming people had to be turned away. At the end of her remarks, Hunton received what she reported to be the greatest ovation of her life. But the struggle was far from over as the next day the black teachers who attended her talk were not allowed into their school building and "the principal was beaten." These experiences meeting with everyday people throughout the country emboldened Hunton. Not only did she provide the NAACP with detailed reports on the state of the organization and the race climate in local communities, Hunton helped with the transformation of black consciousness into one that was less abiding to patience and providence and more attuned to deliberate protest, no matter the cost.[47]

Hunton's NAACP work also afforded her the opportunity to continue her leadership and fellowship with black women. In her travels for the NAACP, Hunton furthered the work of the Anti-Lynching Crusaders. In May of 1919, the NAACP sponsored a National Conference on Lynching attended by twenty-five hundred people. Out of the conference, black women launched the Anti-Lynching Crusaders—a national network of black women who sought to "arouse the consciousness of the women of America, both white and black."[48] Many involved in organizing the Crusaders, women like Mary Talbert, Alice Dunbar-Nelson, and Helen Curtis, were themselves recently involved in drumming up black support for the war. The group created a fifteen-woman board of directors who oversaw the work of seven hundred women organized in a nationwide network. They raised thousands of dollars, generated substantial press coverage, and publicized the fact that black women as well as black men were lynched.[49] During her work for the NAACP, Hunton helped bring women from across the country into the network of Anti-Lynching Crusaders. The detailed financial records Hunton kept documented the efforts of everyday women who dug deep into their purses to help put an end to lynching. Though many were not women of means, they were determined to do their small part on behalf of the race. In Bayonne, New Jersey, women donated sixteen dollars. In New Rochelle, New York, Hunton collected sixty-seven dollars. And in Marshall, Texas, where twelve lynchings were reported between 1903 and 1917, twenty women donated a total of one hundred dollars.[50]

Hunton resigned her post as NAACP field secretary in January 1924. Although it is not exactly clear why, a number of explanations are possible. The extensive travel and relentless meetings had been taking a toll on Hunton's health. In August of 1923 after she had attended a multi-day ICWDR meeting and after a rigorous trip for the NAACP, Hunton landed in the hospital for three days. It is also possible that she was feeling hampered by her NAACP employment—perhaps in part because of gender issues. In a March 1921 letter to Mary White Ovington, a board and staff member of the NAACP, Hunton shared, "How I miss you when I come in from the field. There is always so much to tell . . . and of course nobody understands a woman's point of view like a woman." When writing to James Weldon Johnson about her resignation, Hunton assured him that she planned to remain an active volunteer and that as a volunteer "perhaps I shall have more freedom to espouse the cause in which I so firmly believe."[51]

Hunton's involvement with the Pan-African Congress movement and with the WILPF brought an international element to her postwar politics. It also brought her face-to-face with constant challenges as a black woman. Hunton believed that for peace and black freedom to prevail, black women must contribute to the burgeoning women's peace movement and Pan-African movement. The work was not easy. Hunton's involvement in the Pan-African Congress movement from 1919 to 1927 illustrated the difficulty black women faced establishing substantive intellectual female leadership in mixed-gender race associations. Though they tried, women like Hunton found it difficult to encourage a gender analysis within the politics and structure of the 1919 Pan-African Congress held in Paris. During the Paris Congress, it was left to Hunton to remind the male dignitaries of the "importance of women in the world's reconstruction and regeneration."[52]

Dismayed at the gender imbalance at the 1919 Pan-African Congress, Hunton lived to become one of the few female members of the Pan-African Congress advisory board. Even though few black women acquired roles in the official Pan-African Congress committee structure, it was women who made the immense 1927 Pan-African Congress held in New York City possible. The scheduled 1925 Pan-African Congress never materialized because of the poor leadership of the mostly male committee. In 1926 Addie Hunton, by then a committed Pan-Africanist and peace advocate, was determined to make sure that the announced 1927 Congress took place. To ensure its success, Hunton turned to the black female organization, the Circle for Peace and Foreign Relations. At the time, Hunton was the director and Jessie Fauset was a member. The Circle for Peace and Foreign Relations raised the entire three thousand dollars necessary for the 1927 event. Not only did black women raise all the money, they oversaw all the local arrangements for the four-day congress, which was held in a variety of venues throughout New York City. Five thousand people, including 208 paid delegates from twenty-two states, Haiti, South America, the Gold Coast, Sierra Leone, Nigeria, Liberia, Germany, and India, attended the international congress.[53] Although black women made this massive gathering of postwar Pan-Africanists happen, they were absent from the list of chief speakers who addressed the gathering. Women participated on the executive committee and policy and resolutions committees, but played little public role. A *New York Times* article about the congress listed only men as conference speakers and made no mention of the pivotal leadership of women or the Circle for Peace and Foreign Relations in organizing the entire affair.[54]

Hunton's participation in the 1926 WILPF interracial investigative and friendship mission to Haiti also reflected the contested and controlled involvement of black women in international politics. At the time that she joined the Haiti trip, Hunton was president of the ICWDR. The 1926 delegation traveled throughout Haiti for five weeks investigating the effect of the US occupation on Haitian life. Afterward, they published *Occupied Haiti*, a lengthy report that subsequently guided many organizations' policies on the US occupation. Although, on the one hand, Hunton's trip to Haiti and subsequent work on the 1927 Pan-African Congress suggests significant development in the breadth of black women's influence on world, national, and local politics, on closer examination these developments can also be read as a sign of the limited control black women held over the development of a black-female-centered intellectual analysis of global affairs. Although the *Crisis* reported that the 1927 Pan-African Congress passed a resolution on Haiti that endorsed the findings of the WILPF mission, the article failed to mention Hunton or educator Charlotte Atwood, the other black woman on the mission, as authors of the findings.[55] Likewise, though the Haiti trip resulted in the publication of *Occupied Haiti*, Hunton's specific views are hard to discern as she is represented as only a coauthor, with WILPF vice president Emily Greene Balch, of one of the report's fifteen chapters.[56] Hunton's participation in the Haiti delegations deepened her role in the international women's peace movement and gave her the opportunity to consult with fellow members of the NAACP concerned about Haiti, like James Weldon Johnson, but it also indicated the circumscribed role black women had to constantly negotiate.[57]

A decade after announcing to the 1922 NAACP convention the arrival of black women's new psychology, Hunton took to the convention stage again. In May 1932, at the age of sixty-six, Hunton delivered a lengthy speech to those convened in Washington, DC. This time the dominant concerns were the impact of the Great Depression on everyday black Americans and internal dissension within the organization. Hunton's remarks not surprisingly reflected her internationalist perspective, her commitment to peace work, and her ongoing belief that women were vital to the progress of the race and nation. Hunton acknowledged that the convention was "deeply challenged" at that moment in history. The challenges derived from the dire economic conditions facing so many, the debate within the organization over the role of socialism and communism, and the related internal disagreements between the soon to resign Du Bois and Walter White. In regard to the Depression, Hunton believed that its impact on struggling citizens locally and internationally caused more turmoil and destruction than World War I and the "Massacre of the Innocent." Humanity, Hunton suggested, was "a little less sane and a little more hysterical," making it all the more important for the NAACP to "keep faith and hope alive." She argued that the "despairing conditions" of those who had been "dubbed the marginal workers" called for an "inspired interpretation of right and justice for the colored men and women in the work world." Although Hunton was not advocating an embrace of the more radical politics of the increasingly popular proponents of socialism and communism, she did forcefully talk about human rights. "The Negro," Hunton proclaimed, "has the *right* to food, clothes, and shelter." Faced with the "facts of violence, denial of opportunity, and whole-sale discrimination," the time for "*charitable* consideration" was over.[58]

In the second half of her speech Hunton invoked a more international register. As she reminded her audience, "With all our problems here, as a people within a people, we are still part of a world order." Hunton linked the struggles in the United States with the struggles of "darker peoples" in "India, Africa, and Haiti," who experienced "flagrant violations" of rights. She challenged the NAACP to "re-assume the huge task of educating world opinion" about the humanity, needs, and rights of people of the darker races who, with their "sorrow-lined faces," might yet "rise-up in might." Hunton surveyed many possible strategies for bringing about justice at home and abroad. The core challenge, Hunton still believed, was to "change the restricted attitudes" of whites who still abided by ideas of "race inferiority." Although Hunton held on to what for many was an increasingly old-fashioned belief in the potential of goodwill, she also believed that time was running out. As she shared with her audience: "I am afraid that unless we speedily build a bridge of justice and cooperation the chasm of misunderstanding and distrust may become too wide to be spanned." Though Hunton struck a sober tone at this moment in her talk, she went on to applaud the accomplishments of the NAACP and the risks individuals took in their work to "end wage slavery," "awaken the American consciousness to the sport called lynching," and efforts to "stretch its hands abroad to help in Africa, India, and the Islands of the seas." She concluded her address to the Twenty-Third Annual Conference of the NAACP by applauding the ongoing tireless effort of the "many women" and "some men" who were "struggling desperately to supplant the war worn standards with those of the Galilean." Even though she feared that the world was heading for "terrible cataclysms," Hunton's knowledge of the work done by women kept her hopeful as she believed it would those gathered before her.[59]

Addie Hunton's 1932 speech captures the expanded political subjectivity black women developed after World War I. In her address she made connections between the local, the national, and the international. Her breathless postwar work to secure black women's suffrage, end lynching, promote Pan-African consciousness, procure global disarmament, and model interracial amity represented not a chaotic or haphazard attempt to repair an unstable nation and world, but rather a conscious understanding of the interconnectedness of individual freedom and international peace. Through her leadership in a myriad of organizations like the NAACP, the WILPF, and the ICWDR Addie Hunton sought to stitch together a new political community that would stop making false distinctions between the work for world peace and the work for racial justice and gender equality. Her call for the embrace of new "Galilean" standards was nothing short of a call for progressive-minded white Americans and black men to begin to look at the world through the experienced and sophisticated eyes of black women.

Alice Dunbar-Nelson

Born Alice Ruth Moore in 1875 to Patricia Moore, a former slave, Dunbar-Nelson developed her desire for writing and teaching while living in her hometown of New Orleans. Starting in her youth and continuing throughout her life, Alice Dunbar-Nelson wrote plays, poems, short stories, and newspaper columns. In 1895 at the age of twenty, she received notable attention with the publication of *Violets and Other Tales*, a collection of her prose writing and journalism. Four years later another collection, *The Goodness of St. Rocque and Other Tales*, appeared in print.[60] These would be the only published volumes of her work to emerge while Dunbar-Nelson was alive. Although high school teaching would provide the mainstay of Dunbar-Nelson's economic livelihood, she did venture into paid and unpaid journalism. At the turn of the century she began her career in journalism penning articles for Chicago's *Daily News* and for the *New York Sun*. In Wilmington, Delaware, she attempted to keep the *Wilmington Advocate* running, serving as its associate editor. In the 1920s and the 1930s Dunbar-Nelson's hard copy journalism and syndicated columns appeared in black papers, garnering much praise. In her columns, Dunbar-Nelson refused to be confined to women's issues or the typical society page features. On the contrary, her columns covered a wide range of issues from popular culture to world politics.[61]

Like many African American women with middle-class aspirations, teaching served for years as Dunbar-Nelson's main employment. She graduated from New Orleans' Straight College (now known as Dillard

University), attended the University of Pennsylvania and Columbia University, and received a master's degree from Cornell. Moving to Wilmington, Delaware, in 1902, Dunbar-Nelson taught at the all-black Howard High School for eighteen years. With colleagues in the Federation of Colored Women's Clubs she helped found the Industrial School for Colored Girls in Marshallton, where from 1924 to 1928 she worked as a teacher and parole officer after losing her job at Howard, reportedly for her political activity.[62]

Mine Eyes Have Seen: Black Women and World War I Patriotism

Alice Dunbar-Nelson played a significant role before the war in galvanizing black Americans' pro-war patriotism. Her 1918 play *Mine Eyes Have Seen* and her organizing of a large parade in Delaware underscore her leadership in bringing black Americans into the war preparedness movement. Dunbar-Nelson's efforts to convince black Americans to elevate national allegiance over the injuries of racism were short-lived as her own experiences of racism during the war as a fieldworker for the War Work Council of the YWCA jettisoned her ability and desire to put patriotism before racial justice. An examination of her early pro-war efforts and her transition to becoming a critic of the war and US domestic and foreign policy illuminates the importance of black women to both projects and the gender dynamics of these developments. Dunbar-Nelson, like Hunton, understood the symbolic centrality of the black male soldier to both the wartime struggle to prove black patriotism and to the postwar project of New Negro protest. Like Hunton, she also aspired to address the issues faced by black women in these troubling times and to legitimate and elevate the perspectives offered by black women on the Gordian knot of race, gender, and militarism.

Mine Eyes Have Seen illustrates both the playwright's importance to the general campaign to cultivate black wartime allegiance and Dunbar-Nelson's explicit use of gender in this cultivation. Concerned about dissension among black Americans, the US government used the 1917

Espionage Act to pressure black leaders and the black press to forestall antigovernment sentiment, and to cultivate patriotism and compliance with the draft. Under these governmental pressures, W. E. B. Du Bois turned the *Crisis* into a vehicle for wartime propaganda.[63] Du Bois's July 1918 editorial "Close Ranks" has been singled out for its significance in bringing the *Crisis* readership in line with the war, yet Dunbar-Nelson's five-page pageant that appeared in the *Crisis* three months before Du Bois's essay also contributed to the fashioning of black attitudes to the war and presaged arguments Du Bois would make in July.[64] With illustrations by artist Laura Wheeler Waring and a closing poem by Georgia Douglas Johnson, Dunbar-Nelson's piece exploited black female moral agency to rally black patriotism and forestall the appeal of socialist antiwar arguments. It also served to extend the popularity of all three women.[65]

The three central characters in the play are the parentless siblings Lucy and her two brothers Chris and Dan. Jim Crow racism killed their parents—their father was lynched and their mother died from overwork. Additionally, their family home was burned to the ground by angry whites, forcing the siblings to move on their own to a Northern industrial city. Dan, the older brother, is exempt from the draft because he was crippled by an industrial accident. Chris, the younger brother, has just been drafted but initially refuses to go. Dunbar-Nelson uses the two brothers to represent the opposing black perspectives about participation in the war. The position represented by Chris placed racial identity and the history of racism before national identity. As Chris asks early on in the play, "must I fight for a nation that let my father's murder go unpunished? That killed my mother?" He followed this question with the assertion: "these white people, they hate us." Dan, on the other hand, elevated the history of black military service and a collective national identity over the persistence of racism. Dan reminded his brother that "our men have always gone," and that the "love of humanity is above the small considerations of time or place or race or sect."[66]

Throughout the play, Lucy serves as a mediator though her sentiments are with Dan and the pro-war position. She assures Chris that his first responsibility as a man of the family is to serve his nation. By serving his nation, he would be fulfilling his masculine duty as a protector of the innocent and a fighter for democracy. Dan uses masculinity to weaken Chris's initial impulse to refuse the draft. He calls Chris a slacker, a weakling, and wonders if he is "big enough" to understand that as a man he must protect the women and children of his race and must also be "of one blood" with the mothers of Europe. By the end of the play Chris realizes the importance of obeying the draft. Dunbar-Nelson's play, though it calls for support of the war, keeps the history of racism central to the narrative and embeds military service into the strategy of racial uplift. She asks readers of the *Crisis* to rally behind the war because, as she states, "It IS our country" and all black men should be "proud to be numbered with the darker ones, soon to come into our inheritance."[67] Dunbar-Nelson, like many others, wagered that this time military service would uplift black Americans' position in the country. Her play, which ran three months before Du Bois's oft-quoted "Close Ranks" editorial, presaged Du Bois's claim that through military service the race made "no ordinary sacrifice."[68] Readers of the *Crisis* were well prepared for Du Bois's call to patriotic military action because Dunbar-Nelson, through her play about black domestic life in the time of war, had already warmed the magazines' readership to the understanding that the role of black women was to support the sons, brothers, and husbands who would be called to duty. And the role of black men was to support the race through military service.

Dunbar-Nelson would continue to serve as a mediator of the vicissitude of black perspectives on the war and its race and gender dimensions. Her reputation as a supporter of black participation increased with the publication of the play and would continue to grow. A few months after the play appeared in the *Crisis*, the *Philadelphia Tribune* applauded Dunbar-Nelson for organizing a Flag Day parade in Delaware that drew a massive crowd of six thousand black citizens. The newspaper labeled the parade the "greatest day in the history of colored people . . . where the loyalty of the Race to the American flag was the gist of many brilliant and patriotic addresses."[69] From her strong support of the war to her transformation into an antiwar activist, Dunbar-Nelson would use her skill as an organizer and a writer to keep people engaged in examining the political implications of US militarization.

Reporting on Black Women in War Work

The war presented black women with a number of questions, including what would be their role in the war effort and what would be the implications of the war on their status in society? Many, like Dunbar-Nelson, hoped the war would bring positive developments including new employment opportunities and expanded leadership roles. And for Dunbar-Nelson and others, although the war did open up new job opportunities, the advantage of the jobs was ultimately outweighed by the troubling race politics of the war. Dunbar-Nelson worked for the Committee on Women's Defense Work and authored the 1919 report "Negro Women in War Work." The report was one of the first detailed assessments of the war's impact on black female life.[70] Her findings along with observations by other women who would become associated with the WILPF, namely Mary Church Terrell and Nannie Burroughs, concluded that although the needs of the home front opened up new employment opportunities, the persistence of racial segregation negated the gains offered by these jobs. The mistreatment of black women during the war lessened their allegiance to the United States and compelled many to become outspoken critics of the country and its policies of militarized racism.

As historian Dorothy Salem observes, black women's wartime patriotic services "were not selfless sacrifices for the American war effort;" instead they represented a desire to take "advantage of opportunities to demonstrate ability and responsibility, showing themselves worthy of equal treatment."[71] Dunbar-Nelson's life exemplified the complexities Salem describes. One major arena for black women's wartime participation was the Committee on Women's Defense Work of the Council of National Defense. The committee allocated four hundred thousand dollars to organize war work among black women. Dunbar-Nelson was selected as one of fifteen women designated to organize across the country. Other noteworthy participants included Anna Julia Cooper and Mary McLeod Bethune. Bethune created the Mutual Protection League of Working Girls to help young women in the transition from domestic and agricultural work to their new wartime work as bellhops, elevator girls, and factory workers.[72] Home front war work involved a range of activity. Women established canteens stateside to provide for black servicemen housed in training camps. Women made bandages and other medical products. They supervised the work of women in industry. Many organized well-baby care services and raised victory gardens. Some organized patriotic parades to keep up morale. Dunbar-Nelson noted in her report that African American women were particularly well equipped to meet these challenges because of their long history of racial uplift work. Segregation had forced black women for decades to set up and run employment agencies, schools, and health clinics in order to deliver the services blacks were denied in many cities and towns across the country.[73]

Reporting on her travels throughout the South, during which she visited women who were participating in war work, Dunbar-Nelson captured the chaos of the time period. She also presented black women as stoic and well equipped to meet the challenges of the time:

> Into this maelstrom of war activity women of the Negro race hurled themselves joyously. They asked no odds, remembered no grudges, and solicited no favors, pleaded for no privileges. They came by the thousands, hands opened wide to give of love and service and patriotism. It was enough for them that their country was at war; it was enough for them that there was work to do. Centuries of labor had taught them the love of labor; a heritage of service had taught them the beauty of giving of themselves, and a race record of patriotism and loyalty had imbued them inherently with the flaming desire to do their part in the struggle for their native land.[74]

Dunbar-Nelson balanced this description of black women's abiding national pride and patriotism with a discussion of white behavior during the war and how black women negotiated it. As she observed: "the problem of the woman of the Negro race was a peculiar one. Was she to do her work independently of the women of the other race, or was she to merge herself into their organizations?" The answer to the question varied throughout the country. Yet in most cases, North and South, East and West, black women had to contend with segregation and racial prejudice.

But as in her play, *Mine Eyes Have Seen,* Dunbar-Nelson used the persistence of wartime racism as an opportunity to champion black moral fortitude and humanity. Reflecting on the deportment of the black women she had met during her work for the Committee on Women's Defense, Dunbar-Nelson observed that:

> They accepted without a murmur the place assigned them in the ranks. They placed the national need before the local prejudice; they put great-heartedness and pure patriotism above the ancient creed of racial antagonism. For pure, unalloyed unselfishness of the highest order, the conduct of Negro women of the United States during the war stands out in splendid relief, a lesson to the entire world of what womanhood of the best type really means.[75]

Yet black women did not merely accept mistreatment. And, in fact, the resilience of white racism caused acts of defiance. In her travels for the Committee on Women's Defense Work, Dunbar-Nelson was charged with measuring the level of black women's wartime efforts as federal and state officials worried that black women's contribution level failed to meet the standards required by the war. As Dunbar-Nelson's report indicated, many black women offered stellar contributions, but wartime racism did indeed dampen the interests of some men and women. A poignant example Dunbar-Nelson recounted was the case of a woman in Vicksburg, Mississippi. The woman, whose husband was serving in the US Army in France, was tarred and feathered for reportedly "acting out of line." Dunbar-Nelson observed that when news of the woman's mistreatment spread through town, the "colored brass band" refused to "lead the colored draftees to the station seeing no cause for making music."[76]

Clubwomen turned the stories of women who withstood mistreatment yet who continued to support the war into examples of black women's stalwartness and superior character. In reporting on her own wartime activity, Mary Church Terrell shared her outrage that even the "best [white] citizens . . . unilaterally opposed" hiring black workers because they believed that they were "so bad on general principle that it was useless to try and improve them."[77] Even in the face of such attitudes, the NACW underwrote the war through its financial support, raising and donating fifty-one million dollars. Behind this money were the selfless actions of numerous women who banded together to make donations. For instance, ninety-one thousand dollars was raised by poor black women working in Norfolk, Virginia, tobacco factories.[78] And in the face of wartime Jim Crow, the women of the Josephine Gray Colored Lady Knitters association proudly adopted a "definite" policy of "no color line" as they "knitted for all American soldiers regardless of race, color or nationality."[79]

Clubwomen and church women at times tempered their wartime patriotism. In a September 1918 presidential address to the Women's Convention of the Black Baptist Church, S. Willie Layten encouraged the gathered women to grow victory gardens and conserve goods, yet she also acknowledged that women were "restless and discontent when their rights are abridged at home."[80] During the same conference, Nannie Burroughs, who would later become a supporter of the WILPF, called on the women to continue their work against lynching and segregation. She also dared President Wilson to apply his slogan "make the world safe for democracy" to the United States. The convention voted to have Burroughs's speech, which was critical of the US president's hypocritical stand on war, race, and democracy, sent to Wilson. At the following year's convention women continued their critique of war and racism as they joined together and sang "We've Fought Every Race's Battle but Our Own." Burroughs's antiracist and defiant patriotism caused her to be investigated by the War Department.[81]

Dunbar-Nelson found the restrictions placed on black women during the war deeply frustrating. Unlike white women, black women's opportunities to travel to Europe and provide wartime assistance were severely limited. Dunbar-Nelson met with disappointment on a number of occasions as she attempted to find a way to work overseas. She was distressed not to be one of the limited number of black women chosen to deploy to France to take care of the black troops. She was also angered when her request to the white-owned *Philadelphia Public Ledger* to be assigned as a war correspondent was also denied. In her 1920 poem "I Sit and Sew," Dunbar-Nelson lamented the fact that the double burden of her race and gender curtailed her patriotic options.[82] She captures this exasperation in the following stanza of her poem:

But—I must sit and sew.
The little useless seam, the idle patch;
Why dream I here beneath my homely thatch,
When there they lie in sodden mud and rain,
Pitifully calling me, the quick ones and the slain?[83]

This deceptively simple poem testified to Dunbar-Nelson's ongoing political transformation. Although she initially applauded black women's stoic patriotism and encouraged her *Crisis* reader to "shut her eyes to past wrongs and present discomforts and future uncertainties," when the racial structures of the nation-state refused to abate Dunbar-Nelson championed the New Negro movement.[84] She encouraged African American women to use their "more serious mind" and "new inner consciousness" kindled by the war, to create a "community consciousness among our people."[85] The initial patriotism promulgated by women like Dunbar-Nelson dissipated as the war reignited black women's double consciousness, or in Dunbar-Nelson's language, "double problem."[86] The question now before Dunbar-Nelson was how to live as a black woman in a nation that denied her humanity and access to full citizenship.

Forming of a Postwar Peace Identity

In response to the postwar rise in racism, Dunbar-Nelson turned her attention to electoral politics, antilynching reform, and interracial peace work. Through these projects, she hoped to encourage in the general public an understanding that antiracism needed to be a core aspect of the work for peace. In 1920, Dunbar-Nelson became a member of the Delaware Republican State Committee, the first African American woman in the country to hold such a position.[87] Dunbar-Nelson coupled her knowledge of the electoral process with her work to try and secure the passage of federal antilynching legislation. The early focus of her antilynching work was the Dyer Anti-Lynching Bill, initially introduced in 1918 by Representative Leonidas C. Dyer, a Republican from Missouri. By the early 1920s passage of the bill seemed hopeful and African American women, with Dunbar-Nelson as a key leader, founded the Anti-Lynching Crusaders to galvanize black women's financial and grassroots support for the bill.[88] Dunbar-Nelson led the Delaware branch of the Anti-Lynching Crusaders. In 1922, on the heels of the unfortunate defeat of the bill, Dunbar-Nelson directed a successful campaign to unseat Republican Congressman Caleb R. Layton for his nonsupport of the Dyer bill. She helped register twelve thousand new voters; Layton lost his reelection campaign by seven thousand votes, equal to the number of black voters who cast a ballot for his democratic opponent.[89] In the fall of 1921 Dunbar-Nelson joined thirty other prominent black leaders, many of whom had supported the war, to convince President Harding to grant executive clemency for the sixty-one black soldiers serving life sentences for the 1917 Houston race riots. Though the delegation, led by James Weldon Johnson, was not successful their efforts symbolized the growing militancy of the postwar New Negro and the entrenchment of national racism.[90]

Like other leading clubwomen who had organized black women's wartime contributions, after the war Alice Dunbar-Nelson became a peace advocate and leading critic of US foreign policy.[91] Her peace advocacy took root in her journalism and in her work with the WILPF and her employment with the American Interracial Peace Committee (AIPC) of the American Friends Service Committee (AFSC). In 1925 WILPF president Hannah Clothier Hull notified Dunbar-Nelson that she had been elected to the WILPF national board. The board elected her hoping that she would help them "educate for peace in all groups of women."[92] Three years later, in 1928, Dunbar-Nelson was hired to be the paid executive secretary of the AIPC. The WILPF and the AIPC placed Dunbar-Nelson in the spotlight of peace advocacy and enabled her to influence the opinion of white peace advocates on the role of race in the peace movement. Although the AIPC folded in 1930, Dunbar-Nelson maintained close ties with the WILPF, supporting the Philadelphia WILPF Interracial Extension Committee until her death in 1935.

"Une Femme Dit"

Dunbar-Nelson reached large numbers of people through her journalism and her work with the WILPF and AIPC. In 1928 alone she addressed ten conventions, including women's clubs and a gathering of seven hundred teachers.[93] And in 1930 the AIPC sent her on a ten-thousand-mile speaking tour during which she spoke to college students, YWCA and YMCA conventions, and civic clubs. The AIPC reported that through her travels Dunbar-Nelson reached twenty-three thousand people in one year.[94] Her newspaper columns also provided her with a predictable avenue for informing black readers on a range of issues. She frequently used her columns to advance her analysis of the racial politics of US foreign policy. The *Pittsburgh Courier* ran a number of different columns penned by Dunbar-Nelson. "From the Woman's Point of View," later renamed "Une Femme Dit," ran from January to September of 1926. From January to May 1930 the same paper ran her column, "So It Seems to Alice Dunbar-Nelson." Another column by Dunbar-Nelson, "As in a Looking Glass," appeared from 1926 to 1930 in the *Washington Eagle,* the national newspaper of the Improved Benevolent and Protection Order of the Elks of the World.[95]

Through her journalism and speaking tours Dunbar-Nelson continuously proffered that race and gender mattered to the form and shape of black women's peace consciousness and analysis. Until her death, she would stitch together an analysis of war that used the mistreatment of black Americans during World War I, and people of color the world over, as the fulcrum for her antiwar message. Though in her speeches and writing Dunbar-Nelson would reference masculine icons like the soldier and folk hero John Henry to animate her New Negro analysis on war and peace, she still insisted on the centrality of black women to all efforts to design successful and sustainable movements for peace and racial equality.

If during the war Dunbar-Nelson helped to create a "same as" sensibility in the name of patriotism, after the war she sought to develop a "different from" perspective. During the war she encouraged black Americans to put their Americanness first and to set aside the injustice of American racism. After the war she encouraged black Americans to embrace their racial difference as a place of moral exceptionalism and as a place from which to build political kinship with other people of color. Dunbar-Nelson now regularly derided the United States and warned members of the black diaspora of the dangers of US power. In a 1926 newspaper column Dunbar-Nelson observed that "the dark nations are [was] having a hard time" at the expense of US foreign policy. Writing about developments in Liberia, Haiti, and the Virgin Islands, Dunbar-Nelson used the apt image of a sea creature as a metaphor for US actions. She asked rhetorically, "is it not true that the octopus is a white fish—reptile, creature of prey?" Like an octopus, US foreign policy, with its "slimy *white* tentacles" was busy "gripping, plunging, exploring, seizing, devouring all in its reach." Dunbar-Nelson closed her observations about race and foreign policy by reassuring her readers that the octopus, "surely . . . is white."[96] In order to not be devoured and strangled, Dunbar-Nelson encouraged her readers to intensify their understanding of the intention of US policies and to deepen their Pan-African consciousness.

Dunbar-Nelson regularly wrote and spoke about the racial economy of war, the appeal of Pan-Africanism, and the limits of white racial consciousness. Dunbar-Nelson also frequently used the history of black servicemen as a template for her observations. In a 1930 speech to a capacity crowd at the Los Angeles Civic Center, Dunbar-Nelson declared over and over again that war had nothing good to offer black citizens. The postwar Dunbar-Nelson now preached that war was not a ticket to freedom. War was the antithesis of freedom: "Clear-eyed, the Negro stands now and sees war for what it is,—an economic conflict. Greed and capitalism, reaching out to acquire more and yet more—and little ones of the earth, the peasant and the proletarian—and the mass of Negroes is both—[are] but the infinitesimal grains of black powder which fire the big Bertha of commerce."[97] In her Los Angeles speech, Dunbar-Nelson invoked a more radical and populist tone. She called for African American and white workers to unite through a shared history of wartime mistreatment. She ridiculed the greed that contributed to the Great Depression and the continued profiteering of arms merchants.

In order to explain why military participation did not produce racial equality, Dunbar-Nelson deconstructed how whites portrayed and treated the black soldier. One tactic used by the United States was to completely erase the history of black bravery. In her April 1926 "Une Femme Dit" column she pointed with humor to US efforts to deny Revolutionary War hero Crispus Attucks's blackness. She noted sarcastically about the Attucks debate: "Indian or a Spaniard . . . or a dark Yankee . . . But a Negro? A historical error. Let us draw a deep breath of relief. The supremacy of the white race has been saved."[98] Three months later in another column Dunbar-Nelson compared the treatment by France and the United States of its service men. "France," she wrote, "praises her black troops, and gives them full credit for their valor and heroism." The United States, on the other hand, "lynches hers, and tearing the uniform from their crippled forms, bids they forget they were once men."[99] Dunbar-Nelson devoted substantial time to the misrepresentation and mistreatment of black military men because she wanted to forestall black interest in war. In a March 1928 "As in a Looking Glass" column, she observed that "down to the bed rock it would seem that the country does not wish to arm Negroes, does not want Negro soldiers." This rejection, she concluded, was "a very fine thing for the Negro," because, "who wants to lay down his life" for the "white man's many quarrels."[100] The black citizen who was once enchanted by the call of military service would now seek a new duty as a citizen of the world and guardian of the peace. Dunbar-Nelson applauded the New Negro who "begins to see that what affects humanity of the darker skin everywhere, must affect him here on this continent"[101] and who would "keep the keel of the ship of state steady and true."[102]

"Harlem John Henry Views the Airmada"

Dunbar-Nelson combined peace advocacy and world-mindedness in her 1932 poem "Harlem John Henry Views the Airmada." Dunbar-Nelson wrote the poem, which is laced with black spirituals, in a mere two hours while she waited for a bridge game with fellow clubwomen to begin. Dunbar-Nelson remarked in her diary that writing the poem left her "limp as a rag," though the highballs served during the bridge game refreshed her.[103] Printed in the *Crisis* on the eve of the 1932 Geneva Disarmament Conference, her poem was hailed as an "epic Negro peace poem."[104] Peace advocates hoped that the much championed Geneva

Disarmament Conference would place strict limits on the building of new navy and air fleets and forestall the practice of war profiteering. Dunbar-Nelson's verse served as a paean to those universal goals. It also set the fight for disarmament squarely in the realm of black concern and history.

In the poem Dunbar-Nelson transforms the mythic black folk hero John Henry into a critic of the postwar arms race. Folk ballads about John Henry usually portrayed him as a superhuman, hardworking, steel-driving railroad worker. These images aimed to bring pride and glory to the backbreaking contributions of black workers to the building of America's infrastructure. Through her writing, Dunbar-Nelson relocates John Henry's fame and glory in his ability to see through the subterfuge of modern industrial capitalism and war. When "Harlem John Henry hears the sinister drone of sextuplets of planes" it makes his "soul flow to the past." Harlem John Henry reviews the history of slavery and war and warns black workers against once again becoming cogs in the wheels of the military machine. The jarring sounds of the warplanes, "the fierce horse hiss above the sky," resurrect not memories of patriotism but "cruel corsairs of foul, slave-weighted ships" and "deep-throated wails from black, stench-crowded depths." Harlem John Henry remembers "Crispus, Smiting a first wild blow for Liberty," and the "jingo jabs" of the Spanish-American War. As the airmada of warplanes "make dark the air" over the Hudson, "Harlem John Henry stands with lifted face" and memorializes those who "stumble[d] . . . from France and Flanders Field, Back from the mire and rats and rotting dead." He asks, "was that in vain?"[105]

Alice Dunbar-Nelson clearly feared that it could be. She worried that Americans in general and black Americans in particular could too easily forget the costs of war. As Harlem John Henry laments: "Must beauty die once more, slain o'er and o'er in stupid, senseless rage?" With her poem Dunbar-Nelson redeployed the icon John Henry in order to set a new path for black manhood and, in this way, a new direction for interwar era politics of racial justice and peace. She hoped to erase any remaining thought that war could be fruitful. Black Americans' gallantry was now to be measured based on the courage to look at war with a sober mind and pronounce it inimical to humanity. To never let war again "insult the quiet of spring."[106]

Improving the odds that peace-mindedness could supplant war-mindedness required that Dunbar-Nelson also turn her attention to the attitudes of white peace women. In a fall of 1928 "As in a Looking Glass" column, Dunbar-Nelson reported the unwillingness of white women, in attendance at an interracial meeting in Pennsylvania, to talk with honesty about race. In relief to white women's reticence to speak forthrightly, Dunbar-Nelson made clear that "it was the colored women . . . who kept the conversation on a frank and open plane, who struggled the hardest to prevent the conference from degenerating into a sentimental admiration society." Praising the work of black women who were in attendance at the conference, Dunbar-Nelson indicated that without black women's scrutiny and supervision, such gatherings could become shams. As Dunbar-Nelson observed, "it takes real courage . . . to stick to the cold, hard unsentimental facts, and to pay homage to the God-of-Things-As-They-Are."[107]

Dunbar-Nelson's courage, her transformation from a war patriot to a war critic, did more than mimic the overall postwar move of black Americans away from militarism. Dunbar-Nelson's writing, speeches, and organizing directed the trend and kept the role of women in it alive. Dunbar-Nelson hoped that by providing the nation with a looking glass that reflected the reality of middle-class black women's experiences and thoughts on war, a sharper and clearer picture of the path to peace and freedom would emerge.

Jessie Fauset

Jessie Fauset was born in 1882 in Camden County, New Jersey, and raised by her father, Redmon Fauset, a circuit minister with the AME church. An honors graduate from the select Philadelphia High School for Girls, Fauset's entrance to Bryn Mawr College was blocked by Bryn Mawr president M. Carey Thomas, who feared that "Southern girls" would withdraw from the elite private school if Fauset was matriculated.[108] "Exiled" from Philadelphia, Fauset graduated Phi Beta Kappa from Cornell in 1905 and then taught at the famous M Street High School in Washington, DC, from 1905 until 1919 when she began her paid employment with the *Crisis*.[109]

For more than fifteen years, Jessie Fauset contributed to the life of the *Crisis*. Her leadership in the magazine, behind the scenes and as a regular contributor, gave Fauset influence over the many thousands of readers drawn to the publication. And as one of the few African American women who actually traveled to Africa during the 1920s, Fauset helped to bring the continent to her readership, framing Africa as both a growing symbol of race unity and strength and of American and European excess and imperialism. In 1919, *Crisis* editor Du Bois recruited Fauset, whom he had known since 1903 and who had been a contributing writer since 1912, to be the magazine's first literary editor. For the next eight years, Fauset identified and promoted the leading writers of the Harlem Renaissance, including Langston Hughes, Jean Toomer, Countee Cullen, and Claude McKay. In this way and others she influenced the literary taste and caliber of the *Crisis*. Although the job of literary editor was significant, scholars now concur that Fauset's role was even wider as she regularly took on the day-to-day running and promotion of the magazine. For instance, when Du Bois was called to France to investigate the conditions of the black troops, Fauset took over as general managing editor for the duration of his five-month absence. During the time of Fauset's tenure, the *Crisis* reached the homes of 110,000 readers.[110]

A reading of Jessie Fauset's writing for the *Crisis* from 1915 to 1925 and her 1924 novel, *There Is Confusion*, reveals how African American women influenced New Negro consciousness on war and peace and Pan-African dialogue. Fauset helped develop postwar ideals of engaged internationalism and her writing conveyed the complexity involved in African American women's rethinking of their place in the postwar world. Not surprisingly, World War I influenced Fauset's writing for the *Crisis* and provided the context for her first novel, *There Is Confusion*. Starting with her September 1915 essay "Tracing Shadows," *Crisis* readers traveled with Fauset as she exposed the racialized parameters of the war and the new possibilities and new limits it presented African Americans in their search for democracy and a place to call home. In Paris on a scholarship when Germany declared war on France, Fauset was on a train when she first heard about the outbreak of war from "a polyglot lady of no fixed nationality."[111] From this point on Fauset became an analyzer of the impact of war on ideas of national identity, race, and gender. She chronicled and championed the Pan-African Congress movement, which was revitalized by the war. And through her frequent and far-ranging book reviews, she brought the literature of and about black nations like Haiti and Liberia to the black imagination.[112]

Fauset's contributions to children's literature, like her contributions to the *Crisis*, sought to formulate an appreciation of world-mindedness. Soon after the war, Fauset, Du Bois, and Augustus Dill launched a *Crisis* publication for young adults—the *Brownies Book*. A magazine "designed for all children, but especially ours," twenty-four issues were published from 1920 to 1921. Fauset wrote hundreds of pieces for the magazine, from reviews of global children's games and songs to her regular column "The Judge." In one typical column, the Judge reprimands a young African American member of the Court of Children for arrogantly stating that he was better than a delegate from China. "But I am an American. I'm better than they are. I'm the way they ought to be." The Judge responds, "What you are saying is the kind of thing that sets the world by its ears, that makes war, that causes unspeakable cruelties."[113] Fauset's work on the *Brownies Book* represented a spirited part of her postwar desire to help shape black peace and transnational consciousness. Fauset's subsequent writing continued to examine African Americans' relationship to US nationalism and to propose new alliances of belonging with people from non-Western worlds.

"Nationalism and Egypt": Gender, Race,
and Pan-African Consciousness

Fauset's April 1920 six-page essay "Nationalism and Egypt" published in the *Crisis* was one of her first articles to examine the war's influence on the future of black nations and to promote a Pan-African ideal. It also signaled her effort to analyze women's connections to postwar political developments. In the article Fauset reports on the struggle between Egypt and its colonial ruler, Britain, over the issue of representation at the 1919

Paris Peace Conference. The British insisted that only delegates selected by the British government be officially acknowledged. Egyptians, who had elected their own delegation of Muslims and Christians from various class backgrounds, protested the actions of the British. The United States, Fauset reported, supported Great Britain's position. The British responded to public protests by brutally attacking the popularly elected Egyptian delegation. Most interesting in Fauset's essay is how she situates women in the struggle against European empire and in the postwar construction of Egyptian nationalism. Fauset designates a street protest by three hundred upper-class Cairo women who supported the banned delegation as the most poignant symbol of the relationship between British imperial power and the eruption of Egyptian pride. By reporting on Egyptian women surrounded by bayonet-wielding British soldiers, Fauset connects colonial rule with efforts to restrict and suppress women's freedom, movement, and self-expression. After educating her *Crisis* readers on the Egyptian struggle for self-rule, Fauset beckons them to new consciousness as she asks: "who doubts that Egypt is really speaking for the whole dark world?"[114] With "the scene being staged for the greatest and most lasting conflict of people," Fauset posits women as central to the act of resisting empire and demonstrates that struggles for national liberation can transform women's roles.[115] Fauset honors the daringness of "women of the darker races" as they break with the class-laden social codes of public propriety. With this brief yet instructive mention of Egyptian women's protest, Fauset momentarily encodes Pan-African unity and political will with the face of female agency.[116]

Reporting on the 1921 Pan-African Congress

In 1921, Jessie Fauset attended and reported on that year's Pan-African Congress proceedings, which took place in London, Brussels, and Paris. Her lengthy essay, "Impressions of the Second Pan-African Congress," captures the continuing development of Pan-African consciousness and black critiques of World War I and colonialism. As Fauset states early in her essay, the "basic motif" of World War I "had been the rape of Africa." And the portion of the congress held in Belgium proved to be particularly illustrative of the historical and ongoing exploitation of black nations for white gain. Fauset described her visit to the Congo Museum and how "for the first time in my life I was able to envisage what Africa means to Europe." Viewing the museum's collection from "edible plants," to "fine grained mahogany as thick as a man's body is wide," to "skins, and furs, gold and copper" and musical instruments, Fauset saw with her own eyes "the sources from which so many Belgian capitalists drew their prosperity."[117]

But, of course, the Pan-African Congress sought to contest the continued misappropriation of black lands and peoples. Two years after the Versailles Peace Treaty and the 1919 Pan-African Congress, it was increasingly clear that the war and the Wilsonian pledge of self-determination were not intended to end European colonialism or American racism. This failure of the war, though, did help generate the growth of a transnational black political consciousness and a "black and yearning world." As Fauset wrote at the finish of the London portion of her trip, during which "men from strange and diverse lands," like South Africa, Jamaica, Sierra Leone, and Largos, "came together": "Not one of us but envisaged in his heart the dawn of a day of new and perfect African brotherhood." In her essay's conclusion, Fauset considered the work left to be done at the end of the days of meetings. She talked about the need to continue to build a strong organization. She urged Americans to learn more languages so that people could converse more freely. She called for patience, noting that nothing "can be righted in a day nor in a decade." Most interestingly, in her closing summation Fauset endorsed the development of an aggressive Pan-African community that might, paradoxically, generate cosmopolitan understanding:[118] "All the possibilities of all black men are needed to weld together the black men of the world against the day when black and white meet to do battle. God grant that when that day comes we shall be so powerful that the enemy will say 'But behold these men are our brothers.'"[119]

Fauset's reporting illuminates the dominance of male leadership in the Pan-African Congress of 1921. In previous congresses, African American women from Anna Julia Cooper to Addie Hunton had admonished male Pan-Africanists to remember that women must participate in the movement if it was to be successful. Interestingly, Fauset's own writing on the congress undersells the presence of the women who participated. Masculine constructions of Pan-Africanism, of the bringing together of a "spectacular brotherhood," seemed to cloud even Fauset's ability to champion the participation of women in the 1921 congress as she had earlier championed the participation of Egyptian women in freedom struggles. Although the central goal of Pan-Africanism was the development of a transnational black community and consciousness, the construction of that consciousness upon the measurement of manhood seemed to result in the sidelining of women. The participation of ICWDR member Helen Curtis and white Hull House founder and NAACP advisory member Florence Kelley received scant mention in Fauset's reporting. Fauset, herself a delegate representing the Delta Sigma Theta Sorority, made no mention of her own speech in Brussels in which she chronicled the achievements of black educational institutions in the United States. Nor does she acknowledge her talk in Glasgow in which she proclaimed that black women's clubs were the "great moving force behind all the movements for emancipation."[120]

Visiting Algiers

The absence of African women from the 1921 Congress required Fauset to ask the male African delegates to "carry a message of friendship and encouragement to African women."[121] By 1924 she had her own opportunity to create a communion between North African women and black women in the United States. As part of a six-month study and leisure trip to Europe, Fauset and artist friend Laura Wheeler Waring visited Algiers. From this trip Fauset produced two articles. The first article, "Dark Algiers, the White," appeared as a two-month serial in the *Crisis* accompanied by sketches by Waring. Through this article Fauset sought to bring her readers "behind the veil" by sharing her and Waring's experiences as "dwellers in Africa," a place they reached after a twenty-eight-hour boat ride on a "sea that smiled and faintly rippled." According to Fauset, the boat ride began to "roll back the curtain which separated our known from the unknown."[122]

Whereas in her reporting on the 1921 Pan-African Congress Fauset had emphasized the exchanges of men, in Algiers, by contrast, Fauset sought to create a Pan-African understanding for her readers through centering her reporting on the lives of women. At first when she arrived in Algeria, Fauset recorded disappointment because she found Algerian streets full of "children, boys, and men, men, men."[123] Yet, upon closer examination and foot travel into the streets of the Kasbah, Fauset finally found the Dark Algiers she was looking for, the women of North Africa. Fauset strives through the sketches of the diverse women she meets to transform Africa from a "dreamland" to a reality. She gives her readers images of veiled and unveiled women; young and old; poor and prosperous; women who venture into public and ride the bus unescorted; women traveling under the watchful eyes of men; women adorned with ankle bracelets; and collectives of women gathered around cooking fires attending to the day's news and household chores. As well, she attempts to move her reader past the cliché of exotic orientalism that often accompanied the image of veiled women. To do so Fauset used the trope of domesticity to try and establish a bond between an elderly veiled woman she met on a bus and her *Crisis* readers. Fauset writes of the interaction on the bus: "Before we ourselves descended an old woman came and sat opposite and we found a chance to examine her face veil. It seemed to be made of a piece of soft embroidered muslin shaped very much like the white apron a good American housewife sometimes assumes on a leisurely afternoon."[124] Through this use of the trope of domesticity Fauset hoped to extend Pan-African unity and community more directly to middle-class African American women. In attempting to foster a community of likeness of mind between the women who occupied the unfolding Pan-African world, Fauset questioned the masculine framework of Pan-Africanism. Yet, as symbols of women's domestic sphere, the muslin veil and the housewife's apron at the same time represented the limits of women's influence.

Fauset's descriptive act, in fact, gestures toward the very dilemmas black women faced as they attempted to fashion a role for black womanhood in the international movements of the time. On the one hand, Fauset's trips to Europe and North Africa symbolized the possibility to her readership of expanded female mobility; on the other hand, Fauset's reference to the domestic sphere through the image of the apron points to the very tentative nature of a Pan-African female ideal. For decades, middle-class black women had used the language of domesticity and social motherhood to authorize their role in the social and political advancement of the race. They argued that because they were entrusted to raise the future leaders of the race, then they should also be entrusted to participate more directly in other political arenas. Black women had also employed the language of domesticity to challenge white America's insistence that black women were not capable of achieving maternal virtue or true womanhood. Fauset's incorporation of the apron and the veil, then, signals the ongoing need middle-class black women felt to lay claim to the domestic sphere even as they sought active and equal participation in the increasingly international protest politics of the interwar period. With the prominence of the masculine language of Pan-Africanism and the political purchase of domesticity, black women like Fauset struggled to figure out how best to situate women in this shifting, expanding, and treacherous social and political culture.

There Is Confusion: Searching for a Public Stage

The Gordian knot of gender, race, and nation surfaced again in Jessie Fauset's 1924 novel *There Is Confusion*. Released shortly before Fauset's trip to Europe and North Africa, the novel, the first of the Harlem Renaissance to draw wide public circulation and acclaim, received favorable review in the *New York Times Book Supplement,* the *London Times,* and in various publications of the black press. Its publication was also the catalyst for the large formal gathering of black and white intellectuals that many deem the symbolic launching of the New Negro literary movement.

There Is Confusion concerns the postwar coming to consciousness of Joanna Marshall, a young middle-class black woman hoping to find personal fulfillment as a classical dancer and performer. The novel explores how the Great War changed Joanna's outlook and the lives and expectations of the African American men and women around her. Joanna's love interest, Peter Bye, goes off to war where his dignity is assaulted by the long arm of American racism. The other female characters in the novel,

Maggie Ellersley and Vera Manning, come to new race consciousness through the war. Maggie, like the real-life Addie Hunton, is one of the few black women allowed to go to France to take care of the black American Expeditionary Forces. This experience amplifies her love of her race and her conflict with America. Similarly, the experience of the war allows Vera to realize that the value of her ability to pass for white was not to be found in the act of assimilation, but in her ability to go underground in the South and investigate the racist rampages set off by the war.

Joanna's desire since a young age was to "dance the dance of nations." To fulfill this dream, Joanna shoulders the abuses of Jim Crow as she moves through New York City and Philadelphia in search of the best teachers and venues for her pursuits. Finally, Joanna receives her break when she performs the starring role of America in the District Line Theater production of *Dance of Nations*. Joanna gets the job as a last-minute replacement for a white recalcitrant dancer. The only hitch is that Joanna is required to wear a white mask. On opening night the white audience, suspecting that Joanna was black and hence unfit to represent America, demanded that she pull off her mask and reveal her *real* face. In response to this demand, Joanna attempts to claim her place in the nation through lecturing her audience on the history of African American male military service. She admonishes the audience: "I hardly need to tell you that there is no one in the audience more American than I am. My great-grandfather fought in the Revolution, my uncle fought in the Civil War and my brother is 'over-there' now."[125] At this moment the limitations of the public stage for black women began to unfold for Joanna. Even though the audience rewarded her with a standing ovation and the show moved to Broadway, the public demand that she legitimate her claim to American citizenship and nationhood dismayed her. Subsequent interactions with Jim Crow theaters and white performers confirmed Joanna's growing belief that her authenticity would always be contested on the national stage. Joanna's youthful determination that individual black female exceptionalism could prevail over the color line weakened as she awakened to the insidious power of Jim Crow. Her claim to citizenship through the wartime patriotic contributions of the men of her race proved insufficient in melting the color line. At the conclusion of *There Is Confusion*, Fauset has Joanna walk off the stage and turn her back on the white nation. Joanna, who throughout the novel resists marriage to Peter Bye, marries him in the end, refocusing her energy and talents on the private sphere of the family.

Through the character of Joanna Marshall, Fauset inspects the dilemmas black women faced as they attempted to rethink postwar America and their role in it. Fauset, who became increasingly "disenchant[ed] with a United States that could not accept 'difference in its citizenry,'" returns Joanna to the sphere of the black home in an attempt to create a concept and experience of citizenship, nationhood, and belonging that respected black womanhood.[126] Read together, Fauset's journalism on Egypt, Algeria, and the Pan-African Congress movement along with her first novel presented postwar readers with the details of the Gordian knot of gender, race, and nation faced by women of color. As Fauset chronicled, the war along with the protest movements that developed from it refigured and complicated the ever-shifting puzzle of black female independence.

Fauset spent much of her life, through her literary and political career, her studies and international travel, attempting to envision forms of black independence that worked for women as well as men. And through female protagonists like Joanna, Fauset looked to bring attention to the war's impact on women. Central to these efforts was the issue of home. In her reporting on the evolution of postwar Pan-African consciousness, Fauset helped foster the understanding that for African Americans the experience of home, belonging, and freedom might be most likely to occur in a transnational context and outside of white scrutiny. Writing about the 1921 Pan-African Congress, Fauset rejoiced that "the rod of common oppression had made them feel their own community of blood, of necessity; of problem." In the postwar world race could be a tool of oppression, but it could also create new possibilities. Again remarking on the postwar rise in Pan-Africanism, Fauset asked, "What can be more fascinating than learning . . . that the stranger across the seas, however different in phrase or expression, yet knows no difference of heart?"[127]

At the end of her novel, when Fauset reunites Joanna with Peter, she seems to conclude that black women can only experience love and personal fulfillment within the sphere of black home life. This return to the domestic sphere can be understood in many ways. Some may see it as a retreat.

Others may see it as a measure of the harm caused by postwar racism on the lives of black women. Though it may seem as if Joanna's world and her mobility are shrinking, if we read the home to which Joanna returns as being the transnational and Pan-African home Fauset experienced and reported on throughout her career, than Joanna's world beyond the white stage is a potentially expansive and joyful one. In writing about meeting delegates from throughout the Pan-African world, Fauset exclaimed: "We clasped hands with our newly found brethren and departed, feeling that it was good to be alive and most wonderful to be colored."[128] Like the muslin veil and the apron, the conclusion to *There Is Confusion*, Joanna's marriage to Peter Bye, is a complicated symbol. Although Joanna seems to finally experience the wholesale acceptance of her black womanhood she was looking for in Peter's love of her, the reader is left to reconcile on her own Joanna's departure from public life. This domestic move, then, symbolizes both the postwar significance of national and transnational black unity and community building and the potential circumscription of black women's lives. Through Joanna, Fauset mobilized black women's wartime experiences to make the point that war does not resolve questions of race, gender, democracy, and citizenship or deter the spread of colonial power. What war does is complicate black women's desire for and obtainment of freedom.

Like her protagonist, Jessie Fauset found the postwar world to offer both opportunities and restrictions. The war and its aftermath gave Fauset opportunities to travel and the responsibility to shape black thought on national and transnational issues. At the same time, Fauset herself found her life circumscribed and her right to occupy the social and political spaces of the nation contested. In her March 1922 essay, "Some Notes on Color," Fauset wrote that as "a colored woman, neither white nor black, neither pretty or ugly . . . of fair manners and deportment . . . in brief the average American done over in brown," she did not receive even common courtesy from white men on the subway, and she was unable to dine in restaurants of her choice.[129] Perhaps more significantly, after she left her *Crisis* position in 1926, Fauset was unable to secure a job in publishing even though she offered to "work at home" if her race was a problem.[130] In the end she was forced to return to teaching, an occupation she did not like. And unlike Joanna, Fauset did not marry until she was forty-seven years old.

Although Fauset's relationship with the WILPF was not as extensive and direct as Addie Hunton's and Alice Dunbar-Nelson's, she did support the organization in various ways as exemplified by her welcoming remarks to the 1924 International WILPF Congress held in Washington, DC. Throughout the years, Fauset offered to lend her name to the WILPF and to write pieces of literature for various WILPF campaigns. As a writer for the *Crisis*, Fauset's perspectives on race, war, peace, transnationalism, and gender would be familiar to the many WILPF members who helped to found the NAACP and who held memberships in the interracial organization. As a daughter of Philadelphia, her observations on the racial restrictions of the city would be of potential interest to those inclined to be concerned about the practice of Jim Crow in the North and in the city of the national WILPF office. And when her third novel, *The Chinaberry Tree*, was to be published WILPF member, author, and Fauset friend Zona Gale was asked to write the introduction to it. Fauset and her ideas, in other words, would be no stranger to many white women in the WILPF. Additionally, as a contemporary of Hunton and Dunbar-Nelson, Fauset's ideas and friendship with both women would no doubt influence them. Dunbar-Nelson and Fauset were known to play bridge together. And Hunton and Fauset convened over issues facing the NAACP, worked together in the Circle for Peace and Foreign Relations, and shared a commitment to make the Pan-African movement a success.

Addie Hunton, Alice Dunbar-Nelson, and Jessie Fauset spent the postwar years attempting to create an awareness of the relationship between the mistreatment of black women and the politics and culture of war. When Dunbar-Nelson wrote, "Cano, I Sing," the poem cited at the beginning of this chapter, she sought to place the history of black women into the collective memory of war and the unfolding movements for peace. Through their persistent struggle to create openness for the participation of African American women in the social and political spaces of the nation and world, Hunton, Dunbar-Nelson, and Fauset raised important questions about the practice of democracy, the experience of war and citizenship, and the path to peace and freedom. They worked to open the postwar public sphere to the equal participation of African American women for they believed that black women's perspectives were vital to the success of the search for peace and freedom. To win, as Addie Hunton called it, the Galilean struggles before the world, black women's experiences of the multiple injuries of war needed to be recognized and addressed.

2

Race and the Social Thought
of White Women in the WILPF

THE WORK of Rachel Dubois, Emily Greene Balch, and Anna Melissa Graves demonstrates that many white women of the interwar WILPF also consciously and constantly negotiated race as they constructed responses to war and national strife. Although their thinking differed at times, they held in common the understanding that unenlightened Victorian racial attitudes played a significant role in maintaining the conditions that created war and hindered efforts to establish domestic as well as international peace. The white women of the WILPF who challenged scientific racism employed a range of counter-ideas about race as they moved to create a new, more equalitarian and peaceful world order. They endeavored to replace the nation's allegiance to nativism and Anglo-Saxon superiority with a new attachment to the concepts of world-mindedness and cultural pluralism. They hoped to diminish the idea that race was biological and a determining factor of intelligence and morality by moving people toward a more cosmopolitan approach that believed in the collective humanity of the world's people.

The Rise of Scientific Racism

According to John Higham, by the turn of the century two currents of regressive race-based thinking dominated the intellectual foundations at work in the United States. A defensive form of racial nationalism aimed to control the "enemy" within the nation—immigrants and African Americans—whereas an aggressive racial nationalism worked to rally and validate US expansionism abroad.[1] With a new wave of immigration under way in the 1890s and US military intervention in Cuba and the Philippines, the nation recommitted itself to using race to explain and legitimate domestic and foreign policy. Scientific racism most often served as the scaffolding that both the defensive and aggressive forms of racial nationalism clung to. Proponents of scientific racism believed that race was a measurable and quantifiable biological fact. Race, they proposed, determined and explained everything about a person or a society from intelligence and temperament to fitness for civilization. With race a fixed and unalterable quality, proponents of scientific racism stood firmly in their observation that the superiority and inferiority of the races were objective and natural facts. They used this "science" to argue for limitations on immigration, state-endorsed eugenics programs, and US military and economic expansionism abroad. To scientific racists, slums were products of poor breeding, not products of complex economic factors. Immigrants were feared because they might "pollute" the Anglo-Saxon stock.[2] Sociologists and economists like Madison Grant, author of *The Passing of the Great White Race or the Racial Basis of Europe History*, Lothrop Stoddard, author of *Clashing Tides of Color*, and Edward Alsworth Ross, leading proponents of scientific racism, promoted a conflict-ridden social Darwinian model of social relations.[3]

During the 1898 Spanish-American War, Theodore Roosevelt used the language of social Darwinism and Anglo-Saxon superiority to encourage and manage the US takeover of the Philippines from Spain. According to this logic, a race-based hierarchy would always exist and those located on the highest rungs of the ladder needed to take charge of those less capable. "Fitness," Theodore Roosevelt believed, was not a universal human quality but an achievement attainable by only a select few. In championing US expansionism Roosevelt argued, "Fitness [for self-government] is not a God-given, natural right . . . but comes to a race only through the slow growth of centuries, and then only to those races which possess an immense reserve fund of strength, common sense, and morality.[4] The language of Anglo-Saxon superiority and masculine benevolent responsibility was exemplified in Rudyard Kipling's famous 1898 poem "The White Man's Burden" and embraced by leaders like Roosevelt. Though writing within a British context and with an ironic tone, Kipling's work created a moral argument suitable for US expansionists who wanted to soften, though not necessarily completely reverse, the use of scientific racism. According to the masculine benevolence argument, the United States was a nation made up of selfless white men, willing to do the protectionist work that other nations were not manly enough to consider.[5] Although perhaps a little softer in its rhetoric, underlying the idea of the white man's burden remained a belief in Anglo-Saxon superiority—a chauvinistic reliance upon white middle-class American ideals of civilization, progress, and competence as the yardstick by which other nations were to be measured and controlled.

Modernists like Dubois, Balch, and Graves turned to culture to challenge the claim that race was a quantifiable, scientific, and biological category of difference. Many anthropologists, sociologists, economists, and philosophers "interpreted character, morality, and social organization as cultural, rather than racial, phenomena."[6] By shifting frameworks, people like Franz Boas and Ruth Benedict sought to remove the negative signifying power of race and interrupt the belief that there existed identifiable "pure" racial groups.[7] Less willing to see the world in Victorian grand binary narratives of male and female, good and evil, savage and civilized, modernist social scientists disputed the view of race as biology and as a prescriptive determinant of social relations. Women like Dubois, Graves, and Balch advanced the culture paradigm as a component of their vision of an interdependent world humanity. As peace historian Sondra Herman writes, peace progressives of the interwar period "combined a dynamic interpretation of human nature with a rejection of conservative Darwinism and competitive individualism."[8] Peace progressives believed that the formula for creating a world of peace and freedom rested upon the ability to, at least in part, redirect people's adherence to racialized hierarchies. This change in racial thought had to occur in the day-to-day interactions of people as well as in the workings of nation-states. Cosmopolitan theories of interdependence and mutuality directly contrasted with and contested scientific racism's adherence to a conflict-ridden social Darwinian concept of social relations as promoted by people like Teddy Roosevelt and Madison Grant.

The critique of race as science did not produce one coherent new understanding of race. Instead, as Peggy Pascoe argues, it helped foster a consortium of new ideologies that she labels "modernist racial ideologies."[9] Although they shared a criticism of scientific racism and wanted to form a "dissident consciousness" that was critical of "race-coded civilizations," racial modernists' alternative understandings were constantly in formation and not always internally coherent.[10] The necessity to address the writings and power of people like Madison Grant and Lothrop Stoddard was clear. What it meant to promote race as culture, instead of race as biology, was not as clear. Modernists did not necessarily get rid of the concept of race, but they tried to denaturalize it and remove its power to stigmatize and oppress. Like other racial modernists, Dubois, Balch, and Graves's ideas about race developed and shifted over time and in response to the specific context of the issue under study. As racial modernists and peace activists, their critical race consciousness developed with, through, and as a part of their embrace of community internationalism. Collectively, the community- and internationalism-based racial modernism projects they engaged in encompassed four oftentimes interdependent projects. First, they challenged national legislation that used scientific racism to maintain racial hierarchies. Second, they deconstructed the idea of the natural superiority of Anglo-Saxons by shifting scrutiny from the practices of racialized ethnicities and racial minorities to the practices of whites. Third, they suggested a link between the promotion of race-based thinking and the development of hawkish nationalism. And finally, they advanced the humanist concepts of interdependence and world-mindedness.

In her study of the role of race in the development of feminist thought from the 1840s to the 1920s, Louise Michele Newman reminds us that for many white women in Western Europe and the United States the language and practice of imperialism or expansionist racial nationalism proved useful to their advancement. Newman argues that "imperialism provided an important discourse for white elite women who developed new identities for themselves as missionaries, explorers, educators, and ethnographers as they staked out new realms of possibility and political power against the tight constraints of Victorian gender roles."[11] Newman concludes that these Victorian era feminists embraced the ideology of Anglo-Saxon superiority in order to argue that white women were fit for citizenship and equality with the men of their race. These women joined their male counterparts in advancing the concept of the white man's burden and used colonial projects to open up spaces for white middle-class women's move into a variety of public spheres. Women like Dubois, Balch, and Graves believed they had a different burden. As critics of nationalism and imperialism, their burden entailed exposing the paternalistic racism in which the white man's burden was moored while galvanizing people to contest the drums of war and to promote a vision of a new world steeped in a race-sensitive humanist mutuality.

The women in this chapter responded to the overtly racist discourses of the early part of the twentieth century in a variety of ways as they went about their work as educators, reformers, political agitators, and internationalists. At times some of them advocated cultural pluralism and the celebration of the varieties of racial/ethnic groups as a counter discourse to the 100 percent Americanism movement.[12] They all advocated forms of transnationalism, the replacement of nationalism with a dedication to world-mindedness. As community internationalists they believed that social and economic adjustments were central to the building of a long-lasting faith in human unity. In this way they supported the cultural anthropologists' claim that what were understood to be biological race differences were in fact signs of social/cultural differences and economic disparities. Conflict in society was not inevitable but the result of flawed thinking that led to a belief in social hierarchies.

If we are to understand the lives of individual women and the project of peace and freedom that consumed so many during the interwar years, we must consider white WILPF women's relationship to the looming race issues of the time period. Without such a consideration we will continue to develop an incomplete understanding of the motivation and intent of women who involved themselves in the women's movement for peace during the interwar years. The efforts of Dubois, Balch, and Graves to transform the way Americans thought about race after World War I indicate that the women's peace movement was much more self-conscious about the relationship of the structures of race to the future of peace than most historians have thought. Their intelligent and methodical challenges to early twentieth-century American racism reveal that the women's peace movement, at least the WILPF, was a key partner in interwar era projects to contest racism in the nation and to advance new ways of thinking about the heterogeneity of the nation.

Rachel Davis Dubois

Rachel Davis Dubois is considered by many to be the initiator of intercultural education and its "most prominent champion."[13] In the aftermath of World War I, Dubois designed school programs intended to create a new generation of students interested in cross-cultural and cross-racial friendships. Through the achievement of world-mindedness, Dubois believed that students would best be able to resist future calls to war. In the racist and nativist climate of the postwar industrial society, Dubois promoted the idea that culture could serve as a safe "mediator of social relations and structures."[14] To convince students that all human beings were equal and valuable contributors to society, Dubois championed the "cultural gifts" educational model. Through increased familiarization with the accomplishments of different racial and ethnic groups in the areas of music, science, and literature, students would learn to appreciate and trust people who differed from them. As Dubois was well aware, the fear of difference was sanctioned around the country. Searing and angry debates roared in her home state of New Jersey over black children's efforts to integrate public swimming pools. At the same time, Catholic teachers were being fired from schools, and twenty-two states banned the teaching of "foreign" languages in primary school. As an antidote to this fear, Dubois felt that public educational institutions must lead efforts to change adolescents' beliefs about ethnic and racial difference.[15]

Progressive Era reformers placed significant value on the role that education and middle-class values could play in the transformation of society. This investment in the power of education extended past the Progressive Era as antiprejudice education reform took shape in the 1920s and 1930s. As historian Diana Selig documents, the teaching of tolerance emerged at the same time as and in response to the increase in nativist and racist sentiment and legislation—witnessed most stunningly in the passage in 1924 of the National Origins Act. Pluralism, she documents, came into fashion and the teaching of the "cultural gifts" of immigrant groups and African Americans served as an "antidote" to the expansion of nativist attitudes.[16] Concomitant with the theories of cultural anthropologists like Franz Boas, behavioral social scientists placed increasing interest in the psychological development of children. Studies by researchers like Bruno Lasker emphasized that racial prejudices were not innate, and hence that children could be taught to appreciate, not fear, the heterogeneity of the United States. The science of child development and the promotion of cultural pluralism converged in the endeavors of people like Rachel Davis Dubois. Selig emphasizes that the concept of cultural pluralism did not appeal only to a small group of the intellectual elite, but rather became a part of popular culture. The rise of the Parent Education Movement helped secure an avenue for the dissemination of this new thinking and practices. The 1926 inaugural issue of *Parents Magazine* endorsed the teaching of tolerance to children. Immigrant groups and African Americans paid particular attention to the content of public school texts and agitated for curriculum reform in hopes of improving the representation of the cultural, political, and intellectual achievements of the people they represented. In 1926 Dr. Carter G. Woodson instituted Negro History Week, which marked one of the concrete developments that emerged out of interwar era educational reform.[17] "Resistance to racial prejudice," Selig writes, "became an emblem of the modern mother or modern teacher."[18]

The promotion of internationalism in schools was also supported by various segments of postwar America. Female peace reformers worked with schools and educators to establish an appreciation of world-mindedness among young people. Women like Dubois designed educational resources that offered educators strategies for adopting and implementing the more globally minded curriculum. At the 1919 International Congress in Zurich, the women of the WILPF spoke boldly about the role of education in inculcating a new worldwide value system. In their drive to "establish a new basis for human civilization," they believed that peace women "must begin with the education of the people." This global educational reform with the aspiration of "creating an international spirit" would begin with removing from textbooks all materials that "injure national pride" and that "arouse hate and scorn for foreign people." In its place material that "makes the young" familiar with the "evolution of peoples," and that develops a "world consciousnesses" including the "duties of world-citizenship" should be taught. The WILPF women encouraged the use of comparative studies and the teaching of literature from around the world. They proposed that the "sacred task" of reeducating the world could only be entrusted to "men and women of high moral and intellectual standing."[19] As one of those entrusted with the responsibility of reeducating the world citizenry, Dubois's educational reform work placed an examination of ethno-racial difference at the center of education for peace-mindedness.

Dubois was born in 1892 in Woodstown, New Jersey, to a family of devout Quakers. Raised on her family's farm, Dubois notes in her autobiography that her interactions with the Italian immigrants who worked for her family provided her with one of her earliest forays into the study of immigrant cultures. Dubois attended a local Quaker high school until 1910 when she left to attend Bucknell College. Immediately upon graduation in 1914, she was hired to teach algebra, biology, and United States history at Glassboro high school, located not too far from her hometown. She served briefly as the acting principal of Glassboro High after the standing principal was enlisted into World War I. In 1915 she married Nathan Dubois, a man she had been acquainted with for many years. In the summer of 1920 Dubois decided to take a hiatus from teaching in order to gain real-world experience, and dedicated her time and talent to the cause of peace. Upon her return to teaching she launched into her public career as an innovator in intercultural and antiprejudice education.[20]

In the summer of 1920 Dubois attended the All Friends Congress in London and in December of 1922 she participated in the Conference for a New Peace, sponsored by the International WILPF and held at The Hague. These two events gave Dubois an exceptional opportunity to become acquainted with the postwar campaigns under way to meet the needs of war-torn Europeans. She learned about the prevalence of child hunger, the spread of tuberculosis, and the impact of the blockades on Germany's citizens. Dubois remembers the London Quaker Congress for awakening her to the impact of the war on European citizens and for raising her awareness of the racial dynamics of colonialism. The harsh criticism the Indian Yearly Meeting representative delivered about British colonial power in India advanced Dubois's consciousness about race, imperial power, and war. At the same time, the derogatory remarks delivered by the white representative of the South African Yearly Meeting about black South Africans drove Dubois to think more critically about the dynamics of race within her own political milieu.

The 1920 and 1922 conferences also brought Dubois into contact with renowned women peace activists. Dubois's introduction to the workings of the WILPF began on her boat travel to Europe. Though Dubois and her friend Clarinda Richards were traveling second class, Jane Addams ignored the ship captain's admonishment that second-class passengers were not allowed entrance to first-class staterooms. And Addams insisted that Dubois attend the daily meetings held in Addams's first-class quarters. Participation in these confabs, during which the US delegation prepared for the congress, introduced Dubois to the politics and personalities of the movement. Once at The Hague, Dubois was greatly impressed by the "tone of harmony" and "mutual acceptance" she observed among the 350 Hague delegates who gathered from various countries.[21]

Yet it was a trip to the American South in 1921 that Dubois credits with most significantly shaping her emerging educational philosophy and her thinking about the role of peace, race, and ethnicity in US and global education. The Philadelphia Friends Yearly Meeting sent Dubois to the South to visit a black high school for which they were considering raising funds. It was a life-changing experience. This trip began Dubois's introduction to the dire conditions under which poor Southern blacks lived and it expanded her understanding about how the systems of racial hierarchy worked in the United States. She, for instance, witnessed the ubiquity of segregated bathrooms and segregated train cars. Once she arrived at the Martha Schofield School in Aiken, South Carolina, Dubois was asked if she would make an address the following day to the school's five hundred students. Having recently returned from the International Friends Congress in London, which included a side trip to Germany to visit the feeding stations erected to alleviate the poverty and hunger of Germany's children, Dubois decided to speak on the horrors of war. Davis remembers that at the end of her talk, the students applauded her speech by singing "Ain't Gonna Study War No More." As moving as her time was at the Aiken school, according to Dubois her real transformation took place during her return train ride to Philadelphia. On the train, she read an article by W. E. B. Du Bois in which he insisted that racism was the underlying cause of war and that "the damn pacifists don't know it." Du Bois's article, the "Dilemma of the Negro," published in the *American Mercury,* brought the strands of Dubois's interests together and offered her a way to combine her work for peace and her growing concern about racial and ethnic strife. Dubois now understood that if racism was the root cause of war, then she could best advance the cause of peace through challenging the nation's attachment to xenophobia and antiblack attitudes. Raising better educated children would assure a better chance at social cohesion for future generations.[22]

A dedicated pacifist, peace activist, and feminist, during her hiatus from teaching Dubois donated her time to emerging organizations including the WILPF. In particular, Dubois assisted the WILPF in expanding its membership and appeal among the nation's youth. Dubois guided the WILPF as it embarked on a series of peace education programs for grade schools and high schools and she took charge of organizing Junior International Leagues for the organization. In the first year of her youth campaign, she reportedly spoke to ten thousand children and young adults about the importance of the peace movement and its relationship to their future. She also helped create a Washington, DC, clearinghouse for youth groups interested in peace reform. In 1923 Dubois became a member of a three-woman Auto Peace Caravan that traveled throughout Maryland, New Jersey, Pennsylvania, and Virginia, making "quite a stir" as they promoted disarmament and internationalism. In the single town of Shamokin, Pennsylvania, the women delivered their message to three thousand people gathered in the town's theaters and silk mill.[23] Fueled by the energy and excitement of the Auto Peace Caravan, that same year Dubois collaborated with WILPF executive secretary Amy Woods to write an eight-session high school program entitled "War and Its Consequences."[24]

After her four-year break from teaching, Dubois returned to her vocation with new goals and a new emerging educational philosophy. She began her work to popularize school assembly programs in world-mindedness and cultural pluralism, now believing that such work was vital to the cause of peace and racial harmony. As part of her efforts to encourage cross-cultural thinking, Dubois designed programs for use in high schools, including two programs published by the national WILPF office, *Education in World-Mindedness: A Series of Assembly Programs* and *Contributions of Racial Elements to American Life,* which were published in 1928 and 1930.[25] Dubois's influence, though, went beyond the students in her classrooms and the women of the WILPF, who used her pageants on world-mindedness in their branches. During the 1930s and 1940s, she became a leading figure in nationwide efforts to popularize intercultural education.

Education in World-Mindedness

Dubois premiered her cultural educational approach in 1926 when she launched the first of her two morning assembly programs at her Woodbury, New Jersey, high school. These innovative programs would come to be known as the Woodbury Plan. She tested the *Contributions of Racial Elements to American Life* project from 1926 to 1929 and in 1927 she unveiled her second program, *Education in World-Mindedness.* Through requiring students to participate in regular school assembly programs and auxiliary classroom assignments over the length of the school year, Dubois believed teachers could alter the prejudicial attitudes of their students. She prompted educators to revolutionize the psychology of their students, who Dubois feared without intervention would go "out into life with ready-made associations between the concept of race and those of moral value."[26] Anecdotal evidence from high school teachers illustrated to Dubois that educational intervention was needed. As one Buffalo, New York, teacher reported, by the time her students reached high school they demonstrated an attitude of "'one-hundred percentism,' an attitude which takes the idea of Nordic supremacy and our own national superiority simply for granted."[27]

The *Contributions of Racial Elements* program aimed to kindle in students "sympathy," not "pity" or "toleration."[28] To accomplish this goal, Dubois immersed students in the histories, customs, and accomplishments of racial/ethnic groups overlooked or misrepresented in educational environments. This approach, it was believed, would mediate students' drive to ostracize and stigmatize racial and ethnic groups. Believing that the average student was "wandering, culturally speaking, in a No Man's land," Dubois wagered that with intense immersion in the cultural contributions or "cultural gifts" of the nation's diversity of people, students would be less inclined to develop racist and nativist attitudes.[29] Although Dubois designed her programs primarily to rehabilitate the attitudes of white students, she also hoped that the programs would contribute to the self-esteem and pride of students who were members of stigmatized racial/ethnic groups. In her efforts to dislodge the social Darwinist discourses of racial hierarchies, Dubois devised programs that she anticipated would illustrate to her students that "no one race is any better than any other race." Dubois combined the elements of cultural immersion, participatory democracy, and student-led experimentation through her assembly programs with the aim of establishing an "ethical tone" and a "tradition of solemnity."[30]

The programs consisted of three approaches offered to generate a synergy that could lead to attitudinal transformation. The intellectual approach involved acquainting students with new knowledge about the contributions of marginalized peoples. The second approach—what Dubois labeled the emotional approach—was intended to hook students' interest through their observance of demonstrations, readings, or performances by special guests invited to the schools. And the third element, the situational approach, looked to give students an opportunity to practice and apply their new knowledge and new attitudes. Schools were encouraged to intensely focus on about five racial/ethnic groups during the school year. Each selected group should receive at least one month of designated study. In the spirit of pragmatism and efficiency, Dubois anticipated that schools would select groups to study based on the degree to which particular racial/ethnic groups were the targets of discrimination. In a 1934 program published by her Service Bureau for Education in Human Relations, Japanese, Chinese, Jews, and African Americans were selected as the groups most in need of attention, whereas, for instance, the study of the cultural contributions of the Norwegians and the Greeks could be forgone.

To be effective, the programs encouraged all school departments to take part. Students in geography made detailed maps of the countries under study. The music department taught students songs relevant to that month's area of focus. Students listened to Italian operas, black spirituals, and Native American chants. In the domestic arts students made peanut bread using flour supplied by George Carver of the Tuskegee Institute. The same students might also be introduced to the history and art of Japanese flower arrangement. A history class might study the genesis of the Seder, an art class might make Seder plates, and each homeroom might participate in a Passover dinner. Guest speakers and performances featured prominently in the programs. Students at the morning assembly programs might hear lectures on the history of Japanese sports, view a flower-arranging demonstration, or watch a Chinese opera. Dubois wanted her students to hear from the people she believed were the best representatives of each group. In order to control the content of the material presented by guest speakers, she screened the guests herself to make sure they matched her criterion. Dubois brought to her New Jersey school many of the inspiring talents of the Harlem Renaissance. Author Jessie Fauset talked about her work, painter Aaron Douglas discussed his art and inspirations, and poets Gwendolyn Bennett and Georgia Douglass Johnson read from their works and discussed the craft of poetry. To move students from intellectual knowledge to improved social aptitude, students hosted teas for all the visiting guest performers. The teas ostensibly gave students opportunities to "practice . . . the social amenities" involved in civil cross-cultural interaction. Further practice in interracial or cross-racial sociability occurred as students participated in field trips designed to introduce them to new communities and neighborhoods. For instance, students took trips to synagogues, attended dinners held by the Japanese-American Young Peoples Group, and watched a Chinese puppet show at the Chinese Community School in New York City. A Washington, DC, school using Dubois's program visited the art department at Howard University.[31]

At the end of the 1934 Woodbury Plan program in Englewood, New Jersey, high school teachers surveyed seniors to assess if the year of cultural immersion made a difference. The students' reports indicated at least a general improvement. Their remarks ranged from surprise that "foreigner[s] could be quite so human," to the more cosmopolitan attitude that "we are all human beings." Some students stated that although the programs had not exactly convinced them to see their "foreign neighbors as brothers," it had given them a "swell start." From the faculty's perspective, the programs improved the atmosphere in the classroom. The lecture by Jessie Fauset, reported the chair of the literature department, improved the interracial climate in the classroom, produced "increased confidence of the Negroes in themselves," and led to increased interest by all students in reading black literature.[32]

Dubois's "cultural gifts" programs placed primary focus on the psychology of racial attitudes. One criticism of the programs was that they gave little attention to the issues of political power, legislation, or the history of race politics in the United States. The closest her programs came to addressing the political context of race was in her instruction that homeroom teachers lead discussions about "American concepts" like "fair play" and "justice."[33]

Teaching Through Pageants

Dubois tested her second school assembly program, *The Education in World-Mindedness*, in Woodbury, New Jersey, from 1927 to 1928. This program promoted Dubois's understanding that race antagonism was a root cause of war. Engaging W. E. B. Du Bois's challenge to pacifists, Rachel Dubois instigated a program that linked enlightened racial awareness to the production of a belief in a common humanity and the practice of peace. In the introduction to the published program, Dubois outlined her lofty goals. She believed that the pageant could lead students to create "a new faith in man; a new social justice at home and abroad; a new conception of the democracy of nations, and a new belief in World Brotherhood."[34] To match the high idealism of her world-mindedness program, Dubois opened the school year with a pageant. Pageants were distinguishable from plays by their epic and flamboyant nature and their unabashed attempt to propagandize. As propaganda, pageants were popular among suffragists, black activists, and peace activists for their effectiveness in promoting causes. Along with historical figures, pageants often featured characters that represented large ideals like "Truth, Freedom, and Beauty."[35] The 1927 inaugural pageant performed at Dubois's New Jersey high school was indeed extravagant and epic. The three-scene pageant, entitled "World Unity," sought to explain the causes of war and racial strife. Central to it was an exhortation on race and physical difference. The prologue to the play announced the vast intentions of Dubois's undertaking:

> Then know all ye students of High School, in this year of Assemblies,
> We shall unfold the story of Man through the countless ages
> How he was torn and divided through war and misunderstanding;
> With Good-will and Education, how he must be re-united,
> To guide him back to *World Unity,* in her garden of Peace and Plenty.[36]

The pageant's featured characters included Mother Earth, Education, Good-Will, Hunger, Ignorance, Superstition, and five Primitive Men. In the opening scene of the pageant, Mother Earth and her five "brown-skinned" male children play happily and fearlessly as they enjoy the bounties of nature that surround them. This peace and unity ends when Hunger enters the stage and rips the children from Mother Earth, scattering each of them to different corners of the world. Forced to adapt to their new environments, the children's physical features transform and over time they change from brown-skinned men into a "Chinaman," an "American Indian," an "East Indian," a "Nordic," and a "Negro." Once separated and scattered, the men lose their moral compass. They are taken over by Ignorance and Superstition, and begin to engage in warfare. But, just when things look bad, two young sisters, Education and Good-Will, dressed in majestic white robes, ceremoniously enter the stage and reform and reunite the brothers. Yet before true peace can be achieved there is one more piece of work still to be done. As the East Indian exclaims: "Brothers! But how can we be brothers who are not alike? . . . This man is white, this red, this black! I cannot understand."[37] At this moment in the pageant, the Nordic and the Negro step forward to explain the changes in their appearance—how they transformed from two brown-skinned bothers to one who was white and one who was black. The Nordic explains:

> I am a *Nordic!* When gaunt Hunger tore Us from our Mother's side he bade me go North for my food where snow lies thick and white . . . My brown skin whitened, my dark hair grew fair, and my nose lengthened, that the frozen air might be made warm in passing through my nostrils.[38]

And the Negro explains:

> I, too, have changed from him whom once you knew, for Hunger pointed South, I went forth into the Jungle and the heavy heat of the earth's fertile places where the sun burned my brown skin to black . . . my nose grew short, the nostrils wide and flaring, so the scant and feeble air might reach me easily.[39]

Cowritten with her sister, Ruth Edward Davies, the pageant approaches the issue of racial difference from a cultural anthropological perspective. By explaining perceivable racial differences as simple physical variations that developed as a result of migration and environmental adaptation, race becomes a benign marker, not an indicator of intelligence or morality. In keeping with the modernist approach to race, Dubois directed her students to comprehend the physical differences and heterogeneity of the world as nothing to be feared and as nothing more than environmental necessity. By selecting the *Nordic* and the *Negro* brothers to deliver the message that differences in skin color and facial features were benign, Dubois made clear her assessment that the most important attitudes to alter were those held by white students about African Americans. In order for the world to return to its original state of peace, the brothers needed to be enlightened that race was not a sign of evolutionary status or a legitimate ground for division or violence.

Gender also factored into the pageant. On one level, the gender politics of the pageant are obvious: men make war and women make peace. When race is coupled with gender, the gender contours of the pageant deepen. By adorning the sisters in white robes, the pageant encourages a strong connection between the moral qualities needed for peacemaking and the image of the white female reformer and peacemaker so present in the popular culture of the 1920s. By having the sisters represent Education and Good-Will, Dubois relies upon and furthers the ideals of a racialized social motherhood. White women are allowed into the public spaces of society because they promise to act as teachers and nurturers of the civic soul and mind. By dressing the sisters in the solemn and gallant white robes, Dubois memorializes the fifteen hundred white women who marched through the streets of New York City in 1914 announcing their claim to the moral high ground by standing up and calling for an end to war. Dubois came of age under the shadow of esteemed white women like Jane Addams and felt firsthand the self-empowerment gained by rallying people across the country to stand up for peace. W. E. B. Du Bois may have inspired Rachel Davis Dubois to become committed to the fight against racism, but for Dubois white women remained, consciously or unconsciously, central to the project for postwar progressive achievements.[40] In spite of her promotion of white womanhood, Rachel Davis Dubois gave children and teachers new and groundbreaking tools, opportunities and outlooks that they could put to work in their interpersonal efforts to resist the anti-immigrant, racist, and nativist sentiments alive in the United States in the 1920s.

Dubois's leadership in antiprejudice education brought praise from many, but it also brought threats of job loss and censure. The harsh attitudes held by some about her educational philosophy reflected disdain for her promotion of pluralism and her involvement in the peace movement. She was red-baited by the Woodbury American Legion and the Daughters of the American Revolution for her promotion of peace ideals among high school students. Her commitment to teaching students respect for all people brought the charge that she promoted "disloyalty" and "sexual promiscuity." In response to her work, the Board of Education and American Legion attempted, unsuccessfully, to have her fired. Though she was not fired, local scrutiny of her programs did result in the canceling of a black history program. The night before its premiere, Dubois's principal announced that the school board refused to allow the program, which was designed by and was to showcase the school's black students, to take place. In particular, the school objected to the proposed recital of James Weldon Johnson's "God's Trombones" by Ed Davis, a senior student. The censuring and ostracizing Dubois and her students received did not go unnoticed. The *New York Times* covered the story and she received letters of support from, among others, W. E. B. Du Bois and A. Philip Randolph.[41]

Dubois left her teaching position at New Jersey's Woodbury High School in 1929 to pursue a doctorate degree at Columbia University's Teachers College and in 1934 she founded the influential Service Bureau for Education in Human Relations and became its first executive secretary. The Service Bureau served as a clearinghouse for teacher education materials and teacher trainings designed to improve the antiprejudice approaches used in schools throughout the country. In 1933, in preparation for opening the Bureau, Dubois taught the first course in the country on intercultural education to students at the Harvard extension school. The Service Bureau was endorsed by a range of organizations, including the AAUW, and received funds from the Works Progress Administration to hire people to interview students about their racial beliefs.[42] Starting in the mid-1920s she regularly attended the national meetings of the NAACP, which helped her form enduring friendships with key people in the struggle for racial equality. Among the people who became her compatriots were Crystal Bird Fauset, James Weldon Johnson, William Pickens, and A. Philip Randolph. James Weldon Johnson, among others, served on the advisory board of the Service Bureau. In the mid-1920s Dubois and W. E. B. Du Bois began a lifelong friendship that would entail numerous opportunities for them to collaborate on educational projects. In 1927 she participated in the Pan-African Congress held in New York City, organized by Addie Hunton. In 1931, at the behest of Du Bois she was elected to the editorial board of the *Crisis*. In 1935, she became the first national director of the Progressive Education Association's Commission on Intercultural Education. During the New Deal era she was a lead consultant on the twenty-six-part CBS Radio series *Americans All—Immigrants All*. From 1935 to 1945 she published two books on intercultural education.[43] In 1941 she helped found the Workshop for Cultural Democracy. In later years she would join the board of the American League for Puerto Rican

Independence. And in 1965 Martin Luther King Jr. hired her as a member of the Atlanta staff of the Southern Christian Leadership Council. He strongly believed in the model of interracial dialogue she had developed over the past four decades and thought it would be a useful tool for the civil rights movement. Dubois lived to be 101 years old. She kept up her commitment to peace reform and racial unity throughout her life, hosting multiracial group discussions in her home and staying active in issues like housing justice.[44]

Differences of opinion existed among social scientists and educators about the best approach to use when educating students about race and ethnicity in the 1920s and 1930s. Those who disdained the melting pot approach, assimilation, and scientific racism held varying ideas about the content of the alternative approaches that should be offered. Bruno Lasker, Rachel Dubois's friend and at times harsh critic, offered that although there were "unending texts" about neighborliness, world friendship, and "adventures in brotherhood," much of the material was overly sentimental, religious, and pedagogically untested.[45] He also calculated that many school plays trafficked in "unmitigated snobbery," where "America" is performed by the "prettiest and most popular pupil."[46] Lasker's biggest concern was that the cultural pluralism or cultural gifts approach did little to raise students' awareness or concern about the actual structures of racism in society. Lasker found the educational approach championed by Dubois potentially dangerous because it usurped attention from the politics and history of discrimination, leaving untouched, for instance, the segregated school systems and English-only laws that encouraged bigotry. Selig offers that Dubois's "softer approach" may have been a result of the political prosecution she faced during her early advances to teach about peace and cultural diversity. It may also have been a pragmatic decision driven by her need to secure funding for the work of her pioneering agency, the Service Bureau for Education in Human Relations.[47] Another warranted criticism of the cultural pluralism model is that it reified particular paradigms of race, class, and gender. The focus on "great achievements" and middle-class values central to the *Contributions of Racial Elements Program* left no room for championing the histories of the working people filling the factories and neighborhoods of America in the 1920s. In reaction against the erasure of ethnic identity promoted by nativists, cultural pluralists often sentimentalized immigrants and erased all signs of intragroup difference. And the promotion of group particularism inherent to the pluralist approach increasingly came under scrutiny during the era of Nazi fascism as progressives raised concern about promoting static ideas of "ethnic particularism" and called instead for a promotion of the idea of "democratic citizenship."[48] Even with these criticisms, Dubois's work marked a radical departure from the calls for immigrants to assimilate and the efforts to limit immigration all together. Her promotion of African American history and culture in public elementary and high schools was a direct affront to the insidious idea that girded so much of US interwar racism—that African Americans had not contributed and were incapable of contributing anything of value to what was understood to be the best of American culture. Her cultural gifts project sought peace through the dismantling of scientific racism and through the building into a new generation of youth a yearning for connectedness, not conflict.

Emily Greene Balch

"[A] social age, an age of fraternal relations between men, an age in which exploitation of class by class, of rivalry of nation with nation is outgrown, an age in which the unlikeness of other races will be conceived as much of an asset as the unlikeness of wind and string instruments in a symphony." Emily Greene Balch offered these anticipatory words to the female student body of Wellesley College assembled for her 1916 Presidents' Day speech. In her speech, "What It Means to Be an American," Balch outlined her utopian vision of a world cradled in harmony, respect, and understanding.[49] To achieve this utopian vision, Balch engaged in the complex work of questioning the meaning and function of race in the United States during the first half of the twentieth century. Balch's tireless efforts to expose US imperialism and racialized nationalism mark her as a key interwar era critic of US trends and policies. Over the next decades Balch would tackle the role of race in US domestic and foreign policy. Her work represents a sophisticated effort to expose the racial structures of

US nation building. Balch represented the vanguard of WILPF leadership committed to voicing concern about the racial superstructure of US history, culture, and politics. In collaboration with women like Jane Addams, Dorothy Detzer, and Addie Hunton, Balch looked to educate the WILPF membership, the nation's citizens, and the nation's leaders on the folly of race-tainted politics.

In her article "Miscegenation Law, Court Cases, and Ideologies of 'Race' in Twentieth-Century America," Peggy Pascoe argues that the twentieth-century transformation from the discourse of scientific racism to the modernist discourse of race was not the smooth, complete, unified, or overnight accomplishment depicted by many historians. Pascoe is concerned that historians' treatment of challenges to biological theories of race approach the period in an oversimplified manner, as if "when modern social science emerges, racism runs out of intellectual steam."[50] As a corrective, Pascoe calls for more case studies of the ways in which people confronted and reshaped the language and landscape of racial thought. The early twentieth-century and interwar era women's peace movement offers a compelling and underexamined example of the shifting ground of American racial politics for which Pascoe calls. In particular, the life of Emily Greene Balch deserves attention. Balch, a Wellesley College professor, lifelong member and president of the WILPF, and Nobel Peace Prize winner, attempted throughout her career to redress the legacy of racism in the United States and to replace scientific racism with ideas of cultural pluralism and world-mindedness. From her 1910 pro-immigrant book, *Our Slavic Fellow Citizens,* to her diplomatic work on US policy in Haiti and Liberia in the 1920s and 1930s, Balch scrutinized and criticized the influence of racialized thinking on US domestic and international politics. For Balch, thinking critically about race was often a vital part of thinking about peace and social transformation. Her efforts were deliberate and persistent. Balch's work to expose the presence of racism in US domestic and foreign policy marks Balch, and by extension the US WILPF, as key contributors to the modern era challenge to race-based US expansionism.

Balch's ideas on race were stimulated by an alchemy of influences and confluences as the conditions of the pre–World War I years found many progressives engaged in intellectual and political exploration. Balch's thinking about race developed through her involvement with fellow progressive social reformers, her training in the new social sciences, her early socialist associations, and her leadership in the women's peace movement.[51] Like many community internationalists, Balch applied the ideals of the social settlement house movement to her work on international arbitration and transnational community building. Balch witnessed in social settlement houses the proof that ethnic, racial, and national differences need not result in strife. And she shared with Jane Addams a strain of cosmopolitanism that believed in the human potential to peacefully negotiate differences. Four hundred social settlement houses existed in the United States during the first decades of the twentieth century. Weekly, nine thousand people used Hull House, the Chicago settlement house run by Balch's fellow WILPF leader Jane Addams.[52] The daily work of the social settlement houses appealed to Balch's pragmatism and suggested that the social ills of war, nativism, and racism could be overcome. Balch knew that "goodwill, high purpose, [and] devotion to great ends" was not enough. She worked with others in the WILPF to develop "concrete devices" and "elaborate arrangements" that could produce achievable forms of world community.[53] The community building undertaken by social settlement houses proved to Balch and others that race was social, not biological, and that world harmony was achievable.

Balch is frequently memorialized for her Kantian cosmopolitan transnationalist vision captured in her oft-quoted motto, "Lovers of Our Land, We Are Citizens of the World."[54] Balch's transnational dream is usually linked to her involvement in the gendered women's peace movement, namely, the WILPF. Yet, although the internationalism central to the WILPF and to many middle-class women's associations that developed during the Woman's Era indeed shaped Balch, that transnationalism or community internationalism was also deeply steeped in conditions of race that embattled the United States. In other words, Balch's internationalism was not just a product of the women's peace movement. Balch's world-mindedness celebrated the potential of women united in fellowship and activism, but it also contended that the economic and racial structures that produced divisive nationalism needed to be examined and eviscerated.

Born to a well-established Unitarian New England family two years after the end of the Civil War, Balch's educational path followed that of many bourgeois women of the time period. She attended Bryn Mawr College and in 1890 received its European Fellowship, which allowed her to study the French charity system. She studied at the University of Chicago, a leading institution of the newly developing social sciences, and also at the University of Berlin, where she was required to petition the male professors and student body for permission to attend. In 1896 Balch participated in the International Socialist Workers' and Trade Union Congress in London. Back in the States she pursued workers' rights and socialism further. In 1903 she helped found the Women's Trade Union League. Three years later she publicly announced herself a socialist and in 1909 organized the "Socialism as a World Movement" conference with Vida Scudder. Though she helped found the Denison House, a social settlement in Boston, in 1892 and served as its first director, Balch was not content with philanthropic efforts. She believed that "the point of leverage" was to teach "social economic subjects."[55] Her belief in education over social service or good deeds work set her path for the remainder of her life. As a researcher of immigrant life, a professor at Wellesley College, and an intellectual leader of the WILPF, Balch strove to shape the intellectual mind of the nation.[56]

Emily Greene Balch's training as an economist and sociologist along with her almost half a century membership in the WILPF provided her with ample opportunities to examine the racial foundations of anti-immigration sentiment, economic imperialism, and colonization. She served as president of the US section of the WILPF from 1929 to 1933 and as a member of its International Executive Committee from 1919 to 1922 and from 1929 to 1932. In 1946 she received the Nobel Peace Prize for her work exposing the tenets of nationalism and for promoting transnational community building.

Race, Immigration, and Nation

Balch's first scholarly monograph, *Our Slavic Fellow Citizens*, published in 1910, established Balch as a leader of Progressive Era struggles to disentangle notions of racial fitness from the requirements of citizenship.

The content of her five-hundred-page study of Slavic immigrants also announced Balch as an advocate of unrestricted immigration, intermarriage, and the emerging concept of race as culture. Balch researched the book for two years, traveling throughout the United States and Austria-Hungry in a journey to understand the originating cultural practices and values of the new Slavic immigrants arriving and settling in the United States, the impact of immigration on those practices and values, and the social and political conditions Slavic immigrants faced once they reached the United States. In the United States her travels took her to mining villages in Pennsylvania and Colorado, tenements in New York City, Texas and Connecticut River Valley farm communities, and industrial centers like Pittsburgh and Bridgeport.[57]

Our Slavic Fellow Citizens was one of the very first detailed immigrant studies. As such it helped establish the model for future works on immigration and it continues to be referenced as a significant intervention in the debates over immigration that captivated the United States during the early twentieth century. One reviewer in 1911 hailed the book for its ability to appeal to both academic and popular audiences and praised it as "one of the most sympathetic and interesting studies of immigration."[58] A 1973 review essay, "How Historians Have Looked at Immigrants in the United States," pointed to Balch and *Our Slavic Fellow Citizens* as one of the key works that helped institute the "friends of the immigrant" approach to immigrant studies in direct contrast to the restrictionist and assimilationist writing that was popular at the time of Balch's pro-immigrant publication.[59] Writing in 2005, Robert W. Dimand called Balch one of the "outstanding American economists" and credited *Our Slavic Fellow Citizens* and a 1912 speech Balch delivered to the American Economics Association with redirecting the discourse on immigrants and immigration dominant within the field of economics.[60]

Balch's study of Slavic immigrants appeared in the middle of a national maelstrom over the role and future of immigrants in the United States. A steady rise in immigration began in 1897 and reached its zenith in 1907 with the first decade of the twentieth century witnessing nine million new immigrants entering the country.[61] This period of immigration was marked not only by the pace of immigration, but also by the national origins of the new arrivals. The overwhelmingly Southern and Eastern European heritage of the new immigrants provoked a racist backlash. This new round of immigration stimulated a comingling of racial "science" and racist nationalism into an effort to pass restrictive anti-immigrant legislation and forestall the adoption of ideas of cultural pluralism or "friends of the immigrant" sentimentality. Racial nativists wanted to keep the nation "one-hundred percent American," which meant white, and white meant of Northern and Western European origin. Under the guise of Anglo-Saxon superiority, scientific racism, and nativism, restrictionists like Madison Grant argued that unlimited immigration would lead to the literal demise of the so-called white race. If the new Eastern and Southern European immigrants, many of whom were Catholic and Jewish, were allowed to mix with the "natural stock" of the nation, Grant argued, a new "lesser race" would be produced, resulting in the death of the "Anglo-Saxon."[62]

From the 1870 Naturalization Act to the 1924 Johnson-Reed Immigration Act, legislation was used to define the racial shape of the nation. The 1870 Naturalization Act limited citizenship to "white persons and persons of African Descent." From 1887 to 1923 there were twenty-five federal court challenges to the Naturalization Act, including two Supreme Court cases by defendants who claimed that they were white, although the courts ruled that the defendant's national origin and so-called commonsense knowledge would deem them not white. The 1882 Chinese Exclusion Act reversed the patterns of Chinese immigration and legitimated generalized anti-Asian sentiment. The 1924 Johnson-Reed Act limited European immigration to 2 percent of the national origin group in the United States in 1890. This meant that "Nordic" or Anglo-Saxon Europeans who made up the major immigrant groups before 1890 were favored, and those perceived to be nonwhite and hence unassimilable, that is, the Eastern European, Slavic, and Mediterranean immigrants of the 1890s and 1920s, were restricted.[63]

Through *Our Slavic Fellow Citizens* Balch set out not to prove that Slavic immigrants were good candidates for assimilation, but to challenge the biologically based concept of racial or ethnic type central to anti-immigrant sentiment and politics. She reasoned that the most endurable

way to kick open the door to full citizenship for immigrants was by shut-
ting the door to the scientific racism that underpinned restrictionists' and
racial nativists' arguments. At the very same time that *Our Slavic Fellow
Citizens* captured in rich detail the daily customs of the Polish, Hungarian,
and Ukrainian immigrants she lived with, she warned her reader against
equating these practices with a knowable racial type or essence. Balch
attempted to disrupt the practice of ranking Europeans in a hierarchy of
racial desirability when she proclaimed that "there is no such person as
a Slav any more than there is such a person as a Teuton or a Celt."[64] With
these words she expected to forestall her reader's desire to glean some
essential truth about, for example, Polish coal miners in Pennsylvania, at
the same time that she directed her reader to question the popular assump-
tion of a stable transhistorical "Nordic" ascendancy. She shared with her
readers that she "[felt] a profound skepticism as to the value of generaliza-
tions in regard to the character of nations or races, more especially if it is
assumed that such characters are inherited and unchangeable."[65] Balch's
"profound skepticism" was of course rooted in her understanding that the
nation justified its disdain for the new immigrants hailing from Eastern
and Southern Europe, the Mediterranean, and Asia by arguing that non-
Nordic immigrants possessed inherently dangerous "racial qualities" that
would, if not restricted, dilute the quality of the so-called native stock and
result in race suicide.

The race suicide argument called upon popular fears of both a decline
in the family sizes of "Anglo-Saxons" and of potential increased sexual and
social intimacy with the new immigrants. Leading University of Wiscon-
sin economist and sociologist Edward Alsworth Ross helped establish the
concept of race suicide at the turn of the century. Ross warned that "Latins,
Slavs, Asiatics, and Hebrews"[66] were causing the "the submergence of the
'American' pioneer breed." In true scientific racism form, Ross used physical description when referring to the immigrant "threat." He warned of
people with "sugar-loaf heads, moon-faces, slit mouths, lantern-jaws, and
goose-bill noses" who allegedly swarmed the streets of industrial cities
driving down wages and threatening the future of all around them.[67] In
Our Slavic Fellow Citizens Balch addressed the popular contamination and
race suicide narratives by proposing that Anglo-Saxons would improve in

quality as a result of close contact with the new immigrants Ross demonized. Intermixing, Balch proposed, would rejuvenate the "rather sterile and inbred [Anglo-Saxon] stock" by adding "valuable varieties of inheritance to a rather puritanical, one-sided culture rich in middle-class commonplaces."[68] Balch's advocacy of intermixing was a bold position to take given the historical context. It pushed against the logic of scientific racism and it refused to endorse the less charged politics of assimilation gaining traction at the time. In their place, Balch dared to suggest that the qualities of the self-proclaimed dominant race would be better served not from less contact with the new immigrants, but through more contact. The nation, Balch theorized, would grow stronger in character and quality through the active promotion of racial/ethnic equalitarian social interaction and in the process destabilize the very idea of the Anglo-Saxon and Anglo-Saxon superiority.

With *Our Slavic Fellow Citizens* Balch began to advance the idea of race as culture. She believed this position would allow her and others to epistemologically and pragmatically contest forces like the Immigration Restriction League and supporters of Madison Grant. Her book established her as "a friend of the immigrant" in a time when labor unrest, urban chaos, and the demise of the so-called Anglo-Saxon were all blamed on the presence of non-Northern and non-Western European immigrants. Yet, even in the most radical of her proposals, like her support for intermixing, we see the residue of a science-based notion of race. Although Balch wrote in 1907 that "[g]roup types are perhaps quite as much products of social development and imitation, determined by historical causes economic and other," she left open the possibility that group types were also in part "the expression of innate qualities."[69] Still, even though she sometimes used words associated with racial science, words like *stock, breed, and inheritance,* Balch disputed the concept of a natural Anglo-Saxon superiority.

Balch aimed to reconfigure the dominant race ideologies adopted by everyday citizens, union organizers, eugenicists, college presidents, her fellow social scientists, and political leaders with her detailed descriptions of Slavic life in all its variation in Europe and in the United States. She aspired to help lay the foundation for a pluralist nation in which all people were equally welcomed and equally valued, not based on a demand for sameness, but on an appreciation for the unending variations of lifestyles produced by social and historical forces. In its very title, *Our Slavic Fellow Citizens*, Balch situated immigrants on an equal footing with all other people who were working the land, sweating in factories, and debating the future direction of the nation. Yet at times, Balch also ceded the moral high ground to the very immigrants who were so feared and maligned at the turn of the century. For instance, she challenged Americans to heed the conclusion of one Slavic leader who observed, "My people do not live in America. They live underneath America."[70]

Race, Gender, and National Character in Wartime

In her 1916 Presidents' Day address "What It Means to Be an American," delivered to Wellesley College students, Balch continued her attack on the nativism and racism that she felt left "poison . . . in our minds."[71] The speech expanded on themes she outlined in *Our Slavic Fellow Citizens*, and it linked the growing national dislike of racial and ethnic difference and growing class unrest with the war being waged in Europe. Addressed to the young white college women in her audience, Balch's words compel, in part, because she used the injury of race rather than gender as the nation's Achilles' heel. Balch challenged her female students to understand how racism worked and urged them to take up its eradication with the same conviction she felt. Though woman's suffrage was not yet a federal achievement, Balch understood the rising power available to educated young white women like those in her audience. She glimpsed the potential for their imprint on the future course of the nation and the world and hoped to persuade her students to turn their civic participation and dreams of democracy to the eradication of anti-immigrant sentiment and lawless racial violence.

Central to Balch's speech was the contention that democracy, freedom, and liberty were not accomplishments to be memorialized on Presidents' Day, but instead were contested and dynamic ideals yet to be achieved. Balch suggested to her audience that the task before the nation was to create a "liberty that is not a matter of form but substantial and real."[72] To prove that liberty, freedom, and democracy are a mirage for many living in the nation, one only needed to turn to the plight of the nation's poor and racially stigmatized. Balch pronounced that members of the working class were only "half free." They had the political rights of citizenship, but were forced into an industrial caste system that robbed them of social freedom and control over their labor. Compounding the demeaning and liberty-robbing conditions of industrial labor, Balch observed that racialized ethnic stereotypes further limited the promise of democracy and liberty for many. Americans, Balch lectured her female students, should be "mortified" to live in a country that mistreats Chinese and Chinese Americans and continues to promote "prejudice and class feeling for the newcomer." From the ridicule of Slavic immigrants for going barefoot in the house and the shunning of Irish women for wearing a shawl, to the embrace of racialized anti-immigrant epithets like "Dago," "Wop," and "Sheenie," Balch concluded that such attitudes compromised the nation's character and warranted radical transformation.[73]

Balch reserved her strongest criticism for the discrimination and violence that targeted African Americans. In her remarks she invoked the history of lynching to punctuate her point that the nation "harbor[ed] the ugliest types of racial prejudices and brutality and insolent lawlessness."[74] In the year preceding Balch's Presidents' Day speech, D. W. Griffith's landmark film *Birth of a Nation* appeared, grabbing public attention for its advancement of film technology and for its racist subject matter. The NAACP demanded the banning of the film because the film celebrated the Ku Klux Klan and depicted the KKK as the saviors of white womanhood. The film also portrayed black men during Reconstruction as shiftless, primitive drunkards unfit for the political rights won at the end of the Civil War. Griffith's racist version of the Reconstruction period garnered President Woodrow Wilson's approval and praise and a private White House screening. Ten days after the film opened in New York City, an interview with Jane Addams ran in the *New York Evening Post*. In her remarks, Addams protested the film for depicting African Americans as "grotesque and primitive and contemptible" and for its "glorification" of the KKK.[75]

Balch's speech extended Addams's critique of *Birth of a Nation* by calling for public accountability for the crimes of lynching and for unity and alliance building between African American men and white women. Instead of promoting a defensive racism through a narrative that promoted fear of black men, Balch lectured that the nation needed to ask African Americans for "forgiveness" for the bloody history of slavery and for ongoing white vigilantism. She directly contested D. W. Griffith's depiction of black male character as rapacious by recalling to her white female students that during slavery "white women and children were safe" in the hands of slaves "when the masters were away at the war."[76] Instead of fearing African Americans and black men in particular, Balch urged her students to work as allies in shaping a true democratic nation based upon "equal opportunity" for all. To build meaningful democracy and freedom, as Balch understood it, required that the history of lynching not be "overlooked or minimized." Balch lectured her audience that in the previous two decades almost thirty-five hundred people had been lynched in the United States and that "in the first nine months of 1914" twenty-seven lynchings had occurred, including the lynching of three women. In case her students thought the practice of lynching rested in the hands of a few renegade men, she made them aware that US railroads frequently "ran special trains—crowded with eager sightseers—to the place where a man was to be burned alive by the mob."[77]

In the conclusion to her Presidents' Day speech, Balch linked the ongoing race, ethnic, and class wars in the nation to the war raging in Europe. "How far is the tragedy enacting itself across the seas today due to the same evils which abound among us today?" she asked her audience.[78] This theme, the linking of local conditions of inequality to the global forces of war, echoed the founding principles of the WILPF: that peace and freedom were inextricably linked goals and attributes. In a 1915 article Balch wrote for the *Survey* she directly explored the impact of racial thought on the war in Europe. She concluded that "national vanity and national greed" stemmed from a philosophy of racialized exceptionalism and that this defensive and aggressive nationalism was one source of the war in Europe. This need to strengthen national borders and promote "contempt for those who differ from us," Balch proposed, "takes on a thousand forms."[79] One of those forms could be found in the domestic race politics saturating the United States. For Balch and the fledgling

WILPF, the unchecked nationalist qualities that produced domestic racial violence were the same qualities that promoted war.

In the United States Balch worried that citizens had become complacent not only about the antiblack, anti-immigrant, antiworker sentiment of the country but also about the "high responsibility" before the nation to help bring peace. She condemned the fact that the nation exported weapons and "made money out of the necessities of others."[80] Though the majority of her speech soared with harsh assessments of the state of the nation, she brought her thoughts to a close by invoking her pragmatist belief that another way was possible and necessary. Similar to D. W. Griffith, Balch believed the nation and the world were experiencing a new birth out of the combustion of war and racial and ethnic strife. Unlike Griffith, Balch sought reconciliation, a "newer and warmer tone," and a realization that we can bring "inspiration and joy" to each other.[81] Balch hoped that the female students in her audience would take up the work of reconciliation and build the "substantial and real" liberty she believed the time period called for. If African Americans had "a heavy count against the white man,"[82] perhaps white women could redress the sins of the founding fathers. Balch concluded that there was no "golden past" to celebrate on Presidents' Day and that answers to the race problems she outlined in her address were not to be found in the past, but in the potential of the young white women sitting before her.

Investigating Haiti: White Masculinity as the Black Man's Burden

In her Wellesley speech Balch hoped to inspire her white female students to use their education and sense of civic responsibility to help lay the foundation for a new world order free from the man-made rivalries of nation, class, and race. A decade later, Balch's investigation of the continued US occupation of Haiti served as a strong reminder of the depth of US investment in maintaining a corrosive race-based foreign policy and the complexity of the task she placed in the hands of the nation's women. In 1926, under the auspices of the WILPF and the leadership of Balch, an interracial group of five women and one man traveled through Haiti for three weeks. In 1927 a report of their findings, *Occupied Haiti*, was published.

The trip confirmed for Balch that race continued to strongly influence US foreign policy. She used the investigative mission, the subsequent report, and a meeting with President Coolidge as opportunities to challenge and recalibrate the nation's thinking about race, masculinity, and foreign policy. The WILPF's work on Haiti contested both the defensive and aggressive forms of racism and showed their interdependence.

In her book *Taking Haiti*, historian Mary Renda argues that the US occupation of Haiti powerfully influenced American culture, producing "new ways of understanding race, gender, sexuality and Americanness."[83] From white marines' and soldiers' letters home to family and friends to Eugene O'Neill's *Emperor Jones*, Haiti became an important symbol through which and against which Americans vetted their ideas about race and gender. For many the preponderance of writings generated by the occupation, which equated Haiti with voodoo, the primitive, and beastly lust, served to justify the US expansionist spirit. The occupation and the cultural fascination with Haiti facilitated by it emboldened a spirit of American exceptionalism and steeped that exceptionalism in the myth of benevolent white manhood. For others, including Balch, the intense political and cultural obsession with Haiti had the opposite effect, as it ignited "challenges to domestic relations of power" and produced anti-racist political alliances.[84] The occupation precipitated the formation of interracial alliances, dramatized the influence of Jim Crow racism on the US military machine, and accelerated critiques of the influence of race on US policy making.

Peace women recorded their concern with US intervention in the Caribbean and Central America more than a decade before the 1926 WILPF mission sailed for Haiti. In July of 1915, members of the WPP publicly protested the presence of US troops in Haiti along with US aggression and colonial aspirations in Nicaragua, the Dominican Republic, and Puerto Rico.[85] Emily Greene Balch began making requests in 1915 for a mission to investigate US activity in Haiti. In 1920, the US WILPF executive board officially went on record calling for an investigative mission to Haiti and stipulated that the mission include African Americans.[86] The 1924 WILPF International Congress held in Washington, DC, called for a New International Order and generated increased momentum for a thorough accounting of US economic and military aggression in Haiti and the Western Hemisphere.[87]

The interracial mission that traveled through Haiti for three weeks in February of 1926 built upon the interracial alliances and antiracist analysis trumpeted during the 1924 International WILPF Congress. The investigative team signaled the WILPF's deepening ties to black internationalists and the development of a female-based interracial internationalism. The Haiti mission included Addie Hunton and Charlotte Atwood. Charlotte Atwood, a teacher from Dunbar High School in Washington, DC, represented black clubwomen. The more famous of the two, Addie Hunton, joined the mission as a representative of the ICWDR and as national vice president of the NACW.[88] As a leader of the ICWDR and NACW Hunton fashioned the development of black feminist internationalism and encouraged alliance building with like-minded white women in the WILPF.

As the interracial WILPF investigative team traveled around the island meeting with officials and laypeople and studying the state of agriculture, health care, infrastructure, and US military practices, the WILPF group modeled a form of transnational diplomacy grounded in mutual respect and the principles of community internationalists. As community internationalists, women like Balch and Hunton believed that the lessons they learned as they attempted to work across lines of racial difference in the streets of Philadelphia or in the hills of Haiti held the nucleus to world peace. These local lessons of mutual respect and understanding, if adopted by national leaders, could help walk the world away from aggression and toward peace.

Balch realized that mutual respect seemed a distant hope when the military and political occupation of the island rested upon racist stereotypes. As she traveled through the island and met with white officials, Balch concluded that the "traditional" attitudes of white men stationed in Haiti were "intensified." White marines, especially those from the South, believed in white superiority and black inferiority.[89] In 1926 the status of US race relations continued to be embattled and bleak. In the South where most African Americans lived, lynching remained a national pastime, black economic outlooks stalled, and voting rights were provisional. Haiti, on the other hand, had for more than one hundred years been an independent nation led by French-speaking black elites. In the face of this evidence of black fitness for self-rule, Balch found that the occupying forces escalated their use of racial stereotypes. As she wrote in the opening pages of *Occupied Haiti:* "Of all the black man's burdens perhaps the most tragic is that the uncultivated white man finds him funny. All peoples who have known oppression suffer something of this—the Jew . . . , the Irishman, the educated Hindu (compare Kipling's Babus), but none in such measure as the Negro."[90]

Through her announcement and description of the black man's burden, Balch makes clear that the occupation served not only as a mechanism for expanding US economic and military strength but just as importantly as a mechanism for revitalizing and legitimating a transatlantic racist discourse. By finding black Haitians funny, the US occupying forces were invoking the vaudevillian stereotype of the middle-class dandy used during Reconstruction and in *Birth of a Nation.* The stereotype aimed to challenge and forestall the growing economic and political power of free blacks.[91] Balch knew that to end the occupation Haitians and their US allies not only needed to turn back the military and economic claws of the occupation, but also needed to turn around the race discourse. Balch calculated that in order to rescind the racist attitudes of the US military machine, the focus of scrutiny needed to shift from Haitian behavior to the behavior of the US occupying forces. To do so, Balch questioned the purported civility of white manhood by linking it with antimodern parochialism. She observed: "There are many white men who conceive of themselves as men of the world who yet find it impossible to take seriously any man of a darker race than their own."[92] With this comment, Balch elevated the status of black manhood, distanced white women like herself from the provincialism of US policy makers and military men, and advanced her belief in humanist internationalism.

The WILPF mission attacked the character of the occupying forces in a number of ways. In its report it documented the illegal imprisonment of Haitians, the use of forced labor in US reconstruction projects, and the indiscriminate killing of civilians. But it was the discussion of sexual conduct that Balch and others presented to unravel the myth of white benevolence and black criminality. In the early pages of *Occupied*

Haiti, Balch cited the congressional testimony of Helen Hill Weed to establish that before the occupation white women traveling alone in Haiti were safe. In her testimony Mrs. Weed reported that she frequently traveled by horseback "all through the mountains" and "found the Haitians always kind and courteous."[93] Haitian women of all classes, on the other hand, experienced the racial politics of militarized sexuality. During the occupation, Port-au-Prince recorded a rise in the number of saloons and dance halls with 147 registered businesses that were known to cater to prostitution. Balch and Hunton also reported a rise in the number of "illegitimate children" and compared those findings to the same developments in the Philippines, a US protectorate since the Spanish-American War.[94] Although Jim Crow attitudes did not forbid white marines from having sex Haitian women, white marines who desired to formalize their relations with Haitian women were sanctioned. In the race relations chapter of *Occupied Haiti* Balch and Hunton noted the hypocrisy of the case of a white marine who, when he married into a prominent Haitian family, was shunned by the marines for performing an act "unbecoming to a soldier and gentlemen."[95]

Balch maintained her approach of rebutting white racial attitudes as one tactic for ending the occupation. Upon release of *Occupied Haiti,* Emily Greene Balch received a private meeting with President Calvin Coolidge.[96] The granting of the meeting acknowledged the power of the female peace lobby, though the mission's findings and interracial model were not enough to bring the occupation to a quick end. A number of years later, Balch seized the opportunity to draft a five-page memorandum to President Hoover's Haiti Commission in which she returned to the issue of the role of US racial attitudes in the occupation. Balch warned the Hoover Commission that unless it retracted the "Massa in Niggerland" attitude from its diplomacy the administration would never be able to reach a "real understanding, from the inside out" of the Haitian claim for the restoration of self-rule.[97] Scientific racism, Balch believed, kept US policy makers from viewing Haitians as equals, civilized, and fit for sovereignty. Echoing her argument on immigration, Balch advised the Hoover administration that it would gain in character and outlook if it could begin to empathize with and learn from the Haitians it sought to control. Balch knew that the commission would not take up her plea for a new foreign policy based in humanitarian mutuality. Yet she warned the commission that continuing a foreign policy laced with white paternalism and scientific racism would cause the United States to perpetually "live in a fools' paradise."[98]

From her work on immigration to her efforts to contest the US presence in Haiti, Balch engaged the modernist's burden of exposing the racism, oftentimes cloaked as science, used by everyday people and politicians to restrict citizenship rights within the nation and expand US power abroad. Balch's steady efforts to confront anti-immigrant sentiment and Jim Crow politics at home and in Haiti indicate that she helped direct twentieth-century transformations in race discourse and politics. To achieve the new social age of interdependence and cosmopolitan world-mindedness Balch aspired to, she understood that the scaffolding of scientific racism needed to be dismantled. To dismantle the scaffolding, Balch increasingly turned to culture and history, and away from science, as explanatory frameworks. Clearly for Balch, to work for peace mandated a commitment to work against racism.

Anna Melissa Graves

The adventurous life and writing of Anna Melissa Graves, the daughter of a Southern plantation owner, represents yet another way in which white peace women attempted to shift the racial dynamics that defined the United States during the first half of the twentieth century. Starting in 1917, Graves spent more than twenty years of her life traveling the world and publishing collections of letters and memoirs based on her journeys. Through her writing and travels, she aimed to "build up a belief in the oneness of humanity" and "expose and discredit all propaganda which tends to separate" in an effort to prove "that this propaganda which separates is not disinterested and it is not scientific."[99] As a method for discrediting race-based stereotypes, Graves felt that the content of the letters she published—people's discussions about their families and their hopes and fears—would reveal that individuals from disparate locations shared a common set of basic concerns and desires. By focusing on what she hoped would be interpreted by her Western readers as familiar daily struggles from people from places like China, Peru, Armenia, or West Africa, for instance, Graves endeavored to loosen her reader's attachment to race-based allegiances and encourage new, more transnational allegiances based on what she identified as universal yearnings and practices. Graves did not necessarily want to deny the diversity of the world's people, but she did want to weaken the argument that in difference one found proof of variation in levels of human development and worth.

As Louise Michele Newman notes, historians of gender need to analyze "white women's embeddedness within the racial discourses of abolition, benevolence, suffrage, missionary ideology, civilization, imperialism, progressivism, and feminism."[100] As we see with Graves, although she is a critic of colonialism, imperialism, and racism, she is attached to the idea that select Western white women held a particularly advanced capability to advocate for and protect racially persecuted peoples and nations. In other words, within her antiracist positions Graves can at times be seen as positioning some white women as exemplars of civilization. In addition, although Graves condemned the use of race as a method of separation when deployed by imperialists, she advocated its use as a form of oppositional consciousness and political community building when it came to the campaign to secure Liberia's independence from outside influence. With Liberia, Graves championed the formation of a strong Pan-African consciousness, or as W. E. B. Du Bois called for, a "new racial philosophy."[101] Graves's support of Pan-Africanism is not necessarily an endorsement of the idea of race as a biological or static category. Graves remains consistent in her belief that race is a political and malleable category; only in the case of Liberia does she find its strategic use by the racially oppressed both acceptable and necessary.[102]

Graves was born in 1875 to a formerly slave-owning Confederate family. She began her life of travel in 1917 at the age of forty-two when she went to London to do social work in the city's slums with children crippled by the war. She then moved to France and associated herself with the Working Women's Club of a French munitions plant. For the next two decades, Graves moved around the globe, financing her travels in part through teaching English and history. Her stays in each place generally varied in length from eight months to two years. Her longer travels included visits to China, Peru, Mexico, Russia, Syria, and Palestine; Armenia, Georgia, and Azerbaijan; Liberia and Sierra Leone; Portugal and Brazil. She also spent four months "exploring" ten land-grant black colleges in the United States. Shorter trips included visits to Korea, Bolivia, Chile, Argentina, Germany, Italy, England, and Switzerland.

Graves used her world travels in a practical manner to help expand the WILPF's international membership and to appraise organizational leaders on the political issues in different countries. She served as an eyewitness and investigative reporter in places like Mexico, Peru, and Liberia. With Central and South America and Mexico prime targets of US intervention, Graves assisted in strengthening WILPF's presence on the Pan-American continent. During her ten-month visit to Peru in 1922, she networked with Peruvian feminists and established support for the WILPF. Additionally, she became an advocate for the leftist resistance in Peru, participating in campaigns that demanded the return of exiled leader Victor Raul Haya De La Torre. In 1923 Graves assisted the Women's Peace Union in establishing contact with the Consejo Nacional de Mujeres Mexicanas (National Council of Mexican Women) and helped Zonia Baber, the chair of the US WILPF's Pan-American Committee, make contacts in Mexico. In the early 1930s she traveled to West Africa, during which time she spent three and a half months in Liberia. Shortly afterward, Graves moved to Geneva and became a consultative member for the WILPF on the League of Nations' Liberia commission.[103] In the discussion of Graves that follows, I will first focus on her writings about her stay in China in the early 1920s. I will also discuss her publication of *Benvenuto Cellini Had No Prejudice Against Bronze: Letters from West Africa* in 1942. In the final section I will explore her work with Emily Greene Balch to derail US support for economic and potentially military intervention in Liberia.[104]

Graves's zeal and passion for her work was rooted in her identity as a feminist and her family's missionary roots. In a ten-page advice letter Graves wrote in the early 1920s to a Peruvian woman who expressed interest in feminist peace work we can detect the influence of these two forces.

Buy and borrow and lend books, read at least one book or five articles a week on matters connected with men's relation to man, and directly with war . . . but even before one informs one's self, before one starts at all, one must have the conviction that all this is necessary—one must realize the seriousness of the call to women—one must literally be possessed by this duty to the exclusion of everything else—because it includes everything else. Almsgiving is foolishness if one is doing nothing to prevent that which when it comes makes all the almsgiving in the world as a drop of water in a desert of the famished.[105]

Graves's advice to this woman reverberated with the missionary fervor and righteousness so familiar in her own family. The language of conviction and devotion mirrors the linguistic strategies employed by missionaries. Similarly, Graves's call for women to be self-sacrificing, though in the name of peace, also reveals the similarities in the character traits both feminists and missionaries hoped to foster and advocate. Though similarities in emotive strategies abound, the difference appeared in the political project. If missionaries served as the front people for the exploitation of colonial subjects, then, according to Graves, feminist peace women functioned as the antipode. Yet, although women peace internationalists situated themselves as the antithesis of missionary and imperial projects, their own personal histories were often intimately intertwined in such projects. Graves's own early childhood years were influenced by the evangelizing missionary tales of her uncle and the children's books she loved to devour by British colonial author Flora Shaw.[106] In her preface to her own book, *The Far East Is Not Very Far*, Graves evokes an early childhood memory of China as an example of the influences she was working against during her own travels around the world. Remembering a missionary uncle who lived in China during the mid-nineteenth century, Graves recounts the songs and lessons he taught her:

When about five, I could sing "Jesus loves me, this I know, for the Bible tells me so" in Cantonese, and still remember the words. (But, the Cantonese don't understand my pronunciation.) Though my uncle's visits were not frequent there were three or four between 1880 and his last in about 1904 and many other missionaries came to our home. Of course what I learned was rather uncomplimentary to the Chinese who weren't "converted"; girl babies thrown into the "baby tower," hobbling women and drugged men.[107]

This framing passage from her book of China correspondence underscores the centrality of the missionary narrative to Graves's anti-imperialist project and the centrality of gender to her efforts to make the Chinese more knowable to her Western readers. Graves wanted to save the Chinese from the likes of her missionary family and in so doing save herself from the racism and misguided religious fervor of her own familial heritage. Although she was highly critical of the missionary past of her father and uncles, she financed portions of her travels by working as a contract teacher for missionary associations. In her critique of her family's portrayal of China and its inhabitants, she laments the lack of historical and political context offered her as a child. As she notes she had "no knowledge of its suffering from the West, no knowledge of opium wars . . . and of course had never been told of the part missionaries played in China's subjugation and disintegration."[108] Graves made her own first expedition to China in the tumultuous year of 1919. Her travels brought her into the middle of Chinese upheaval, marked by resistance to Japanese imperialism and internal political strife. With her uncle's orientalist stories resonating in her head, Graves traveled to China with a "background divided between a memory of baby-tower stories and a determination to feel, if I could, that the 'Chinee' was neither 'heathen' or 'peculiar.'"[109] Although Graves had been beguiled as a young child by stories of mysterious people in a faraway land, she ambitiously sought through her WILPF associations and her own travels to change the Western orientalist image of China she had learned. Her involvement in the WILPF provided her with the general framework that the key to a future of peace rested, in part, in women's ability to cultivate an awareness of the common humanity of the world's people. As the WILPF spoke out about the dangers of jingoism, Graves looked back upon her own upbringing as a place to begin her personal journey to stitch the world closer together. Through publishing her personal correspondence with people she met in her world travels, Graves sought to prove that the racialized nationalist differences that divided the world into warring parties were false and surmountable.

Critiquing Scientific Racism

Graves's understanding of the need to critique scientific racism is apparent in her 1942 introductory essay to *The Far East Is Not Very Far,* a collection of her fifteen years of correspondence with two young Chinese men, Wang Shou-Ming and Liu Yuan-Lung, whom she met through her association with English-teaching centers and the YMCA. In the introduction Graves declares that she hoped that a "closer more intimate knowledge" of Chinese men would prove the "oneness" of humanity and the "closeness possible between individuals of all cultures and natures and races and geographies."[110] In order to prove that the Chinese were not a "peculiar" people, Graves maintained that it was incumbent upon her to disrupt popular Western stereotypes about the Chinese. She attempted to do this in two ways. First, she ventured to universalize behavior that Westerners had essentialized as indicative of a Chinese nature. Second, she tried to present Chinese men as possessing forms of masculinity that would be familiar and admirable to a Western reader.

As a critic of scientific racism, Graves's overall goal for her collection of letters was to make it impossible for her readers to link the behavior of people who happened to be Chinese with fixed ideas about something understood to be a biological "Chinese race." In her introduction to the collection, she rattled off popular Western ideas about the Chinese. The Chinese were understood to be uncultured—"roughish" and "callous"—and at the same time highly cultured and free spirited—a people who "loved to laugh" and were "innately more beauty loving, more sensitive aesthetically than Western people."[111] As Edward Said explains in his book *Orientalism,* in order for the West or the Occident to understand itself as superior and the emblem of the civilized, it must create in its relief an image of the East or the Orient that traffics in tropes that paint the *oriental other* as mysterious, inferior, and abject.[112] As a challenge to these orientalist and biological determinist arguments, Graves offered numerous examples from her own observations of the Chinese. Of a female schoolteacher who rebuffed a poor begging jinrikisha man, Graves rhetorically asked, "was her callousness Chinese?" In the case of pallbearers who sat down on strike in the middle of a funeral, Graves remarked, "was their behavior Chinese, or for a want of poverty?" Graves concluded her attempt to disrupt her readers' ability to make connections between the day-to-day casual actions of people who happen to be Chinese and the idea of racially marked Chinese traits or values by way of comparison. She asked her readers if the behaviors of the Chinese teacher or pallbearers were really any more inherent or mysterious than that of the foreign rulers responsible for the "absentee control, subjugation and exploitation" of China.[113]

In order to convince her readership that the Chinese were not biologically different from whites or inferior, Graves believed she needed to establish her impartiality. With this in mind, she decided not to feature letters from the Chinese women to whom she taught high school English and history for fear that her own feminism and the discussion of women's issues in the letters would be seen to compromise her appeal to objectivity. Instead she featured her relationship with two men with whom she had corresponded, but with whom she had very little direct contact. She never met Wang Shou-Ming in person and she came into direct association with Liu Yuan-Lung for only six months. Graves felt that Yuan-Lung in particular fit the bill of impartiality because he did not attend American missionary schools. Additionally, much to Graves's chagrin, he became a militarist and supporter of the nationalist movement of Chiang Kai-Shek. Graves used the resilience of her relationship with Yuan-Lung in the face of his militarism as an example of her overall thesis that humans could learn to care for each other across lines of difference. Graves wrote: "His change saddened me but did not create any estrangement whatsoever. There was nothing 'peculiar' in it. I still felt—as he did—that there was no barrier because of race or culture."[114]

The letters from Yuan-Lung that appear in the book deliver to the reader a youthful and earnest man struggling to do what is best for his family. We learn about the responsibility he undertakes to make sure that his younger sister and brother receive an education even in the face of natural disasters, like the floods, inflicting China. We meet his wife and children and follow his struggle to provide for them economically and emotionally while he also tries to expand his own educational horizons. He shares his dreams of going to London to secure a European education.

Financially unable to go, much of his learning takes place through the largesse of Graves, who regularly sends him packages of books often including classics like the *Iliad* and the *Odyssey*. Through the letters that Graves selected for her text, we also learn that Yuan-Lung, like Shou-Ming, expresses deep devotion for Graves and feels compelled to convince her of his good character. In a letter from 1921 to Graves he writes, "I really do not know how to express in English my heart-felt gratitude to you for all your affectionate, kindly concern about my future . . . Let me assure you that I am fully determined to improve,—to develop spiritually and intellectually, I am fully determined to struggle sincerely and unselfishly in some work for the benefit of mankind."[115] As a further example of his character we learn through the letters that Yuan-Lung struggles deeply with the question of militarism as he tries to decide what he believes is best for the future of his family and for China.

Although letters from Yuan-Lung were offered to attest to the so-called psychological and social fitness of Chinese men, Graves also felt compelled to address Western beliefs that Chinese men lacked "vigor" and "virility."[116] By contesting Western interpretations of Chinese masculinity, Graves believed she was defending China against further Western encroachment on Chinese sovereignty. To defend China's fitness for civilization, Graves considered it necessary to replace the popular Western understanding of Chinese men as frail and childlike with images of muscular and brawny men. Graves conjectured that these physically masculine men, presented alongside the intellectual man, like Yuan-Lung, who provides for his family, would provide the Western reader with recognizable and hence admirable forms of Chinese masculinity.

Graves offered as evidence of Chinese men's physicality her trip to the top of the five-thousand-foot Taishan Mountain. To reach the mountaintop, Graves was transported in a chair carried by two Chinese men. These two men, she told her readers, possessed "perfect physiques" and one of them was even reported to be more than six feet tall.[117] Although through this story Graves sought to contest the rote racist images of frail and disease-prone Chinese masculinity, it failed to free Chinese men from racialized gender hierarchies. Graves's tale may have suggested that Chinese men could compete with US muscularity, but if anything was accomplished through the story it was to maintain Graves's own gendered race status. By sharing this story with her Western audience Graves secures her own centrality to the unraveling of Western imperialism at the same time that she maintains her own privilege. And by positioning herself, a white woman, literally above the heads of Chinese men, she in fact also feminizes them. In her zeal to disengage Western attachments to racialized notions of Chinese inferiority, she left unanalyzed her own position as a Western white woman. Graves's efforts to disrupt Western orientalism and challenge scientific racism revealed the complexity and unevenness of such projects. Graves fluctuated between Westernizing the Chinese to make them understandable to a Western audience and encouraging her reader to see Chinese attributes as universal. Like Balch, she understood that masculinity served as a measure of civilization, yet faltered in her ability to question the centrality of Western gender norms and her own exalted position as a white American woman.

Advocating for Pan-Africanism

A decade after traveling to and writing about China, Graves turned her interest to Africa. Her experiences in West Africa, in particular her defense of Liberian sovereignty, generated a change in her thinking about the meaning and politics of race. Although throughout much of her work Graves insisted that discernable differences among the world's people derived from culture, not from some stable or essential racial distinctiveness, in the case of Liberia Graves endorsed the use of racial nationalism as a form of resistance against encroachment on Liberian independence. Her time in Africa turned her into an outspoken advocate of Liberia and of Pan-Africanism and would create an ideological division between her and Emily Greene Balch.

The influence of Africa on Graves's political philosophy can be detected in her 1942 publication *Benvenuto Cellini Had No Prejudice Against Bronze*. Republished in 1960 under the celebratory and Afrocentric title *Africa: The Wonder and the Glory*, the book looked to contest traditional history texts that ignored the accomplishments of Africa and Africans. In her own book Graves detailed African historical, cultural, educational, and political accomplishments and discoveries, in order to promote Africa as a model of a superior civilization. In the introduction to the book, Graves explained her approach to African history as a necessary political intervention. Because Europeans and Americans abide by a "ludicrous" and "panicky fear of losing prestige," Graves observed that they "shy off from giving the world any proof of the outstanding superiority of a man or woman who has any Negro blood."[118] Through her own publication Graves sought to demote the assumed elevated status of Western civilizations and promote Africa as a model society.

The African history Graves provided in *Benvenuto Cellini Had No Prejudice Against Bronze* challenged popular portrayals of Africa as a backward continent. Utilizing previously published African histories, including the works of Franz Boas, Leo Frobenius, "the father of Africanology," and colonial political writer Flora Shaw, Graves published an exhaustive, professional, and richly detailed book that recorded the longevity and complexity of African civilizations. Much to her own amusement, Graves assessed that Shaw's 1907 *A Tropical Dependency* represented some of the best description of life in interior Sudan before the British rule. Although Graves knew that Shaw was an "arch imperialist" and found the political narrative of the book "repulsive," Graves approved of the cultural and material history Shaw recorded of Sudan, finding it untainted by Shaw's colonial perspective.[119] Yet, as a rebuke to Shaw's political views on Africa, Graves used her own telling of African history to trumpet African ingenuity and the centrality of African discoveries, like iron, to the development of modern industrialization. The Sudanese, Graves instructed her readers, designed some of the earliest and most advanced judicial systems, and the Nubians developed four different alphabets. In fact, Graves contended that the "broad and luminous" intelligence of fourteenth-century Ghanaian scholars rivaled that of contemporary Harvard professors.[120] In addition to promoting African history as a vehicle for contesting colonialism, Graves also engaged in direct political advocacy. The best example of this work occurred in the early 1930s when she helped direct campaigns to investigate the Firestone Corporation's role in Liberian politics.

The White Woman's Burden: Graves, Balch,
and the 1930s Liberian Crisis

Considerable tension developed between Emily Greene Balch and Anna Melissa Graves over the Liberian crisis. Their correspondence about Liberia illuminates the shifting ground of racial political thought and its influence on how peace women established their views on key foreign policy issues. At first glance, US intervention in Haiti and Liberia, two independent black nations, might seem to have presented WILPF women with the same set of questions and challenges. But Balch, unlike Graves, found that in the case of Liberia a racial analysis or framework could cloud as much as it revealed. Although US financial ventures in Liberia and the threat of military intervention to secure the financial interests of the Firestone Rubber Company raised alarms for Balch about Liberia's freedom, the behavior of the black Liberian ruling class also troubled her as it did some other anti-imperialists.[121] The black Liberian political elite supported the coerced exportation of Liberian labor to Spanish colonies and exacerbated divisions between the ruling elite and indigenous populations, showing no interest in equalizing political rights or social conditions for the majority of Liberia's people. For Balch the Liberian situation tested the conviction of her belief that drawing a direct line between something understood as racial essence and fitness for national leadership produced dangerous forms of nationalism. In the case of Liberia, Balch contended that racialized nationalism, even when practiced by the black Liberian ruling class, was dangerous and antithetical to the advancement of community internationalism. Whereas Anna Melissa Graves and others unequivocally promoted Liberia as an exemplar of Pan-African promise, Balch refused to condone the behavior of the ruling Liberians. Although Balch remained critical of the racial motivations that influenced US foreign policy in Liberia, she also maintained that ignoring the ruling Liberians' practices against their own citizens meant endorsing the excesses of nation-states. Balch struggled to fashion a political position that could contest both US colonialism and the excesses of the Liberian ruling class. Graves, on the other hand, stood firm in her unequivocal support of Liberia.

As historian I. K. Sundiata details in *Black Scandal: America and the Liberian Crisis, 1929–1936,* Liberia came to represent both a test case of racial capacity, whether blacks were capable of self-rule, and a lightning rod for the continued development of Pan-African politics and consciousness.[122] Yet, although Liberia was a thorny and complicated issue for the US State Department, so too was it for those concerned about the future of Liberian independence. Anna Melissa Graves and Emily Greene Balch both agreed that the free-floating dollar diplomacy that threatened Liberia's sovereignty endangered the future of international peace and the Liberian state. Yet as a series of letters between Graves and Balch illustrate, these two women disagreed on key points. For Graves, Liberia represented first and foremost the issue of black freedom. In contrast, although Balch was aware of the racial parameters and significance of the crisis, she refused to see it as a question easily divided along the lines of white imperial excess and black victimization. Her socialist roots and leeriness of all forms of nationalism caused her to cast a discerning eye on the labor practices of the Americo-Liberians as well as on the activities of foreign business and governments.[123]

Founded in the 1820s by black American freedmen and former slaves, Liberia served from its formation as a symbol of African and African American freedom, independence, and Pan-African possibility. The sovereignty of the new nation, though, soon faltered as economic need led to the establishment of neocolonial economic relations with Western nations. The internal practices of the Liberian ruling class, advanced in large part by the US black emigrants to Liberia (popularly referred to as the Americo-Liberians), also weakened the stability of the nation. Disregard for indigenous tribal practices and the exportation of native labor as a cash commodity exacerbated internal dissention. To some onlookers this labor practice resembled economic slavery.[124]

US involvement in Liberia escalated in 1912 when the federal government, along with Great Britain, France, and Germany, set up a receivership in Liberia to collect trade tariffs and control Liberia's economic and political development. In 1926 the Firestone Corporation strong-armed Liberia into a ninety-nine-year land lease agreement as a way to decrease US reliance on British-manufactured rubber. The terms of the agreement exchanged the leasing to Firestone multitudes of Liberian land at the cut-rate cost of six cents an acre for the promise that Firestone would employ Liberian labor, improve Liberia's infrastructure, and assist in the retirement of the high debt Liberia owed to Western interests. When Liberia soured on the deal, Firestone took its dissatisfaction with the Liberians to the US State Department and instigated what would become a ten-year set of negotiations and maneuvers between Firestone, the United States, Liberia, and the League of Nations.[125]

As a preemptive strike against Liberia, the United States encouraged the League of Nations to investigate the labor practices of the Liberian government and the reported unrest among the native peoples, including the Kru tribe. The League of Nations convened numerous exploratory missions that generated international scrutiny of ruling-class Liberians and little questioning of the practices of white foreign economic interests in West Africa. The US State Department, while endorsing the concerns of Firestone, worried that the United States might be perceived as "playing Caribbean politics in West Africa."[126] To the State Department's chagrin, Liberia did become an issue of concern for some US peace activists and black leaders, who launched campaigns to publicize and protest US economic intrusion into Liberia.

As with Haiti, the US WILPF worked hard to expose the nature of US actions in Liberia. The WILPF's decision to work on Liberia followed naturally from the position adopted by peace women at the 1915 Hague Congress that governments should not diplomatically or militarily support the coercive economic intervention of corporations into sovereign countries.[127] A letter from Anna Melissa Graves to Dorothy Detzer in the summer of 1931 began the more than five-year WILPF campaign to challenge US support of the Firestone Corporation's dealings in Liberia. The WILPF wanted to stop coercive US economic involvement in Liberia, secure a guarantee that the United States would not intervene militarily, and forestall League of Nations' oversight of Liberia as the League of Nations had proposed assigning military and financial advisors to the country. In the almost five years it took to reach an economic and political agreement suitable to the Liberian government, the WILPF served as an aggressive watchdog of the League of Nations' Liberia proceedings.

Detzer, Balch, and Graves organized numerous meetings with officials in the US State Department and with League of Nation officials and kept the pressure on the Hoover and Roosevelt administrations. The WILPF also kept Liberia in the public spotlight through savvy media work and through the building of coalitions with leaders in the NAACP.[128] By January of 1936 Firestone, the United States, the League of Nations, and the Barclay Liberian government reached an agreement on the terms of the 1926 Firestone loan that seemed to secure Liberian sovereignty.[129]

In the intervening years before the agreement was reached, Balch and Graves sparred over the relative harm caused by the Americo-Liberians toward Liberian citizens and by the Firestone Corporation. This debate between the two women developed in response to US circulated reports that broadcast the Americo-Liberians' mistreatment of native Liberians. In part, these US reports served to distract attention from scrutiny of Firestone's presence in West Africa. Upon learning of the US reports, Graves escalated her own efforts to tell the other side of the story. Through letter-writing campaigns, a speaking tour to ten black colleges, consultations with W. E. B. Du Bois, and the support of the WILPF's national and international offices, Graves publicized information about the labor practices of the profit-hungry Firestone Corporation in Liberia. She detailed Firestone's poor wages, use of the abusive company store system, and decreased food rations granted Liberian workers.[130] Aware of Balch's inclination to heed some of the criticisms of the Americo-Liberians, Graves wrote to Balch in 1931 that the Americo-Liberians' actions needed to be kept in perspective. In her letter, Graves likened the Americo-Liberians' behavior to "a little hand roller, not a steamroller" over the rights of the Liberian people.[131] Additionally, Graves sought to put into perspective the appearance of corruption or graft among the Liberian ruling elite, a point that had been used by the League of Nations' investigative team to legitimize a foreign mandate. If political corruption were the grounds for the forced removal of self-rule, Graves wrote to Balch, "is self-government to be taken from Philadelphia, from all of Pennsylvania, New York City, and from Chicago?"[132] As the United States waged a campaign against Liberia, Graves urged the US WILPF to take a leading role in waging a public campaign to "watch over . . . the sinners against Liberia."[133] Graves's most heartfelt message to US students and other interested parties echoed the warning Liberian president C. B. D. King made in Freetown, Sierra Leone, years earlier: "The criticisms that may be leveled upon the Liberian Administration will not be confined to Liberians only but on every black man whether he be of Sierra Leone, the Gold Coast, Nigeria, the West Indies or the United States of America."[134]

Balch was not oblivious to these dimensions of the Liberian crisis. She utilized the Pan-Africanist symbolism and politics surrounding Liberia as a warning in her correspondence with the State Department. As she wrote in letters to State Department leaders in the months previous to one of the many League of Nations arbitrations, "The decision to be taken in May seems to me of very great importance for Liberia, but not only that—of genuine importance to the United States both as a question of principle and for its repercussions among Africans everywhere and especially among Negroes and friends of Negroes in the United States."[135] Yet Balch could not ignore the question of Liberian duplicity in the subjugation of indigenous rights and unfair labor practices. She refused to romanticize or valorize the Liberian elite. To Balch the ends did not justify the means. As she wrote in 1926 in *Pax International*: "'Native' governments are not all-wise and all-virtuous any more than are those of London, Paris and Washington."[136] For Balch, a response to the Liberian crisis premised on an uncritical black nationalism potentially left unaddressed both the complex dynamics behind foreign intervention and the limitations of a politics of resistance postulated on the logic of hypernationalism.

The differences in political philosophy between Balch and Graves surfaced again in the summer of 1934 when Balch shared with a select group of WILPF leaders her impressions on Liberia. Although she warned the women that her letter was "poorly typed" and "badly thought out," its frankness and Graves's harsh response to it prove illustrative. In her letter, Balch shared observations from her meetings with Lord Lugard and Dr. Melville Douglas Mackenzie, both of England. Mackenzie, a medical expert, served as one of three members of a 1931 League of Nations' Liberian Committee that made recommendations on the future of Liberia. Balch reported that she felt that she had influenced Mackenzie to consider the WILPF's perspectives on the question of Liberia and the role of the League of Nations. At the same time, though, she found Mackenzie's discussion of the treatment of the native Kru people by the Liberian government compelling as he "spoke with pain" about the indigenous situation.[137] Mackenzie, it seems, also convinced Balch that in Liberia the League of Nations was motivated by a sense of moral obligation in its efforts to help stabilize the country.[138]

Balch's receptivity to Mackenzie in this matter infuriated Graves, who could not believe that Balch had fallen for Mackenzie, who in Graves's estimation was a mere servant of the League of Nations. Graves wrote her friend Balch that "letters such as yours almost make me want to be a Communist . . . Oh! Emily Balch you are not yet old enough to lose your fearless vigor. Don't for God's sake fear to speak out."[139] In her letter she chastised Balch for seemingly reducing the situation to a match of personalities. She urged Balch not to forget the real meaning of the Liberian crisis. "It isn't a question of Dr. Morais and Mr. Barclay.[140] It is a question of the League having sold itself to Firestone and to the colonial powers who wish to damn Liberia," she scolded Balch.[141] For Graves, Liberia had become a clear-cut example of age-old racist colonial practices and any consideration of any other aspects of the situation merely meant Balch had been duped and misguided. Graves continued to Balch:

> The last bit of Africa comparatively free from forced labour and exploitation and worse still the evil results of being looked down on, of not being able to have self-respect, the last bit of Africa where the Negro race can say: "My foot is on my native hearth and my name is Negro." That last bit is being torn from the Africans and you listen to an old fool . . . I feel like saying: "Ichabod! Ichabod!"[142]

But Balch did not just blindly absorb Mackenzie's views or those of any other League of Nations officials. In her meeting with Mackenzie she presented him with a set of proposed actions that the WILPF considered to be an improvement over the pressure politics the United States was playing with the League of Nations and Liberia. Balch hoped to disentangle Liberia from oppressive foreign intervention and rehabilitate the Americo-Liberian ruling class. Along with many US black leaders, Balch suggested that the Liberian crisis required a multitiered response. Such an approach might include securing some "friendly disinterested aid" in order to get Liberia "out of the hands of Firestone or other financial masters"; US philanthropic involvement, including a Rockefeller Fund project to study tropical hygiene; and the granting of scholarships to US black colleges for fifty "sons of the Monrovian magnates" as a way to reform Liberian governmental practices and launch a new generation of leaders.[143]

Anna Melissa Graves and Emily Greene Balch shared concern about the welfare of Liberia and the effect the Liberian situation could have on black sovereignty and black self-consciousness throughout the black diaspora. But they held differing perspectives on the usefulness of the concept of racial distinctiveness to the reconciliation of the Liberian situation. Graves believed that for Liberia to remain a strong independent nation free from neocolonial influences, Liberia must maintain and strengthen its Pan-Africanist identity and appeal to other black nationalists. It must also build stronger alliances with US black civil rights leaders through the utilization of the Pan-Africanist bond. Though Graves in her other writings and activities hoped to build a world that would ultimately nullify racial types or the use of racial hierarchies, she believed that Pan-Africanist thought was necessary to forestall white neocolonial incursion in Liberia.[144] Balch, on the other hand, found the entertainment of notions of racial distinctiveness in the case of Liberia counter to the project of building international community based in a common humanity. She believed that the potential short-term gains in racial pride and diaspora building were not outweighed by the long-term dangers of a liberation politics based in race.

Although Balch and Graves differed over the overt use of race as a tool for organizing resistance to neocolonial practices, they agreed that as white women they had a responsibility to redress the sins of white men. Liberia, in other words, represented to Balch and Graves a form of the white woman's burden. Both were critics of colonialism and imperialism, but they shared with earlier Victorian feminists who endorsed colonialism and imperialism a racially motivated calling to participate in the debates over nationalist expansionist politics and the position of racialized "others" in these developments. Colonialist or imperialist feminists gained access to global travel and the political sphere by showing that they too could be colonizers. Anti-imperialist feminists aimed to extend the political influence of white women by cleaning up the racist mess colonial feminists profited from. In both cases colonial/imperialist feminists and anti-imperial feminists believed that the world needed white womanhood to take action. As Graves wrote to Balch from Brazil in 1934:

> Sometimes I think perhaps I was wrong in coming here, that perhaps Liberia needed me more than I needed to study Mulattoes in Brazil. For as far as I can see no one is fighting for Liberia with the faith in her that I have and the realization which I have that to expect anything from the Governments which are owned by those who wish to own her, is pure illusion to put it politely.[145]

Emily Greene Balch approached Liberia with less emotional attachment than Graves, yet like Graves, Balch believed that Liberia served as a testing ground of the political and intellectual powers of white peace women. White men had failed at the end of World War I to devise a sustainable peace treaty, an end to colonialism, or a truly functioning international collective power sharing apparatus. The League of Nations floundered in the face of the Liberia crisis. Now the question was: Could white peace women do a better job? Could white women untangle the legacy of the white man's burden they felt challenged to address? As Emily Greene Balch wrote her WILPF associates, "The apparently insoluble question [is] how to build up a decent form of independence capable of evolving into something that will bring out [their] capacity and build up the self-respect . . . to break them down by force and pressure is to begin again to assume the White Man's Burden . . . and to leave them to do as they will is to sit by and see a misuse of power."[146] Balch's comments indicate her continued attachment to the schema of the white man's burden. Balch situates herself and the WILPF as potential brokers of a new approach to race and international relations that ideally would stretch beyond the dichotomous seesaw of white control and black subservience, even while the language she uses belies the idea that Liberians need white assistance in order to develop an independent and sustainable nation. As Newman noted in her study of Victorian feminists and the colonial project, "we must be willing to embrace the idea that opposition movements retain the residue of that which they oppose."[147] Although Balch and Graves retained some racialized attachment to the idea that white peace women maintained a special ability or special burden to set the world on a peaceful racism-free path, the residue of white exceptionalism that can be found in the corners of their work does not preclude us from placing their work in the company of other modernists striving to turn back the tide of scientific racism.

Like Addie Hunton, Alice Dunbar-Nelson, and Jessie Fauset, white peace women after World War I worked to create a new vision of the world. In their pursuit of peace, Dubois, Balch, and Graves aspired to change the way people thought about race and the value placed on national distinctiveness. Though their approaches and arenas of influence differed, the three agreed that a stumbling block to peace existed in the proliferation of racial stereotypes and Western chauvinism. As a counterdiscourse, they tried to paint a panoramic view of a culturally complex world in which the concepts of centers and margins and superiority and inferiority held no meaning or value.

White women of the WILPF provided valuable leadership to many of the postwar struggles against racism and nativism. They struggled to reeducate America's youth away from Anglo-Saxon chauvinism. And they led important challenges to the racist discourses embedded in US foreign policy. At the same time that they contested the worst of modern racial discourses, they found themselves animated in part by the lingering power of Progressive Era ideals that defined middle-class white womanhood as the salve to the nation's industrialized, racialized, and militarized chaos. They repudiated, relied upon, and reconstituted the racialized discourses at play in the early part of the twentieth century. Peggy Pascoe avers that more historically detailed studies of the ways in which modernists confronted scientific racism are needed. The women's peace movement of the interwar years, as represented by the WILPF, offers a vital example of the complex domains in which dominant racial politics and norms were contested and new ideas about race and its relation to gender emerged. As internationalists and peace women, the three women studied here attempted to move the world to believe less in hierarchies based on race, and in the place of these ethno-racial-national hierarchies they wanted a new landscape of transnational allegiances to arise. These women were not mere dreamers or idealists. Balch knew that the project of peace and goodwill, although it needed to be thoughtful and intentional, also needed to help address in an immediate fashion the daily lives of people. She wanted peace women to advance "concrete devices" that produced actual changes in immigration law, foreign policy, and the practice and prosecution of lynching, as well as changes in people's attitudes. Their work showed that they understood that naturalized ideas about race were a constitutive element in the most abhorrent practices of the nation and that it was their responsibility *as peace women* to protest, disrupt, and transform these ideological suppositions. Through their work, Dubois, Balch, and Graves were instrumental in the earliest critiques of scientific racism, and so helped to limit its reach and historical sway.

1. 1926 WILPF delegation to Haiti. *Left to right:* Emily Greene Balch, Charlotte Atwood, Grace D. Watson, Paul H. Douglass, Addie Hunton, and Zonia Baber. Courtesy of the Records of the Women's International League for Peace and Freedom, Swarthmore College Peace Collection.

2. Library at Camp Lusitania St. Nazaire, France, from *Two Colored Women with the American Expeditionary Forces*, by Addie W. Hunton and Kathryn M. Johnson, c. 1920, f.p. 214 Photographs. Courtesy of the General Research and Reference Division, Schomburg Center for Research in Black Culture, The New York Public Library, Astor, Lenox and Tilden Foundations.

3. Postcard from Haiti of men wearing suits and carrying protest signs: "Live Free or Die." Courtesy of the Records of the Women's International League for Peace and Freedom, Swarthmore College Peace Collection.

4. Rachel Davis Dubois, c. 1923. Courtesy of the Records of the Women's International League for Peace and Freedom, Swarthmore College Peace Collection.

5. For the Advancement of the Race: The Fourth Annual Conference of the National Association for the Advancement of Colored People, Chicago, 1917. In the group are Jane Addams, Dr. Du Bois, Bishop Lee, Dr. C. E. D. Bentley, and many other well-known men and women. *Progress and Achievements of the Colored People,* c. 1917. Halftone photomechanical print. Courtesy of the General Research and Reference Division, Schomburg Center for Research in Black Culture, The New York Public Library, Astor, Lenox and Tilden Foundations.

6. Lower Bucks County, Pennsylvania, WILPF members, June 30, 1947. Courtesy of the Records of the Women's International League for Peace and Freedom, Swarthmore College Peace Collection.

3

Philadelphia

Forging a National Model of Interracial Peace Work

IN AUGUST OF 1929 Philadelphia black clubwoman Addie Dickerson attended the sixth WILPF International Congress in Prague. Dickerson joined the US WILPF delegation along with women from twenty-five other countries as they convened for seven days. The deliberation focused on how to make the Kellogg-Briand Pact for the Renunciation of War, which had been signed the previous year by fifteen countries with the Soviet Union and the United States the lead signatures, a viable tool for the enforcement of arms reduction, the end of war profiteering, and the promotion of alternative practices of peaceful arbitration. The cautious enthusiasm generated by the pact and the announcement that the League of Nations would convene its first World Disarmament Conference in Geneva in 1932 compelled peace activists to instigate a massive global petition campaign supporting universal disarmament. In less than three years, the international WILPF alone would gather and deliver six million signatures to Geneva representing the concerns of the world's women. The enthusiasm and dedication to making disarmament possible generated in Prague prompted the development in Philadelphia of the US WILPF's first interracial peace committee. Upon return from Prague, Dickerson joined with influential African American business and clubwoman Evelyn Reynolds in announcing a campaign to convince "1,000 Negro Women" in greater Philadelphia to join the WILPF and the global movement to end the militarization of the land and sea and air.[1] For the next six years, Reynolds and Dickerson would lead, along with Mildred Scott Olmsted, a white WILPF member and executive secretary of the

Pennsylvania WILPF, a group of Philadelphia women in efforts to turn the world toward peace and racial harmony.

The energy created by the Briand-Kellogg Pact provided an enormous spark that invigorated new waves of peace work around the globe, but this enthusiasm alone does not explain why some women turned to inter-racial organizing as a part of the disarmament project. A number of local and national conditions transformed disarmament fever into an interra-cial project in Philadelphia. One of those conditions was the increased participation of African American women in the Philadelphia WILPF. As middle-class black women deepened their commitment to a transnational agenda and searched for spheres of influence beyond the increasingly masculinized black political sphere, their work for peace gained extended purpose and brought Philadelphia women together across the color line. Though short-lived, their work together marked a significant moment in interwar-era women's politics. In this period, women attempted to chal-lenge racism in the nation and in their own relationships as an avowed part of their plan to secure the conditions necessary to achieve peace.

There were many challenges women interested in working interra-cially faced. A central concern was how to build a foundation for racial unity. Women of the Philadelphia Interracial Extension Committee (IEC) used their shared desire for peace and the concepts of noble woman-hood and goodwill as organizational building blocks. The concept of noble womanhood, though it served as a central axis upon which African American and white middle-class women in the WILPF negotiated the interstices of race, class, and gender, was not always sufficient in removing the barriers to black women's full participation and leadership. Another challenge that surfaced concerned the interpretation of the purpose of the IEC. Was the committee charged primarily with increasing black inter-est in the peace movement and campaigns for disarmament? Or was the IEC developed to tackle race relations in the nation and in the WILPF? Although many—primarily black members of the IEC—believed the two concerns, securing the conditions for peace and securing an end to all forms of racism, were interrelated, this analysis was not an evident one for the majority of WILPF members. The most significant challenge was how to secure more support from white women within the WILPF for the work of the IEC and for the full integration of black women's leadership. As the political conditions in the nation and world for African Americans dimmed, intensified by the toll of the Great Depression, the failure of federal antilynching legislation, the advance of Jim Crow, and challenges to black sovereignty in Liberia and Haiti, many black women in the WILPF tired of the slow pace of change in the organization. By 1935, the WILPF experiment in interracialism looked to many black women too much like a buffer against full organizational integration. Although the committee made gains both in the area of peace education and the area of race reform, the pace of change frustrated many involved. In the end, the successes and failures of the Philadelphia IEC during the 1920s and 1930s prepared the WILPF to join the early stage of the civil rights movement that emerged in the shadow of the New Deal and World War II.

The committee's location in Philadelphia shaped its work and elevated its status. Because the Pennsylvania state branch's headquarters were in Philadelphia, the IEC committee had access to the resources of the office and to the national and regional leaders who frequented the headquarters for meetings and events. Philadelphia's large and well-established black communities and history of abolitionism also contributed to the tone and viability of the committee. The committee's foundation rested as much on the depth of black women's political associations in the city as it did on the resources of the women's peace movement. Its location as a mid-Atlantic city meant that women like Balch, Hunton, Fauset, Dunbar-Nelson, and Detzer frequented the Philadelphia WILPF on their coastal travels and willingly conferred with the Philadelphia women as they attempted to increase the ranks of people committed to disarmament and to building better race relations locally and globally.

Noble Womanhood

Early in her role as a leader of Philadelphia interracial peace work, Reynolds publicly declared the white and black women of the interracial coalition "a band of noble women."[2] With these words she consciously bestowed an exalted meaning on the fledgling experiment in women's cross-racial peace efforts. Reynolds's discursive strategy invoked a fabled collective identity. It was not as much a statement of a fait accompli, but instead a signaling to the white WILPF women that African American women expected the committee to perform differently from past and current race adjustment projects. Her declaration claimed a de facto expectation of equality of political voice, authority, and power within the Philadelphia WILPF. She raised the bar on the standard of interracialism to be pursued in the WILPF and experienced by African American women. She also indicted interracialism as an often veiled form of segregation, warning WILPF women that many black women were suspicious of inter-racial programs. These early public statements by Reynolds and other African American women challenged the Philadelphia WILPF to reach beyond complacent forms of interracial alliance building. By announcing the existence of an interracial band of noble women, black women set in motion a high standard for the Philadelphia WILPF.

African American women strategically employed the class-laden title of noble womanhood as a way to secure their passport into WILPF. This discursive action represented a routine precept of racial uplift politics. The promotion of an elite noble womanhood cohered with what historian Evelyn Brooks Higginbotham calls the "politics of respectability." Many middle-class African American men and women embraced it as a strategy for contesting white stereotypes of black Americans. In constructing a working alliance with WILPF women, African American women used middle-class concepts like noble womanhood to disrupt any lingering white suspicion of black women's character and fitness for leadership in the peace movement.[3]

Throughout the nineteenth and into the twentieth century it was believed by many that black women, regardless of class, lacked the qualities of purity and piety and true womanhood. In 1904 Addie Hunton protested this depiction in her essay "Negro Womanhood Defended." In it, she decried the public's lack of knowledge or concern about the difficulties faced by black women. She championed the contributions of black women to racial progress by foregrounding righteous women. She worried that "those who write most about the moral degradation of the Negro woman know little or nothing about the best element of our women who are quietly and unobtrusively working out the salvation of the race . . . The

Negro woman is rightfully making her first effort for purity and truth at her own fireside . . . She is constantly at work for the uplift of her race."[4]

After World War I, middle-class black women still found themselves compelled to defend their reputation and their role in black politics. The continued migration of Southern blacks to urban areas like Philadelphia in search of work and relief from Jim Crow stimulated intragroup tensions and restimulated public discussion about black women's worth. The "politics of masculinity" of the postwar New Negro movement required black female social reformers to redefine and reassert the worth of black women's political leadership to the race. As Hazel Carby observes, "the complex process of urbanization had gender-specific and class-specific consequences for the production of African American culture, in general, and for the cultural representation of black women in particular."[5] This concern with representation compelled women like Jessie Fauset, Evelyn Reynolds, and Alice Dunbar-Nelson to engage in the literary, political, and grassroots refiguring of middle-class black womanhood "as the icon of racial achievement"[6] and influenced their commitment to represent the "best" of black womanhood to the women's peace movement in the 1920s and 1930s. Nannie Burroughs, a nationally recognized black clubwoman and WILPF supporter, declared as late as 1933 that "we must have a glorified womanhood that can look any man in the face—white, red, yellow, brown or black—and tell of the nobility of character within black womanhood."[7]

Many black women who espoused the alchemy of respectability, peace-mindedness, and internationalism joined the Philadelphia and Pennsylvania WILPF. Starting in the mid-1920s the WILPF searched specifically for black women of the "better" class to join the organization. In 1925 Mildred Scott Olmsted wrote to Mary McLeod Bethune, informing Bethune that the Pennsylvania WILPF was "anxious to find a representative and cooperative colored woman to serve on our state board."[8] Seven years later, the Pennsylvania State Education secretary, hoping to increase the general membership among "prominent Negro Women" requested lists of "teachers, wives of professionals, social groups, YWCA workers, and nurses" from the Interracial Committee chair. Yet, many black women who joined the WILPF discovered that not only did they have to negotiate the politics of respectability, they also had to negotiate the politics of receivability. Black women's contributions to peace causes and their efforts to eradicate racism were often monitored and their performance evaluated based on the acceptability of their personal appearance and tone. If whites found a black woman's personal style challenging or disagreeable, then she ran the risk of having her political contributions dismissed. Crystal Bird Fauset, who in 1936 was elected to the Pennsylvania State House, becoming the first black woman in the nation to hold such an office, experienced white scrutiny during her involvement in Philadelphia's emerging interracial peace activism. A 1930s account, for instance, of Fauset's contributions noted that her "manner of dress predisposed one immediately to listen to what she had to say. . . . she speaks with great vividness . . . but without rancor or bitterness."[9] These remarks at first glance may seem laudatory, but they illustrate that Fauset's participation was appreciated as much for her ability to strike a pleasing tone and perform noble womanhood as for the content of her message and activities. If noble womanhood failed at times to equalize women's participation across the lines of race, some believed that the tenets of goodwill might lessen the impact of racism on black women's experiences.

Goodwill

At the 1929 Prague Congress Jane Addams declared goodwill to be the key to the achievement of peace and freedom. Addams's declaration impressed Evelyn Reynolds. In an article Reynolds wrote about her Prague trip for the *Associated Negro Press*, she applauded Addams's observation that the world needed more women who could advance "new solutions born of goodwill and pooled intelligence."[10] Goodwill was a popular theme throughout the 1920s and 1930s. Prominent women of both races invoked goodwill as they addressed audiences about how to achieve global harmony, end militarization, and confront all forms of racism. In January of 1927, WILPF supporter Mary McLeod Bethune appealed to the women of the NACW and the ICWDR to launch an international goodwill mission to Africa to be operated by African American women. Invoking the popular spirit of Ethiopianism, McLeod aspired to advance black women's international experience and Pan-African consciousness. In her annual report she proposed that: "If Ethiopia is to stretch forth her hands then, those hands must belt the seas, and to belt the seas, it is fitting that the women of the NACW should know from actual observation and touch, how to go about their work."[11] Nannie Burroughs's March 1930 WILPF-sponsored appearance at the Philadelphia Union Baptist Church promoted goodwill over legal approaches to race reform and peacemaking. In a speech reported to be full of "passion and elegance," Burroughs encouraged the three hundred people in attendance to step "forward into a new day of interracial freedom, peace and goodwill." Burroughs admonished that "we have enough facts about races; we need more faith in races. We have enough laws, we need more love."[12]

To peace women goodwill bespoke a political agenda committed to fostering transnationalism and a cosmopolitan way of life. Proponents of goodwill taught that the answer to international, national, and local strife existed not only in legislative initiatives and international arbitration, but also, and perhaps primarily, in the fiber of human relations. Through the improvement of relations—the disarming of hearts—the world would find its way to a natural state of international peace and racial harmony. This primacy of social relations philosophy gained resiliency during the interwar years as people hungered for an alternative to the nationalist atrocities of World War I and the hatemongering promoted by nativists and racists. Peace women sponsored May 18 Goodwill Day events and they hosted goodwill pageants in playgrounds, women's clubs, public libraries, and boys and girls clubs. Rachel Davis Dubois, the creator of many of the goodwill pageants used by the Philadelphia WILPF, intended these intercultural community events to bring people together to celebrate the Kantian notion of a oneness of humanity.[13] Philadelphia women hoped to foster in people a renewed belief in humanity through the simple acts of the heart and mind at home, work, and in worship.[14]

The concept of goodwill also provided a malleable philosophical space through which the women of the Philadelphia IEC attempted to secure organizational unity. As Progressive Era women they united under the conviction that education was the key to the future. They also believed that it was their unique duty as noble women to lead the way to disarmament, peace, and interracial understanding. Cloaked in the armor of goodwill they looked to each other across the shaky bridge of interracial sisterhood and waved the flags of knowledge, womanhood, and culture. They hoped that they could extend the same hand of peace to each other that they encouraged others to extend. Yet, as the women of the IEC would come to realize, practicing goodwill was complex. It involved negotiating the interwoven fissures of race, class, gender, and power that dominated interwar America. In other words, practicing goodwill within the Philadelphia IEC would be challenging.[15]

African American Women of the IEC

A financial donation in the winter of 1928 to the Philadelphia WILPF was earmarked to hire a black woman to undertake a month of "special peace work" among the "colored citizens of Philadelphia."[16] This donation signaled the beginning of what would become the Philadelphia IEC. Originally formed to "bring an understanding with the colored group of the League's philosophy of peace," the African American women who took leadership of the committee quickly expanded its purpose.[17] In addition to organizing a black peace constituency in Philadelphia, African American women used the committee to advocate for racial justice and to extend their own political power locally, nationally, and internationally. The shift in the committee's purpose emerged as the title changed from "Special Peace Work among the Colored" to the "Interracial Extension Committee." The original title implied a time-limited project solely focused on addressing black communities. The new title indicated the committee's interest in fostering improved race relations and its intention to be an ongoing entity in the WILPF. With the title change came a change in the committee's stated purpose. In the spring of 1930 the committee expanded its platform to include "program[s] which aim to make people understand and believe in each other."[18]

More than a dozen prominent black women transformed the course of the Philadelphia WILPF IEC during its seven-year existence. They represented Philadelphia's black female talented tenth—educated, professional middle-class women who, for the most part, came of age at the turn of the

century and sought to sway the racial order of America through their propriety, professional achievements, and political skill.[19] They represented
the highest accomplishments of black women in the city in the realm of
business, education, the arts, politics, and the voluntary sector. Their collective influence reached far into the social, political, and cultural fabric of
black Philadelphia. They ushered open the doors of black schools, clubs,
churches, homes, businesses, cultural establishments, and newspapers to
the committee's programs and ideals. Evelyn Reynolds, Addie Dickerson,
Alice Dunbar-Nelson, and Henrietta Mousserone comprised the core sustaining force of the committee. Jointly, they offered an expansive array of
local, regional, and national affiliations as well as interracial experience,
internationalist vision, and the timeworn conviction in the power of organized black womanhood.

Social reformer and poet Evelyn Reynolds chaired the Philadelphia
IEC for most of its existence. She brought to the WILPF prior experience
in interracial reform work, elite social standing, connections with Philadelphia's black political machinery, and, as an artist, the literary flair and
consciousness of the Harlem Renaissance. "Amid the mad rush of earn-
ing a living," Reynolds wrote poetry and made a small mark in the New
Negro literary movement. In his 1937 book *The Negro Genius*, Benjamin
Brawley listed Eve Lynn, Evelyn Reynolds's pen name, as one of the "new
young women of Philadelphia" publishing poetry. In her 1936 *No Alabaster Box*, Reynolds's first collection of published poems, Reynolds strove
to capture the varied experiences and yearnings of urban black Americans—"beautiful as a tea rose" young girls, struggling working-class citizens, and feared and misunderstood black male youth.[20]

While committee chair, Reynolds worked as the Industrial Secretary
for Women of the Armstrong Association, the Philadelphia affiliate of the
National Urban League. Reynolds's work brought her face-to-face with the
daily needs of Philadelphia's working-class and poor black populations.
The Armstrong Association was named after General Samuel C. Armstrong, the white founder of the Hampton Institute, a black land-grant
college established in 1868. The Philadelphia Armstrong Association
was founded in 1906 by Quakers to help meet the employment, housing,
educational, and social needs of black migrants. Like the Philadelphia

Association for the Protection of Colored Women, founded in 1905, the Armstrong Association worked with city agencies and voluntary associations to galvanize material support for arriving Southern black migrants. During her tenure at the association, Reynolds witnessed a substantial drop in the level of social services available in the city to black Philadelphians, a rise in segregation in public accommodations, and the disproportionate effect of the Great Depression on black populations.[21]

Reynolds received political support from her husband, Hobson Reynolds, who was an influential leader in city politics. Hobson Reynolds led the city chapter of the Improved Benevolent and Protective Order of the Elks of the World, a black fraternal organization. In 1935, as a newly elected Republican member of the House of Representatives, Reynolds sponsored the Pennsylvania Equal Rights Law, which was passed by the General Assembly.[22]

Addie Dickerson's accomplishments and community connections matched those of Evelyn Reynolds. The power and leadership Dickerson contributed to the WILPF, though grounded in Philadelphia's black middle class, started in the South and stretched into national and international arenas. Dickerson was born in Wilmington, North Carolina, to "one of the section's best known families" and "while yet young showed signs of brilliant determination."[23] Once in Philadelphia, Dickerson attended Temple University and the University of Pennsylvania and established herself as a businesswoman. As Philadelphia's premier black female real estate broker, Dickerson maintained a suite of offices in Center City from which she handled large real estate transactions in Philadelphia and Atlantic City. Some believed that her business, club, educational, and political work "placed her head and shoulders above all other Negro women in Philadelphia" when it came to understanding the political and civic needs of black Philadelphians.[24] One of five black women to become a life member of the National Council of Women, Dickerson's political and club work reached into traditional black institutions as well as white ones. She was a trustee of the Frederick Douglass Memorial Association, on the advisory board of the Bethune Cookman College, and co-organizer of the YWCA in Pennsylvania. During her tenure at the WILPF, Dickerson also served as the national president of the ICWDR, an organization she joined in 1922. As president of the ICWDR, she attended the 1927 Pan-African Congress held in New York City and the 1929 WILPF International Congress in Prague.[25] Her husband, G. Edward Dickerson, was a prominent Philadelphia attorney for thirty years. He also served as assistant city solicitor in the mid-1920s. Addie Dickerson worked closely with her husband on city affairs and drew him into her circle of work for the WILPF.[26]

Alice Dunbar-Nelson and Henrietta Mousserone were the two other most influential black women on the committee. Dunbar-Nelson brought to the WILPF her ideological critiques of the links between war and racism and her regional and national political influence. In 1925, a few years before the establishment of the Philadelphia WILPF IEC, Dunbar-Nelson advanced from serving on the WILPF Pennsylvania state board to serving on the national WILPF board. Dunbar-Nelson held what were at times conflicting allegiances. Though she contributed to the Philadelphia IEC until her death in 1935, Dunbar-Nelson was also a paid staff member of the AIPC of the American Friends Service Committee (AFSC) until 1931.[27] Dunbar-Nelson lived most of her adult life in Wilmington, Delaware, though she moved to Philadelphia in 1932, just three years before her death.[28] The final significant member of the IEC, Henrietta Mousserone, possessed a less prominent national profile yet she contributed to the IEC exhaustive firsthand knowledge of the inner workings of black Philadelphia. Her grassroots contacts and her exceptional organizing skills garnered Mousserone the only paid position with the IEC.

The black leadership of the committee remained fairly consistent. In 1928 Evelyn Reynolds began her permanent service as chair of the IEC. In 1932 as the Great Depression continued to take its toll, the committee created the position of vice-chair as a way to provide relief to Reynolds, whose energies were divided. Reynolds found she had less time to offer the WILPF as her work at the Armstrong Association intensified in the face of the increased needs of Philadelphia's economically challenged. Leila Walker Jones, a dramatist and founder and principal of the Bryan Academy, a small school dedicated to teaching the performing arts to a multiracial student body, served in the new role of vice-chair. Jones was also a leader in the Philadelphia Federation of Women's Clubs.[29] Mousserone served as the official "special representative" of the committee for the life of the committee. As special representative she also became an officer of the WILPF state branch. Recruited by Margaret Olmsted, Charlene Howard, a recent graduate of Cheyney Teachers College, joined the committee as a full-time volunteer. She assisted Mousserone in the numerous daily tasks of the committee and initiated the creation of the Junior International League (JIL). The JIL focused on fostering interracial and international peace consciousness among grade school and high school girls.[30]

White Women of the IEC

From the start, white women's involvement in the Philadelphia committee appeared more tentative and provisional in comparison to the leadership offered by black women. Though many white women publicly advocated the goals of the committee and would attend committee events, few made its work a priority. Three main factors caused this imbalance. White women's discomfort working interracially and a lingering belief that racial justice work distracted from the more standard or traditional definition of peace work restrained many white women's involvement. Additionally, the strong role of Pennsylvania branch executive secretary Mildred Scott Olmsted in the committee relieved many white women of a sense of obligation to contribute to the daily sustenance of the committee. The absence of dedicated white women from Philadelphia weakened the interracial agenda of the committee at the same time that it allowed African American women more room to shape its direction.

Mildred Scott Olmsted was born in 1890 in Philadelphia. Her father was a trial lawyer and assistant district attorney; her mother, Adele Hamrick, was the daughter of a wealthy North Philadelphia importer. A 1912 graduate of Smith College, Olmsted became a social worker, joining the staff of the Denison House Settlement in Philadelphia. She later worked as a caseworker for the Main Line Federation of Churches and the Girls Protective League in Maryland. Though she married Philadelphia lawyer Allen Olmsted in 1921, Olmsted's life defied the categories of mother and wife. Ruth Mellor, Olmsted's crush throughout college and companion afterward, lived with the Olmsteds for many years. She accompanied them on overseas adventures, and, in most cases, Mellor shared a stateroom with Mildred. Although Olmsted eventually had three children, motherhood and the domestic arts never became Olmsted's primary interest. Instead she placed her first priority on social mothering through her WILPF activities.[31]

Olmsted's interest in pacifism and her desire to join a women's peace organization came together in 1921 while she was working in France and Germany for the AFSC, taking care of people wounded or displaced by war. Introduced to a WILPF member in Germany, Olmsted sought out the WILPF upon her return to the United States. Olmsted quickly established herself as a leader, attending her first national board meeting in 1922. She was hired the same year to be the Pennsylvania state branch's first professional executive secretary, which brought with it a salary of $3,500. As executive secretary, Olmsted canvassed the state, determined to expand the branch beyond the borders of Philadelphia. She approached women's organizations like the WCTU, the Council of Jewish Women, the American Association of Social Workers, and the Birth Control League in her search for peace-minded women. By 1929, in part owing to her leadership, the Pennsylvania state branch maintained six paid workers and seventeen local branches within the state.[32] Olmsted's organizational talents were again rewarded in 1934 when she was hired to be the national WILPF organizational secretary, a position she would occupy until 1965.[33] Olmsted guided membership expansion from ten thousand to fourteen thousand from 1934 to 1937. Though she aspired to create an organization of fifty thousand members, the membership eventually stabilized in the 1930s at about fourteen thousand.

Olmsted's organizational philosophy and position as the paid executive secretary of the Pennsylvania WILPF strongly influenced the shape of the WILPF's interracial work. Olmsted's active support of the committee reflected her mission to expand the size of the WILPF. From her first days as Pennsylvania State executive secretary, Olmsted worked to enlarge the state membership. In her first year she increased the Pennsylvania branch from five hundred to twenty-one hundred. Committed to the belief that "peace must be organized," Olmsted disagreed with elder WILPF stateswomen like Jane Addams who wished to keep the organization a small group of pioneering women. In contrast, Olmsted believed that the WILPF message must reach as many women as possible. Though often alone in her convictions, Olmsted insisted that African American women's networks must be utilized if the WILPF was to succeed.[34]

Olmsted tried numerous strategies to entice white members to join the IEC and help expand the WILPF's appeal to black Philadelphians. In the early summer of 1928 while planning the inaugural meeting of the interracial committee, Olmsted expressed her dream of having "equal numbers of the two groups" in attendance.[35] She succeeded in securing seven "good colored members," but her efforts to convince white members of the merits of the committee failed.[36] In her campaign to get more white IEC members, Olmsted invoked white women's goodwill and assured them that they would not be the only white woman in attendance. In a letter to educator Emily Longstreth, Olmsted informed Longstreth that another white educator had joined and reminded her that "I know how you feel about the contacts with the Negro."[37] When this pledge of white camaraderie and appeal to racial goodwill failed, Olmsted offered Longstreth protection from extensive committee work in exchange for her mere presence. She promised that other than attendance, "there will be no work involved in it for you."[38] Olmsted's appeals persuaded Longstreth to participate in some initial meetings, but she resigned her official affiliation early on.[39]

Reluctant to carry out the day-to-day tasks of the committee, white women contributed in other ways. On the local level, white women joined the speaker's bureau and hosted teas and meetings of the JIL. These events provided white women with a sense of accomplishment, status, and visibility, but did not require much time or commitment. Their work created a public interracial facade, leaving their behind-the-scenes rancor out of the view of most. White WILPF women also traveled as emissaries to black women's conventions, promoting racial goodwill and peace while stumping for support of the WILPF. In 1928, for instance, Mrs. Frances Blanshard, Swarthmore College's Dean of Women, addressed the State Federation of Colored Women's Clubs convention in Chester, Pennsylvania.[40] In 1929, through the invitation of Mary McLeod Bethune, WILPF national legislative director Dorothy Detzer spoke to the NACW national convention. The performance of WILPF member and former suffragist Lucy Ames

Mead's peace pageant in black women's social clubs also helped circulate the WILPF message.

Prominent state and national white WILPF leaders who were already committed to the spirit of interracialism lent their support to the Philadelphia committee. Their public endorsement of the IEC bolstered the committee's legitimacy. Their involvement also deepened the committee's links to other liberal reform organizations, including the NAACP and the AFSC. These women included Rachel Davis Dubois; Hannah Clothier Hull, the US WILPF's president and an Armstrong Association board member; and Ellen Starr Brinton, hired by the Pennsylvania WILPF state branch to expand the organization's membership. Brinton was also a founding member of the interracial Fellowship House. Yet, local white women's contributions to the committee remained inconsistent. In the end, black women in concert with Olmsted produced the committee's accomplishments, longevity, and visibility in the city and nation. Still, throughout its history, the committee looked for ways to institute a racial balance in its membership and activities.

Motivations for Unity

A passion for disarmament and belief that women in particular held a clear understanding of the need for peace brought African American and white women together in the Philadelphia WILPF. Harlem Renaissance writer and interracial committee member Idabelle Yeiser used her regular peace column in the *Philadelphia Tribune,* a black newspaper, to motivate women into action. In 1932 in the shadow of the Geneva conference on disarmament, Yeiser commanded her readers to enlist in what she thought was the most difficult battle women had faced to date, the battle to wrestle power from arms merchants and bellicose nations. She implored: "WOMEN, you fought for suffrage and won. You fought for prohibition and won. But these were minor battles compared with the one confronting you now. IF only from a selfish standpoint you need to fight for Peace and Disarmament."[41] Yeiser and middle-class Philadelphia women of both races believed that disarmament was a high-stakes campaign. They also believed that women's political influence could be the key to victory. This passion, though, was not the only motivation behind the Philadelphia interracial experiment. Women held additional concerns, some shared and some not, that together launched and fashioned the IEC.

White Fear and Fellowship

National WILPF board member Zonia Baber returned from a visit to Fisk University in the summer of 1928 alarmed. She wrote to WILPF executive director Dorothy Detzer that during her meetings with "the educated progressive young Negro," she was "shocked to learn that the radical group has accepted *Force* as the only possible means through which the Negro can secure justice."[42] Baber continued: "They say that the White obtained his power in this manner and is holding it by this means . . . We have put up with the indignities of the White man too long."[43] Though upset by her interactions with the Fisk students, Baber believed that their attitudes could be tempered. She advised Detzer that the WILPF national board should "try to get as many of the influential Negro women as possible to become members . . . [so] that they may obtain a different point of view."[44]

Many Anglo-American and African American progressives shared Baber's desire to mitigate the radicalism of New Negro militants.[45] Though one of the more astute and outspoken WILPF board members when it came to racism, Baber found the Fisk students' advocacy of direct action dangerous and antithetical to her belief in the power of education and liberal reform to contest racism. In searching for a panacea to this changing political landscape, Baber urged the WILPF to open its doors more widely to liberal-minded black female social reformers. Baber, who had recently traveled with Addie Hunton and Charlotte Atwood to Haiti for WILPF, had firsthand knowledge of the organizational resources controlled by black women and of the legion of black women who shared the WILPF's commitment to pacifism and internationalism. She believed that interracial association and fellowship with black women could counter the militancy expressed by the Fisk students and others.

Fear of the rise of black radicalism after World War I had ignited concern among white peace leaders for a number of years. In 1926 Wilbur Thomas, the white executive secretary of the AFSC, made "the exploitation of Negroes by militaristic forces" the top agenda item for the AFSC's first interracial committee meeting.[46] Two years later in 1928 Mildred Scott Olmsted featured the specter of black militancy in her strategy to draw Philadelphians to the premier WILPF interracial peace mass meeting. In publicity materials for the event, Olmsted propagandized the image of a burgeoning aggressive black citizenry. She wrote:

> Are you interested in combating the growth of militarism among the Negroes? Do you want our colored citizens to become militarized? Are they being taught that freedom and justice can be secured only by war? To encourage Negroes to take a more active part in the work for World Peace and to make them feel the fellowship of white people in this cause, an Interracial Mass Meeting is to be held at the Broad Street Theatre on Sunday May 6th at 3 P.M. This is the first meeting of just this nature and we are eager that there shall be as many white people as colored in attendance.[47]

Hence, Olmsted, like Baber, was motivated by the conviction that the shift in black political attitudes as witnessed in the politics of more radical New Negroes was dangerous and a hindrance to building peace and goodwill. In response to this perceived threat, Olmsted encouraged WILPF women to embrace the interracial peace project. She fostered in the white membership a bifurcated consciousness of both fellowship and fear toward African Americans. In the face of middle-class black womanhood, Olmsted and Baber recognized a new pool of potential female peace constituents. In the face of youthful black masculinity, they saw danger in an escalating militant race consciousness. In this context, white WILPF women, in essence, turned to middle-class black women to create a buffer zone between what they identified as the militancy and wrong-mindedness of the more radical New Negroes and the gentility and civilizing nature of white pacifist peace reformers.[48]

Knowledge of rising black militancy alone, though, was not enough to motivate Olmsted to initiate the Philadelphia interracial peace committee. Olmsted's awareness of and prior relationships with reform-minded black women also contributed to her calculation that a WILPF committee designed to stimulate peace work with black Americans was vital. In an

August 1928 letter to Olmsted, Alice Dunbar-Nelson detailed her travels on behalf of the AFSC to organize middle-class African Americans
to join the peace movement. Her report motivated Olmsted to replicate
similar work in the WILPF. Dunbar-Nelson shared with Olmsted tales
of her travels along with her predication of success: "I can hardly say
that I am having a pleasant summer. I covered five hot conventions and
I have five more to cover; but the game seems to be worth the gamble,
if the interest and enthusiasm of the people I meet is any indication."[49]
To Olmsted it must have been worth the gamble. With the backdrop of
black "militarism" and the international petition campaign for universal
disarmament underway, the knowledge that Dunbar-Nelson "got over
some pretty intensive work" by speaking to seven hundred black teachers and spending a week organizing for peace at the NACW convention
invigorated Olmsted to expand the reach of the Pennsylvania and Philadelphia WILPF.[50]

As historian Glenda Gilmore has observed, given the right historical
context white women's knowledge of black political power can motivate
new forms of women's political associations.[51] In the case of the Philadelphia WILPF, Olmsted transformed her awareness of the extensive networks of black women's organizations into inspiration to usher the WILPF
into the realm of interracial politics. In the late 1920s white WILPF women
wagered that forming alliances with black women might vitalize women's
peace efforts and tame black militancy.

African American Women Rethink Place

African American women's motivations for entering into interracial peace
work with the Philadelphia WILPF were, like white women's, multiple and
many layered. The contradictory social and political developments of the
era that sometimes tested and constrained middle-class women's agency
required, as historian Deborah Gray White documents, African American women to rethink their place in the rapidly changing landscape. The
rise of black male political leadership during the New Negro era, dissatisfaction within the NACW about the organization's direction, and the
increased significance of peace issues and international perspectives

caused black women to reconsider how to engage their political concerns during the interwar years.[52]

The practical need to secure and expand political power caused some black women to develop new organizations and to seek a more substantial role within the WILPF. Dwindling interest in the NACW occurred in part because of frustration with the organization's continued reliance on uplift and self-help methods. Many members also wanted the organization to place more attention on international issues and involvement in political party politics. To answer these frustrations, some NACW leaders, including Dickerson, Hunton, and Terrell, helped form new organizations. The development of the ICWDR and the National League of Colored Republican Women was designed to maintain black women's political power and expand their political scope.[53] Although the ICWDR provided black women with a space unencumbered by black male or white female power, its effectiveness was hampered by a lack of financial resources. In part because of the organization's limited resources, some ICWDR members participated in white women's organizations as one way to expand the group's international exposure.[54] As they looked for other organizational affiliations through which they could expand their international interests, the WILPF often surfaced as a promising if sometimes imperfect match. In contrast to the International Council of Women (ICW), for instance, the WILPF offered a more progressive brand of international politics and a more racially hospitable atmosphere. This was particularly true in the mid-1920s. In 1925 the ICW held its International Congress, attended by women from forty-two countries in Washington, DC. During the congress's evening music festival, Addie Hunton and Mary McLeod Bethune staged a walkout because the event's seating was segregated by race. The WILPF, on the other hand, was conscious of the need to arrange its meetings in venues that did not abide by segregated practices.[55]

Mary Church Terrell's attendance at the 1919 WILPF Zurich Congress and Addie Hunton's 1925 WILPF mission to Haiti indicated to the ICWDR that relationships and membership with the WILPF should continue to be cultivated. It is then no surprise that ICWDR treasurer Mary Isenburger joined ICWDR president Addie Dickerson at the 1929 WILPF International

Congress in Prague. In reporting to the press on her and Isenburger's experience, Dickerson noted that the "WILPF afforded a rare opportunity for the two colored delegates to express Negro life and interpret Negro womanhood."[56]

In Dickerson's letters to Nannie Burroughs, chair of the ICWDR executive board, about Dickerson's 1929 WILPF Prague trip, she underscored the need to use the trip to promote black women's internationalism and to bolster the image of the ICWDR. After sharing with her friend details of her "most unusual and wonderful and glorious trip," including her "travel through nine countries" and audience with the Pope, Dickerson emphasized to Burroughs their shared concern, promotion of the ICWDR: "The conference is over and we will be home about October 1 . . . See that the Associated Press has mention of our council being represented and that its President was a delegate. You and I are interested in the council not ourselves so we must give it place in the process."[57]

Black women wanted to influence the international agendas of the women's peace movement and the New Negro movement. In order to do so they needed to secure their participation in the international gatherings of both movements. For instance, while informing Burroughs about the WILPF Prague conference, Dickerson reminded Burroughs that the ICWDR needed to find a way to be represented during the Pan-African Congress planned for December in Tunisia.[58] Because Dickerson knew that "people of vision talk in world terms," she also knew that the ICWDR needed the WILPF.[59] Likewise, as Mary Church Terrell noted in recalling the significance of her presence as a US WILPF delegate to the 1919 Zurich Congress, the participation of women of color made possible the appeal for "justice and fair play for all the dark races of the earth."[60]

Beyond the practical motivation to secure black women's place in international movements, black women in Philadelphia were also motivated by the political desire to promote their perspective on the links between war and racism. Mary Church Terrell sternly warned WILPF women gathered in Zurich in 1919: "You may talk about permanent peace till doomsday, but the world will never have it till the darker races are given a square deal."[61] Equating peace with racial democracy, it was logical for African American women to take control of the Philadelphia

WILPF interracial project. If black women could gain control and influence over the WILPF, they believed they could nudge the powerful white peace movement closer to their position that cultures that nurture and profit from war are cultures that nurture and profit from racism.

Alice Dunbar-Nelson returned to Terrell's theme nine years later. On the cusp of the Philadelphia WILPF interracial project, Dunbar-Nelson wrote in her newspaper column what was obvious to her but not to all involved in the peace movement. Because war is always profoundly detrimental to African Americans' well-being, black freedom required an end to both war and racism:

> No one knows better than the Negro that war is not the kind of thing which will bring about understanding among races, and he must be deeply concerned with inter-racial amity. His fortunes are so inevitably interwoven with the fortunes of everyone else in the nation, that he must deplore all that is wasteful, immoral, subversive of the Ten Commandments, as war is, and welcome all practical methods to bring about international, inter-racial peace, and morality.[62]

Through encouraging and expanding black peace consciousness, women like Dunbar-Nelson aimed to do much more than reverse military spending and imperialist foreign policy. Black women sought the attention of white peace reformers because they believed if the movement was to be successful it needed the political insight and political skill black women had to offer. Warning that the next war "will make the frightfulness of the last one seem like children playing with harmless sparklers," Dunbar-Nelson and other black women turned to the WILPF with large expectations.[63]

"A Thousand Negro Women"

By the 1920s, the black female infrastructure necessary to "secure a thousand Negro women" was in place. Middle-class black women had been working earnestly since the 1880s establishing female clubs, political associations, and educational and relief services. Builders of the infrastructure, black middle-class women like Dickerson, Reynolds, Dunbar-Nelson, and Mousserone, women "trained for the highest level of public work possible,"[64] spun the demands of the interracial committee into the complex and rich fabric of their public and private lives. The community development tasks and leadership roles necessitated by the committee were second nature. Seeing progress for the race in the mission of the committee, black women summoned the religious, benevolent, cultural, and political associations of Philadelphia's black community to the task of securing disarmament and securing a race consciousness within the peace movement.

According to Dunbar-Nelson, the first event of the Philadelphia WILPF interracial committee held jointly in the spring of 1928 with the American Friends Service Committee was a stellar success. The stately Broad Street Theater was packed with hundreds of people assembled to engage the call for interracial fellowship and disarmament. It was decorated with peace posters and premiered an art exhibit. The volunteer staff of high school girls greeted the attendees and later assisted Dunbar-Nelson in collecting the financial donations she solicited. The Sunday May 6 afternoon event featured speeches by the famous W. E. B. Du Bois and J. Finely Wilson, a founder of numerous black newspapers, recent president of the National Negro Press Association, and recent leader of the first black Elks benevolent association. On the Friday before the Sunday gala, Alice Dunbar-Nelson traveled from her home in Wilmington to New York City to give a speech at the Abyssinia Baptist church, returning home on an 11:00 p.m. train. That Saturday she attended a final organizing meeting in Philadelphia, caught a performance of Paul Green's Pulitzer Prize–winning play, *In Abraham's Bosom,* and returned home to begin making some dandelion wine. When she arrived home, she learned that the Wilsons would be stopping at her home on Sunday before the interracial peace event. Dunbar-Nelson bristled at this added responsibility, but the next morning she served the Wilsons rhubarb, grapefruit, deviled kidneys, and corn muffins and gave Finely her final comments on the speech he was about to deliver in Philadelphia.[65]

Although no record of the audience's response to Finely's lecture exists, Dunbar-Nelson noted that her friend made a "good speech." Du Bois, on the other hand, delivered a more memorable and acerbic lecture.

According to Dunbar-Nelson, Du Bois "whacks his Quakers" with his lecture as he linked the desire for peace to the necessity to end Jim Crow's grip on the nation. The nervous anticipation Henrietta Mousserone, the new WILPF "special representative," and Leslie Pinckney Hill, Dunbar-Nelson's fellow worker at the AIPC, struggled with in the weeks leading up to the Sunday event subsided as Du Bois captured the audience's attention. Du Bois's main themes, that racism and war were intimately linked and that the peace movement must work equally to eradicate both social ills, echoed the themes women like Dunbar-Nelson brought to the WILPF interracial project. If the packed audience was not enough proof of public interest and commitment to the interracial plea for peace and disarmament, Dunbar-Nelson believed that the 155 dollars collected directly after her fund appeal signaled the goodwill and commitment of the audience.[66]

The vitality of the May 6, 1928, Peace Mass Meeting forecasted the welcoming if complicated climate the women of the WILPF would find over the next seven years as they canvassed the city for peace supporters. With the success of the Broad Street Theater Peace Mass Meeting behind them and the Geneva Disarmament Conference looming, the committee jumped into action. The easiest work in front of them in some regard was tapping into the power of organized black middle-class societies in greater Philadelphia. The more difficult work would be reconciling the tensions Du Bois's lecture surfaced. Was the goal of the Philadelphia WILPF's interracial project to increase black participation in the disarmament movement or was it also to challenge US racism? And if the two issues were linked, how could women unaccustomed to seeing a link between racism and war be convinced of the necessity to work for the abolition of both?

Because the overall Philadelphia WILPF membership was not yet clear on the link between the two issues, the women of the newly organized IEC realized that the tasks before them were large. To meet the challenge of bringing a thousand black women into the Philadelphia peace movement and to contest racism, the WILPF IEC determined to meet every three weeks with summers off. Their meetings took place in the Philadelphia WILPF office located at 1525 Locust Street and later at 1924 Chestnut Street. Aspiring to "put over" the WILPF peace message to a substantial number of new women, the committee set a furious pace. Mousserone's dutifully recorded reports capture the intensity of the project and the work entailed in launching an event like the one featuring Du Bois. By the end of her first month of work in May of 1928, Mousserone reported making ninety-seven visits, writing thirty-nine letters, and placing thirty-four phone calls as a part of her commission to determine the readiness of black Philadelphians to the message of the women's peace movement. In the following winter, one month of work entailed Mousserone completing 160 visits, ninety letters, and fifty-one phone calls. In addition, she organized four meetings to train new peace recruits to serve as official speakers. In her annual report for 1931, Mousserone estimated that twenty trained Philadelphia WILPF IEC speakers reached two thousand people and that she herself made 405 visits, wrote 196 letters, and placed 249 phone calls. In 1932, the year of the much anticipated Geneva disarmament talks, the group reached forty-eight hundred people, according to Mousserone—more than double the number of the previous year.[67] Mousserone's public log of the seemingly never-ending personal contacts she made with black civic, educational, religious, and political organizations signals many things. Most importantly it indicated the depth of black women activists' commitment to the interracial peace agenda, the responsiveness of Philadelphia's (middle-class) black community to the women's peace movement as championed by known and respected black women, and the depth of black women's community contacts and political skill.

As Mousserone's reports reveal, the committee approached a range of middle-class societies. They canvassed church services, neighborhood teas, public mass meetings, parades, and playgrounds, spreading the message of peace. The women frequently turned to women's clubs and benevolent societies to convert women to disarmament work. As Evelyn Reynolds reminded the committee, clubwomen were a vital resource because they often had "leisure time." Clubs approached by the committee included the Housewives Club; Fireside Group; Mercy Service Club; Women's Art and Literature Club; Blue and Red Dancing Club; and the Hampton, Fisk, and Tuskegee Collegiate Clubs. Women with less leisure also heard from the committee as the committee regularly lobbied professional associations like the Funeral Directors' Association and the Medical, Dental, and Pharmaceutical Conference. The committee also utilized the power and resources of black women's sororities like Delta Sigma Theta and Alpha Kappa Alpha. Under Mousserone's guidance, the committee made a special commitment to galvanize black churches to the peace cause and to foster interracial and international consciousness among the young women of the city. Churches, like sororities, made up a significant part of clubwomen's routine networks, but entailed an active negotiation of gender dynamics not necessary when working with women's single-sex associations. For the duration of the committee, black women made sure not to overlook churches, and they also engaged black men to open doors to the city's and nation's fraternities and benevolent associations like the black Elks Club.[68]

Church Work

Mousserone used the national enthusiasm for disarmament to establish a substantial WILPF presence in Philadelphia's more prestigious black churches. She used the churches to foster the committee's ideals, to secure disarmament signatures and prayers for international peace campaigns, to solicit financial support, and to find new members. From 1928 to 1929 Mousserone reported meeting with 160 ministers and claimed that most churchmen were "generally eager to cooperate" with the program of the committee.[69] She relentlessly blanketed churches with literature and ideas for church-based peace programs. When the United States and Great Britain signed the Kellogg-Briand Pact on August 27, 1928, Mousserone lobbied the ministers to guide their parishioners in "prayers for its success."[70] She encouraged them to consult a WILPF-designed program entitled "The Message of Peace and Inter-Racial Good Will: Suggestions for the Negro Church" for special Armistice Day sermons and year-round study. Mousserone also enlisted Sunday school teachers to stage children's pageants that preached pacifism and global awareness.[71]

Even though the social role of black churches was being eclipsed by movie houses, dance halls, and political and benevolent associations, the committee relied on the churches.[72] A prime reason for this reliance was that many black committee members possessed powerful church affiliations. Dickerson, for instance, was the chair of the National Council of

Church Women. Blanche Anderson was the wife of Matthew Anderson, reverend of the Presbyterian Berean Church. Founded in 1878, the church was a central turn-of-the-century pillar of the uplift and betterment efforts of black Philadelphians. The church ran a medical center, kindergarten, and a building and loan association. In her own right, Blanche Anderson, educated at the University of Pennsylvania and Temple University, served as the principal of the Berean Manual Training and Industrial School from 1929 until the 1940s. The school, founded in 1897 with money from department store magnate John Wanamaker, addressed the vocational needs of the city's black working class. Anderson's other affiliations included the Woman's Christian Union, the Mask and Chance Drama League, the Negro History Club, and the NAACP.[73]

Success in the churches required that Mousserone and Reynolds be astutely aware of the power of black ministers and the gendered dynamics of the church. Though Mousserone believed that it was church women who possessed the real commitment to peace and power in the church, she made specific appeals to male authority.[74] With the help of Reynolds, Mousserone created a gender-sensitive strategy that engaged both the official power of the ministers and the unofficial though substantial power of the women of the church. Starting in 1928 the IEC approached ministers about joining the interracial committee and many gladly agreed to lend their support. Early ministerial committee members included Reverend Joseph Henderson of the Pinn Memorial Church and the Reverend Tindley Temple. Arthur Fauset, a scholar of the city's black churches and husband of Crystal Bird Fauset, also lent his support to the committee.[75] In the winter of 1930 with the London Arms Conference attracting world attention, Mousserone and Reynolds mailed thirty ministers a copy of London's Rabbi Joseph Hertz's "Prayer for the Success of the London Arms Conference." They encouraged the ministers as "leaders of men" to feature the arms conference in their Sunday proceedings. By eliciting the ministers' sense of standing and masculine authority in the black community, Mousserone and Reynolds believed the ministers would take up their request and "pause long enough to think seriously about peace."[76] The wives of ministers were invited to meetings at the WILPF office and encouraged to establish "definite" peace committees in their churches.

Mousserone herself was also a frequent speaker at Friday night and Sunday women's church meetings throughout the city.

The church work of the committee also gained early encouragement from Philadelphia's black press and from white WILPF members as well. The *Philadelphia Tribune* covered one of the first church events of the committee, a lecture by Mildred Scott Olmsted to the black branch of the Women's Christian Alliance. During the committee's first summer, a white committee member spoke about peace before a large welcoming crowd at Reverend Sheppard's Mount Olive Baptist Church and entertained the young members of Reverend Fletcher's church during Children's Day.[77] In the winter of 1931, Mr. Bonsall, executive secretary of the Pennsylvania Sunday School Association and the husband of a white IEC member, gave a talk to the First African Baptist Sunday School.[78] These programs were replicated beyond Philadelphia as Mousserone expanded the reach of the interracial committee into churches in other Pennsylvanian cities and towns like Media and West Chester.[79] Through requests for support to male leaders and the volunteer women's church associations, the Philadelphia IEC accumulated coveted church endorsements and access to large audiences, and helped deepen a peace-focused internationalist spirit in the city's religious institutions.

Junior International Leagues

In addition to church groups, the women of the IEC turned to Philadelphia's youth as another significant constituency to be organized. The committee formed interracial JILs to inspire young girls and teens with the message of peace and goodwill. The committee also intended the JILs to challenge the city's record of racial segregation in city schools. The committee hoped that the increased acceptance among educators and civic leaders of the teaching of world-mindedness might also indicate an increased openness to the fostering of interracial amity among the city's youth. In the spring of 1931, fifty girls from local high schools and the Girl Scouts and the Girls Reserves attended the first JIL tea. Over the next four years the WILPF provided young women with opportunities to learn about world cultures and politics; to attend guest lectures and films; to participate in study groups; and to establish friendships with women they otherwise might not have the opportunity to meet.[80]

Meeting every month, the girls and young women heard numerous lectures on the cultures and politics of countries headlining the news. The study of Japan, India, and Liberia expanded their worldview while spreading a message of peace. The girls were also encouraged to attend events of the main interracial committee. JIL members attended luncheons featuring lectures by Emily Greene Balch and Mary McLeod Bethune on the state of the arms race, the state of the economy, and the state of race relations in the United States. In the spring of 1931, JIL members were invited to attend Cheyney Normal School's commencement. Located twenty-five miles outside of Philadelphia, the school was one of the oldest historically black colleges in the nation. Leslie Pinckney Hill, a committed peace activist and president of the college, invited the JIL members because he supported the WILPF's project and because peace was the subject of that year's commencement speech.[81]

Coverage of JIL events applauded the international and interracial spirit of the gatherings. A *Philadelphia Tribune* society page report remarked at length about the internationalism of a JIL party held in December of 1932. The article emphasized the diversity of the youth who attended by noting the participation of "Russians, Jews, Americans and many other nationalities and races." The article also remarked upon the Mexican decorations in the meeting hall.[82] A few months later the same paper reported on an interracial gathering of young girls from the Wharton Settlement House and the First Day class of the Frankford Meeting House. According to the paper, the girls had "a delightful time playing games, singing and drawing interesting sketches." To the readers of the *Philadelphia Tribune* and supporters of the JIL, the youth involved in the WILPF JIL project represented the prospect that a younger generation could end the legacy of militarism and racism that challenged the nation and the world.[83]

Garden and Tea Parties

Garden and tea parties in some ways represented the adult version of the social gatherings arranged for the young women of the JIL. They were social occasions designed to stimulate support for disarmament and interracial goodwill. Originally planned to encourage "bigger peace propaganda among Negroes," interracial teas quickly became a litmus test for race relations within WILPF and within the city.[84] African American women and some white women understood that for the teas and garden parties to be successful, the WILPF must confront the racialized social codes of the 1920s and 1930s. The teas grounded the discursive promise of interracial and transnational goodwill championed by the committee and the WILPF. The ability or inability of WILPF women to meet as equals over tea and cookies indicated the ability or inability of the world to realign power and move closer to peace. The tensions and successes surrounding the teas reflected the mercurial atmosphere of the Jim Crow North and the high stakes involved in the call by women like Jane Addams and Nannie Burroughs for women to practice goodwill.

Evelyn Reynolds thought of the parties as "harvests." She believed they offered perfect opportunities to plant new interest in the WILPF and to cultivate new women who understood the importance of working for racial equality. The planning of interracial teas and garden parties required much careful preparation by Reynolds, Mousserone and the hosts, especially when the goal was both to lecture on peace and to foster an interracial spirit. A typical party featured musical entertainment, groomed gardens, and catered refreshments.[85] Organizers attempted to encourage an atmosphere of racial understanding by paying careful attention to the racial balance of the speakers, the entertainment, and the guest list. For instance, a tea held in North Philadelphia in February of 1930 in honor of Black History Month headlined an interracial cast of speeches by Mildred Scott Olmsted and Lena Trent Gordon, a special investigator for the city's Department of Public Affairs. Similarly, in the spring of 1929 a Germantown luncheon and lawn party featured talks by national interracial committee chair Addie Hunton and education activist Rachel Davis Dubois. However, offering a racially balanced panel of speakers did not guarantee a racially balanced party, even when hosts expressed the desire to have "equal numbers of colored and white" in attendance.[86] For instance, in the fall of 1929, the sponsor of a tea in Germantown, although "pleased that some very fine speeches" were given, was disappointed that only sixty people attended and that "more Negroes than whites" were present.[87]

For some, the issue was not only if the audience reflected an inter-racial balance, but if those attending shared middle-class status or noble womanhood. In the fall of 1929 Swarthmore music teacher and magazine writer Elizabeth Bonsall hosted a tea at the Swarthmore Women's Club House. Bonsall, a white woman, was a patron of the Black Arts Renaissance. As an arts patron, she helped commission a painting by acclaimed Harlem Renaissance visual artist Laura Wheeler Waring that was featured as part of a national WILPF fund-raiser. Bonsall's tea mirrored the format of IEC teas as it offered a mixture of political speeches and entertainment, including a performance by the Lincoln University Glee Club. Lincoln University, located in Chester County, Pennsylvania, was one of the earliest black universities in the country. But Bonsall registered disappointment with the tea during a follow-up IEC meeting. The committee minutes record that Bonsall regarded the class and educational standing of some of the black guests as problematic. Specifically, Bonsall questioned "the effectiveness of group meetings where the colored group represented is not of the same social and intellectual background as the white."[88] Though the committee minutes do not reveal who the specific women were who attended the tea, Bonsall's remarks revealed the volatility surrounding questions of race and class and the complex and contentious politics of noble womanhood and goodwill.

Debates about who qualified to participate in the WILPF membership were not new. Early field notes filed by WILPF organizers dispatched to expand the organization's membership recorded persistent discussions about whether white working-class women, Catholic women, or farmers, for instance, were suitable for the organization. Bonsall's complaint about the perceived class standing of at least some of the black women attending her tea, and the forthrightness with which she shared her objections, made obvious the ongoing tensions within the organization about the politics of race and class inherent in the informal charter of the IEC. The brief mention in the committee minutes of Bonsall's objections raises at least two questions. Did anyone attending the meeting dissent to Bonsall's comments? To what extent was her complaint in compliance with the middle-class politics of respectability promoted by many of the black leaders of the IEC? Bonsall's tea makes obvious that class remained both a unifying and divisive category in the Philadelphia committee. Middle-class standing sometimes helped bridge the racial divide and could set the stage for interracial coalitions. At the same time class usually closed the door to participation in WILPF to poor and working-class women of any race.

How to use the teas effectively to foster better race relations among peace women and to bring about an end to war remained a question. In crafting the invitation to their North Philadelphia tea held the winter following Bonsall's event, Blanche Anderson and Virginia Sears made it clear that they believed that peace started close to home. In the invitation they exhorted that "unrest, misunderstanding, hate, prejudice—all of these things can be removed if we learn to know each other better."[89] As the IEC staff person, Mousserone promoted the philosophy that global conditions improved when local conditions improved. When Mary Church Terrell turned to Mousserone for advice in the fall of 1930 on the direction her talk at an upcoming tea should take, Mousserone advised Terrell to "talk mostly about . . . the necessity of both groups working together for a better understanding." Mousserone confided in Terrell that better understanding "is in my mind the foundation of world peace."[90]

Although black women turned to the teas as an opportunity to cultivate white women's interracial goodwill, they also used the teas to promote themselves as peace-minded internationalists. Teas and garden parties hosted in the homes of African American women could enhance their public profile and their recognition as peace activists. By holding teas in their own homes, black women diminished the power of white scrutiny while simultaneously elevating their own authority as peace workers within black communities. IEC chair Evelyn Reynolds's hosting of a "Cuban Tea" in the winter of 1933, for instance, received detailed coverage on the society page of the *Philadelphia Tribune*. Declaring it the most successful "Cuban Tea" held in the city, the article highlighted Reynolds's "well appointed house" with its "soft glow from a fireplace" and "fresh flowers in not too gaudy vases." Declaring her the "most popular society woman," the *Philadelphia Tribune* reported that one hundred guests gathered in Reynolds's home to hear the exiled Señorita Porsez speak about political conditions in Cuba.[91]

Large mass meetings served many of the same goals as teas and garden parties, although in a less intimate setting. These events raised awareness of the link between racism and war, advanced the political careers of African American and white women, and announced the Philadelphia WILPF's aspirations to integrate the peace movement. An impressive list of women addressed the Philadelphia committee's luncheons and mass meetings signaling the high profile of the women's peace movement in the later years of the 1920s and into the mid-1930s. Like the teas and garden parties, these events frequently teamed black and white speakers as a strategy for fostering interracial sisterhood as a path to peace.

Lucy Diggs Slowe, Dean of Women at Howard University, keynoted the first annual luncheon of the interracial committee in the fall of 1929. Diggs Slowe was a suffragist, founder of Alpha Kappa Alpha, the first black women's sorority, and lifelong companion of educator and playwright Mary P. Burrill.[92] The next year's luncheon featured Mary McLeod Bethune and Emily Greene Balch. Bethune, a clubwoman, activist and founder and president of the Bethune-Cookman College in Florida, gave a speech entitled "The Negro's Part in World Peace."[93] Mass meetings at the Union Baptist Church continued to advance the link between the eradication of racism and the eradication of war. The poster announcing Crystal Bird Fauset's appearance at the 1932 WILPF mass meeting read: "Out of a Job? Why? Do We Need Bullets or Bread?" In her speech, "Peace from the Inter-Racial Viewpoint," Fauset reviewed the impact of the Great Depression on the lives of black Americans and outlined why disarmament and peace were in the economic interest of African Americans and the nation at large.[94]

Publicity

The committee regularly landed coverage in the major black newspapers in the city and the state including the *Philadelphia Tribune* and the *Pittsburgh Courier*. Coverage in the black press of teas, garden parties, luncheons, and mass meetings extolled middle-class black women in their role as peace activists. As Mousserone explained to Mary Church Terrell, one of her aims in working to integrate black women into the WILPF was to place black women "with those who are nationally known as shining lights of this great movement."[95] The press attention also championed the WILPF as an ally of black Americans in the arena of local, national, and international policy. These papers covered everyday community events sponsored by the Philadelphia WILPF like a campaign to collect "40,000 Pennies for Peace." The *Philadelphia Tribune* also sponsored "Peace Corner," a weekly column by black writer, educator, and WILPF associate Idabelle Yeiser.[96] Yeiser's columns ran in the early 1930s and addressed a variety of peace issues. She wrote about everything from campaigns against children's war toys, to the danger of nerve gas, to the state of US policy in Cuba. The WILPF's interracial projects also received notice on radio shows and in business establishments. Fliers for WILPF events appeared in drugstores, barbershops, churches, public theaters, restaurants, and tearooms throughout Philadelphia's black neighborhoods. In 1929 with the encouragement of the WILPF, WCAU radio station aired the Plantation Quartette singing "Ain't Gonna Study War No More." This musical number announced a connection between the Black Arts Renaissance and the goals and strategies of the women's peace movement.

Coverage of the WILPF in the black press was not exclusive to events sponsored by the interracial committee or only to work accomplished in greater Philadelphia. During the years of the IEC, overall reporting on the WILPF expanded in the *Philadelphia Tribune*. Articles about the WILPF appeared in the domestic and international news sections in addition to the woman's pages. The work of white WILPF members, such as Rachel Dubois, Ellen Star Brinton, and Dorothy Detzer, received regular attention, causing the *Tribune* to state that the WILPF was a "force that promoted goodwill" and global peace. Expanded and friendly press accounts assisted in making the WILPF a more familiar organization to the readers of the *Philadelphia Tribune* and *Pittsburgh Courier*. The coverage also advanced black women's prominence as peace activists. Sponsorship of Yeiser's column, reporting on Reynolds's tea, and the publishing of a quarter-page photograph of Blanche Anderson announcing her WILPF leadership all contributed to the formation of a new black female internationalist peace identity.[97]

Securing favorable press coverage necessitated that the committee actively pursue relationships with the writers, managers, and owners of the city's and state's various papers. Alice Dunbar-Nelson's regular engagement as an *Associated Negro Press* columnist no doubt helped to obtain media coverage for the WILPF. Acquiring equitable reporting of the WILPF's interracial peace work in the city's white-owned news outlets sometimes took intervention. In December of 1930, Mrs. Edwin J. Johnson, secretary of the interracial committee, wrote the editor of the *Public Ledger* complaining about the coverage given to a fall interracial committee luncheon. Johnson questioned why Mary Church Terrell, one of the three luncheon speakers, was not mentioned in the article. She wrote: "There seems to be no reason for having neglected the third person on the program unless you have a ban on mentioning colored people. It is often said that no achievement of a Negro except for crime can get into the papers. Such an attitude we deprecate as grossly unfair."[98]

Race and Disarmament Caravans
in Greater Delaware Valley

The failure of the 1932 Geneva Disarmament Conference did not end women peace activists' efforts to rein in the arms race. Utilizing the popularity of the car caravan that had delivered pro-disarmament petitions to President Hoover in January of 1932, the Philadelphia IEC planned a new set of programs including a regional car caravan. The series of new programs ranged from disarmament speakers in playgrounds on Flag Day to the sponsorship of disarmament-themed card and puzzle parties at women's clubs. The most robust events were the Saturdays in July interracial car caravans scheduled for the most populous black communities. All the programs aimed to educate people in the Greater Delaware Valley on the continued need for disarmament, to promote interracial friendship, and to promote black leadership.[99]

In April of 1933 the black-owned Royal Theater located at Sixteenth and South Street in Philadelphia served as the location for what Alice Dunbar-Nelson billed as a disarmament event featuring "Unusual Three Minute Speakers." The speakers in fact represented many of the most esteemed black men in the city. The event headlined Dunbar-Nelson's husband, Judge Robert Nelson; congressman and state civil rights bill sponsor, Judge John Asbury; and the exalted leader of the Elks, Judge John M. Marquess. Additional speakers included the Reverend Marshall Sheppard of the Mount Olive Tabernacle Baptist Church and Addie Dickerson's husband, lawyer G. Edward Dickerson.[100] To round out the event attendees were treated to the music of the Hoxter Jubilee Singers and the O. V. Catto and Quaker City Elks Bands. This event, organized by Dunbar-Nelson, married the growing power of greater Philadelphia's black politicians and civic leaders with the aims of the peace movement. These "unusual speakers" used the momentum behind campaigns to secure the passage of state civil rights legislation to accelerate support for the disarmament agenda. The event evidenced the continued support by black men of the work of the IEC. In a few months, the men on stage at the Royal Theater along with Leslie Pinckney Hill, Arthur Fauset, and Theodore Penney would lend their endorsement to the Saturdays in July WILPF car caravans.[101]

The miniature peace caravans planned by the Philadelphia IEC for the summer of 1933 differed from the one that had reached President Hoover the previous year. The vision had expanded—the audience to be reached was primarily black, the car caravans were to be interracial, and black men were solicited to join the speaker's podium. The new car caravans also offered an opportunity to cultivate new younger leadership for the IEC. Reynolds and Dunbar-Nelson turned much of the work of planning the event over to recent Cheyney Teacher's College graduate Charlene Howard. As Howard's committee notes indicate, the program was ambitious:

> The business of the moment is this: on the first four Saturdays in July, several cars-full of people under the leadership of one of our Committee members, will go to a different town each Saturday, beginning with West Chester, Wilmington, Atlantic City and ending we hope, with Camden and possibly Lawnside. The purpose of each of these trips is to hold a street-corner speech meeting at one or two thickly populated colored centers. Our speakers will give a simple, short and we trust effective peace message.[102]

In stops along the caravan route, the cars were greeted by IEC members and people were entertained with music. In West Chester, white women met the WILPF caravan at the entrance of the town and escorted it in. In Atlantic City, Dunbar-Nelson's friends in charge of arrangements selected Leslie Pinckney Hill and Theodore Penny as speakers.[103] The occasion of the caravans and street corner speeches marked more than five years since the Philadelphia WILPF announced the beginning of the Philadelphia IEC. On one level the Saturdays in July caravans celebrated the success of black women's contributions to the WILPF and the strength of black disarmament sentiment. But behind the public picture of robust peace activities emerged a different story. It seemed that the WILPF was unable to match black women's commitment with a commitment to rid the WILPF of all vestiges of segregation.

Contesting the Limits of Goodwill in the WILPF

With the changing national and global political landscape came changes in the needs and attitudes of women involved in the Philadelphia interracial committee. The collapse of disarmament talks, the rise of fascism, and the deepening effect of the national economic meltdown caused many activists of all political persuasions to reconsider their priorities, strategies, and political alliances. In the Philadelphia WILPF, debates resurfaced and intensified over two issues. First, did the interracial committees enhance or hinder black women's integration into the organization? Second, did the WILPF believe that ending racism was integral to achieving peace? The answer to these two questions would result in the disbanding of the Philadelphia IEC in 1935. The dismantling of the IEC did not necessarily mean the end of black women's involvement or the complete turning away of the WILPF from projects to contest racism. It did, however, usher in new approaches to the work for racial justice and the building of the foundations for constructive peace.

One early example of these dynamics emerged during the planning of speaking engagements in black and white churches. A successful 1928 outdoor lawn festival at the black Berean Presbyterian Church required negotiations between Olmsted and Mousserone about subsequent church

events. Olmsted and Mousserone both hailed the Berean event as a success because of its large audience and the enthusiastic welcome given to
the white members of the WILPF speakers' bureau who addressed the
church members. On the heels of this success and the generosity of the
Berean congregation, Mousserone proposed to Olmsted that they now
arrange for African American speakers to address one of the city's white
churches. She "felt that we ought to reciprocate by arranging for some of
the colored ministers to speak to white audiences."[104] Olmsted dismissed
Mousserone's suggestion of an equal exchange between the city's racially
divided churches and instead offered a counterproposal. In responding
to Mousserone, Olmsted first "explained the difficulty" of allowing black
speakers to address a white church audience. Next she offered that the
black ministers be guests at a WILPF interracial tea at which time white
members could meet them. Olmsted's offer of "bringing white to black
audiences," and "black to mixed," indicated her summation that white
churches would not accept the authority of a black speaker. Olmsted's
proposed solution accommodated the limitations of white racial attitudes.
In not challenging white churches' Jim Crow practices, Olmsted instead
chose to circumscribe the rules of black involvement in the public activities
of the IEC. This exchange in the summer of 1928 foreshadowed the future
trials black women would experience within the Philadelphia WILPF as
they sought equal access to organizational authority and power.[105]

Still, Mousserone forged ahead, fortified by her commitment to the
twin causes of racial harmony and world peace. Developments on the
state level gave Mousserone and other interracial committee members
reason to believe that perhaps the interracial cause and the importance of
black women's leadership was catching on in the state. Starting in April of
1932 the Pennsylvania state branch took steps that indicated an increased
willingness to endorse interracial projects, black women's leadership, and
the cause of racial justice. These incremental developments encouraged
Mousserone at the same time that they underscored the slow and controlled pace of change in the WILPF and the nation at large.

In the early spring of 1932, upon learning that the Pennsylvania
branch planned to discuss if they should increase their work on the "interracial situation," Mousserone composed a letter to Edwina Johnson, the

Pennsylvania branch chairwoman. In the letter, Mousserone expressed her delight that the topic was to be explored and her deep conviction that the work for interracial friendship and an end to racism was the path to peace. Mousserone wrote to Johnson:

> I see listed in the Topics for Discussion at the Business Meeting: Is the Interracial Situation one which should be emphasized on our program in the next year? Kindly permit me to ask that it will be emphasized. As the special Representative of the Interracial Extension Committee for the past five years, I have been in a position to observe the grave necessity of intensive interest along these lines, both within the organization and the public at large. It has been one of my soul's greatest desires to concentrate more directly on this most interesting subject. So, when I read a few days ago on your program that the Interracial situation was about to be tackled, I felt that one of my largest dreams since having been in the work for World Peace was about to be realized . . . spurring me on in the slow, but sure building of the foundation for World Peace, through better understanding of races.[106]

A few subsequent developments during the following three years suggested to Mousserone that perhaps women in Philadelphia and greater Pennsylvania understood the importance of improving race relations in order to produce peace. The lynching of Claude Neal in Florida in October of 1934 revitalized the decadelong efforts by the NAACP and women like Hunton, Dunbar-Nelson, Detzer, and Hannah Clothier Hall to pass a federal antilynching law. Floridian Claude Neal's lynching, watched by a crowd estimated to number up to five thousand, served as a horrifying reminder of the state of US race relations. Edwina Johnson wrote a letter to United States Attorney General Homer Cummings registering the Pennsylvania WILPF's outrage at this violent act of injustice and called for federal antilynching legislation to be enacted. In her letter to the attorney general, Johnson noted international outrage over the persistence of lynching in the United States. Mousserone sent Johnson a telegram applauding Johnson's swift response and leadership and noted the importance of Johnson's efforts not only to the members of the WILPF, but also to the "219,000 Negroes" living in Pennsylvania.[107]

The increase of black leadership in the state WILPF apparatus also indicated support for a more interracial agenda. In the spring of 1933, in an effort to advance statewide interracial relations, Reynolds and Mousserone traveled to the state's annual board meeting to deliver the Philadelphia IEC report in person. Perhaps because of the limit of Philadelphia branch funds, Reynolds and Mousserone personally covered the cost of their travel to the meeting. They reported back to women in Philadelphia that "our report was well received and the affair was pleasant and successful."[108] The state branch also doubled the number of black women on the Pennsylvania board from one to two. Reynolds, the only black member of the state leadership, was now to be joined in 1933 by fellow Philadelphian Leila Walker Jones. But the process of Jones's ascension to the board also revealed the controls placed on black women's access to WILPF leadership. In a letter to Reynolds, Olmsted apprised her of the state board's willingness to increase black representation and solicited her support in making this happen. Olmsted wrote: "I wish you would agree on some colored woman . . . who would be a good member for our Board . . . *our Board voted . . . a year or more ago that they would welcome having another colored woman*" (emphasis added).[109] The appointment of Leila Walker Jones indicated, perhaps, Mousserone's understanding that the building of "finer race relations" would be a slow process. The Philadelphia board's approach to adding another black woman to the state board can be read in a number of ways. On one hand, by requesting that Reynolds and ostensibly the other black women of the IEC select the new representative, Olmsted indicated her respect of the opinion and power of Reynolds. On the other hand, the pace of black women's integration into the state power structure remained controlled by the white-dominated state board. Still, the presence of black women on WILPF state boards was an achievement accomplished by only a few state branches in the 1930s. By 1935, only five WILPF state branches, including Pennsylvania, retained African American board members. In this respect, then, Pennsylvania was in the vanguard.

Back in Philadelphia in December of 1934, Olmsted believed that the level of activity produced by the city's IEC was declining because of a decline in the quality of Reynolds's leadership. When Olmsted learned that Reynolds had left her job at the Armstrong Association she inquired if Reynolds would now "have more leisure" and thus be able to "get the Interracial Committee under way and really keep them at work."[110] A little more than two weeks later when Reynolds had not replied to her letter, Olmsted wrote Dickerson asking for her "frank opinion" about what to do about the condition of the IEC.[111] On January 7 Dickerson wrote Olmsted with her frank opinion. She informed Olmsted that many African American women in the IEC wanted a change in the quality of their involvement in the WILPF. In her letter, Dickerson also declined to endorse Olmsted's assessment that the perceived downturn in activity indicated a failure of black women's leadership. Instead, Dickerson began the process of educating the white membership about the frustration black women felt about what they concluded was the use of interracial committees to segregate and control them. When Dickerson alerted Olmsted to this changed attitude, she also offered advice about how the WILPF could salvage relations with black women. Dickerson wanted black women to stay involved, but wanted the rules of the involvement to shift. After reminding Olmsted that they had had similar conversations in the past, she advised Olmsted, "it seems most unfortunate that the Committee should go out of existence; unless of course, you are able to secure the interest of every member and place them on [other] committees, so that they might be having the contact and vision of the League and at the same time, the League might have the benefit of their interest and work."[112] In this letter to Olmsted, Dickerson clarified that the future of the involvement of black women actually rested in the actions of the white members. If black women refused to accept their position as corollary members, white members would need to radicalize their commitment to the tenets of goodwill and thoroughly open the WILPF to black women's participation.

Fear and suspicion that interracial committees had become a way to segregate black participation had been mounting in the national WILPF as well. Four days after Olmsted received Dickerson's letter alerting her to black women's request for more integrated participation, Dorothy Detzer released a "Not for Publication" branch report. The report was written in consultation with Addie Hunton, who chaired the national WILPF IEC and who had been involved in the WILPF for years. With the recent developments and suspicions, Hunton advised her friend Detzer that perhaps the interracial committees should be disbanded. Detzer did not call for the disbanding of the committees, but she did issue a stern report on January 11, 1935, to all branch, legislative, and interracial committee chairs. In it, Detzer instructed WILPF leaders on the correct role of interracial committees in the organization. Detzer was to the point: interracial committees and black members were to be treated the same as all other committees and members. Detzer wrote:

> The function of an inter-racial committee should be that of any other committee—namely, to serve the whole group in a special capacity—but the inter-racial committee which would seem to be the most effective would be one whose work was so integrated in the work of the whole group, that there would be no sense of separateness. For example, Negro members should be serving on many other committees, bringing their contributions to the work as a whole, as well as the inter-racial field.[113]

Six weeks after writing Olmsted and after the release of Detzer's national branch letter, Dickerson encouraged African American women in Philadelphia to take it upon themselves to assume new places in the WILPF. In a February 1935 letter, cowritten with Reynolds and Crystal Bird Fauset, Dickerson called for the disbanding of the IEC and the integration of black members into the WILPF. The trio sent the letter with the outlined changes to thirteen other African American associates who had worked with the WILPF, many of them since the original setup of the committee in 1928. The letter declared:

> It is our plan this year to work with the Women's International League not as an inter-racial group, but assuming our places on the respective committees . . . We feel that our contribution in a set up of this kind, will mean first, an added interest to the organization, second, an opportunity for your individual helpfulness, and third, an expression of our group strength.[114]

The liabilities associated with the WILPF's brand of tentative and limited racial segregation had been mounting and increasingly seemed to outweigh the advantages that came with WILPF membership. Keeping black women on the periphery meant, for instance, that black women's participation in the international WILPF remained underdeveloped. Addie Hunton made numerous interventions to expand black women's role in the international WILPF that went unheeded. In the summer of 1932, for instance, Hunton advanced two proposals: (a) a fundraising program to accelerate the WILPF's work among "colored women" throughout the world; and (b) the appointment of an African American woman to serve as an official observer of the League of Nations and at the next session of the disarmament conference. Hunton's suggestions to expand black female international presence, however, did not materialize.[115]

In the summer of 1934 on the eve of the eighth International WILPF Congress, African American women's international prospects were once again curtailed. The invitation to join the September 3 to September 8 congress in Zurich came too late, making it impossible for any of the leading women, like Hunton, Burroughs, or Dickerson, to attend. WILPF president and Philadelphian Hannah Clothier Hull wrote to Dickerson only one month before the congress to extend an invitation to have a "negro" delegate attend. Dickerson, who at that time was also the president of the ICWDR, replied congenially that the women of the ICWDR "should welcome an opportunity to cooperate with our own Women's International League for Peace and Freedom." Yet she also indicated that the likelihood was slim that an ICWDR representative would be able to participate. Dickerson told Hull that because it was the height of the summer and "so many of our women are scattered," the logistics of finding someone able to prepare for the trip and raise the necessary money to cover expenses seemed unlikely.[116]

Olmsted spoke with Dickerson about Hull's invitation and reported back to Hull that Dickerson and the ICWDR would not be able to send their own representative. Olmsted reported to Hull that Dickerson had said that: "Miss Burroughs herself might have gone had they known about it earlier. Of course, they both feel that they would like to be represented." Unable to be represented in person, Olmsted informed Hull about an alternative proposal offered by Dickerson and the ICWDR: "They would, however, be willing, she thinks, if they do not have Mrs. Hunton or herself as a Negro, to have me represent them and to make a report to their Committee upon my return."[117]

In the end, Olmsted served as a proxy for the ICWDR and the African American members of the WILPF. The ICWDR donated twenty-five dollars to support Olmsted's travels.[118] Sixteen years after Terrell's status as a US WILPF delegate to the 1919 Zurich Congress, African American women were no closer to having regular representation at the international proceedings of the WILPF, let alone in the full committee structure of city and state branches. As contingent or peripheral members, African American women missed an opportunity in 1934 to participate in the international Zurich Congress during which women deliberated on how to respond to the spread of fascism.

The quiet revolt in Philadelphia in the winter of 1935, initiated by Dickerson, Crystal Bird Fauset, and Reynolds, spelled the end of the Philadelphia interracial committee and dampened the development of a strong African American presence in the Philadelphia WILPF. The protest called into question the strategy of noble womanhood and signaled the limits of the notion of goodwill. Without some sign that the rank-and-file white members were willing to confront how Jim Crow era racism affected the WILPF and the nation, the cost of continued participation in the organization seemed too great and the benefits too diminished. Over the course of seven years, the appeal and promise of interracialism had worn off, in particular to African American women like Addie Hunton for whom the enduring economic crisis caused by the Depression required a new pace and tenor of political response.

The Great Depression, the rise of fascism, and the slow pace of interracialism caused Hunton and some other middle-class black women to advocate for a more aggressive political perspective that embraced an increased focus on black nationalism through the strengthening of black organizational power. In her 1932 NAACP national convention speech Hunton expressed her concern about the impact the Depression was having on black progress. She also questioned the wisdom of continuing with a gradualist political approach. The Depression, she noted, was "affecting the whole fabric of what we choose to call civilization." And in the face of the "despairing conditions of so many colored men and women," she called upon conventioneers to help her design an "inspired interpretation of right and justice." Further, she encouraged NAACP members and other liberal supporters to end their support of "patronizing panaceas" and charity work, and replace them with "great new solutions born of world justice."[119] The founding in 1935 of the National Council of Negro Women (NCNW) represented a welcomed coalescing of black women's political strength. Hunton endorsed the launching of this new organization and cheered it on with the observation that "we must solidify."[120] The changing political climate did not diminish Hunton's embrace of a multifaceted political agenda. She persevered in her commitment to expose the links between war and racism and to foster a black global political outlook. What did shift for Hunton, though, was the amount of time and energy she was willing to spend challenging the racial attitudes and practices of white women's organizations.

During the interwar years, African American women brought a distinct perspective on peace reform to the WILPF. They maintained a clear conviction that the building of "finer local race relations" was central to the building of world peace. Although the WILPF in principle believed that peace and freedom were two sides of the same coin, for many of the rank-and-file white membership peace and freedom were not as intimately and inextricably connected as they were for African Americans who faced daily infringements on their civil liberties. African American women's use of the strategy of noble womanhood failed to win over the hearts and minds of the rank and file of the WILPF, but it did secure for black women a new platform as peace activists within the social, cultural, and political spaces of the black middle class. This new identity significantly helped to stabilize middle-class African American women's position as vital contributors to the black uplift endeavors during an era in which, as Deborah Gray White has argued, their role was seriously challenged.[121]

The peace philosophy advocated by African American women at the head of the Philadelphia IEC and nationally by Hunton received unequivocal support from some key white WILPF women such as Dorothy Detzer and Zonia Baber. In 1935, echoing Nannie Burroughs's 1930 Union Baptist Church speech in which she called for love and faith to replace legislation,

Detzer and Baber requested that WILPF branch presidents intensify their commitment to end racism and move beyond a strategy of legislative reform. They wanted members to care about tackling race prejudice with the same zeal and conviction they felt for other issues.[122] Yet, even when prospered by white leaders, the encouragement to see the elimination of racism as pivotal to the WILPF's peace mission met resistance. As Zonia Baber assessed:

> There are a few no doubt in each branch who have overcome their color prejudice, but the majority are still governed by it. We have asked our members to read books on the World Court, the League of Nations . . . why should we not have a letter sent out . . . stating that color prejudice is one of the fundamental things that prevents national as well as international understanding and goodwill and recommend that they begin with the home problem. . . . Our people shrink from considering this problem as something disagreeable, something to forget, while they study with zest the German persecution of the Jews.[123]

This unwillingness by white women to see the connection between racism and war became intolerable for African American women who had contributed so much to the WILPF. The reticence of white members to approach racial justice with the same zeal as they approached disarmament convinced white antiracist WILPF leaders like Detzer and Baber to design new political strategies to raise the membership's consciousness about the racial politics of the United States. The frustration of women like Hunton, Reynolds, Detzer, and Baber was real. Although the end of the heyday of IEC was before them, the lessons learned from this interwar experiment helped the WILPF to fashion a more successful involvement in the civil rights movements that would emerge during the next two decades.

In the end, class did not trump race when it came to securing the involvement of women like Dickerson, Reynolds, Burroughs, and Fauset in the ongoing life of the Pennsylvania WILPF and by extension the international women's peace community. As Howard University Dean of Women Lucy Diggs Slowe reminded white women gathered at her college in May of 1935 to discuss the future of peace work in the WILPF: "the difficulty involved in interesting intelligent colored people in a program of peace education" lay in the racial attitudes of white folks, because "oftener than otherwise [colored people] know that they cannot be accepted on the same basis as other people."[124] This unwillingness to accept black women as sister noblewomen became untenable over time and led to the dissolution of the Philadelphia interracial committee.

Yet, the allure of noble womanhood did influence the discourse of interracialism in the city of Philadelphia in the 1920s and 1930s and the position of black women in black middle-class society. The propriety and liberal manner of the IEC became a yardstick by which other forms of interracial activity were measured. The professional middle-class black and white speakers promoted by the Philadelphia IEC found a strong welcome in the many theaters, schools, churches, club rooms, playgrounds, and assembly halls that constituted black society. The *Philadelphia Tribune* regularly lauded the "finery" of the interracial gatherings promoted by the IEC. At the same time, the paper offered noticeably less frequent or favorable reporting to other interracial activities that took place in the city.[125] In 1933, the interracial "frolicking" of "sexual inverts" during Philadelphia's first drag ball angered *Philadelphia Tribune* writers for its display of "sexual transgressions" and for its interracial flair. The fact that the 1933 "pansy ball" received police protection when "the full force of the law" had been used "to prevent the races from mixing on a high social and moral plane" incensed black middle-class political and moral sensibility.[126] Although interracial hunger marches, dances, and drag balls sought to break open the same social covenants against racial mixing that the IEC also opposed, to middle-class black Philadelphians like the women of the IEC these "other fellows" threatened the place of middle-class virtues in the fight against racial segregation.

The dismantling of the Philadelphia IEC meant neither the end of African American women's involvement in the Philadelphia WILPF nor the Philadelphia WILPF's cessation of work on race issues. Blanche Anderson, for instance, who joined the committee in 1928, remained a member of the WILPF into the 1940s. Nor did the push to embrace black nationalism or the rank-and-file WILPF's resistance to integration cause black women to halt the work for peace. In 1935 Dickerson, as president of the ICWDR, appealed to ICWDR members to be active in a new left-ist peace coalition, the Emergency Peace Campaign, designed to respond to the rise of fascism and to keep the United States from going to war.[127] In March of 1940, Nannie Burroughs and Dickerson, both women facing ongoing illness and lessened organizational resources, searched for ways for the ICWDR to "come before the public" and promote organized black womanhood's analysis of "the present situation of the war."[128]

The most stinging indictment of the peace movement's failure to con-tend with racism came perhaps from NACW president Mary Waring in her 1935 annual address, delivered the same year that the African Ameri-can women of the Philadelphia IEC ended their segregated involvement in the WILPF. Waring declared:

> Peace. There can be no peace in spite of the great sums that are spent to promote it unless we are just to all people . . . Ask Pacifists, Philanthro-pists and other groups with similar kind attitudes, how they would like to live in a country where they could neither travel, eat or even purchase the necessities of life without being reminded that they are different, inferior or undesirable. How can we hope to inspire the best effort and build citizenship with double standards and ostracism? Peace? There can be no peace while such practices continue.[129]

In her "electrifying" 1930 speech, delivered before an interracial audi-ence of peace-minded Philadelphians, Nannie Burroughs contended that love, not legislation, would be the balm to the nation's ills.[130] By 1935, in the Philadelphia WILPF at least, it seemed that the promise of racial unity and friendship inherent in the concept of goodwill had failed to material-ize and dissolve the racial barriers at work within the organization and the country. Even in the face of this failure, the formation of the Phila-delphia IEC marked a significant moment in the history of the organiza-tion and the relationship of the racial justice and peace movements in the 1920s and 1930s. World War I and the subsequent disarmament talks had inspired "noble" women to attempt to work across the barriers of race. For a moment the women of the Philadelphia IEC had sparked the hope that

a radical new form of women's political community based in racial justice and world-mindedness could be created and sustained. The escalating political climate that resulted in the walkout by Dickerson and others
also affected the tenor of the conversation among a significant number of
the white leaders of the WILPF. They concluded that what was needed to
address the failures of the WILPF was a redesigned program that worked
on both love and legislation. As the decade advanced, the national organization enhanced its efforts to galvanize its rank and file to address racism
in a more serious and comprehensive manner, including how it shaped
the behavior and attitudes of its own members. The Philadelphia WILPF
persevered, and in the 1940s members joined campaigns to protest racial
discrimination in department store hiring practices and in educational
facilities. Interracial committees were dissolved, and civil rights committees took their place. The Philadelphia WILPF, in large part because of the
lessons learned from the IEC, entered the burgeoning local and national
civil rights movement prepared to work hard on the two-tiered battle for
civil rights: community building and political power.

4

Cleveland, Washington, DC, and Baltimore

Extending the Network of Interracial Peace Work

Bring nearer the social justice in America, so important to world peace.
—BERTHA McNEILL

WOMEN IN CLEVELAND, Washington, DC, and Baltimore criticized interwar America and argued that there was a link between state-sanctioned racism in the United States and the nation's support of militarization abroad. Although the exact design of each branch's efforts to speak out against racism, promote disarmament, and denounce the follies of global politics differed, their work involved the WILPF in what historian Jacquelyn Dowd Hall has identified as the long civil rights movement.[1] Local interracial extension committees prepared WILPF members to help shape and join the antidiscrimination battles of the 1940s and the civil rights movement that firmly took hold of the nation in the 1950s.

The interracial committees in Cleveland, Washington, DC, and Baltimore contended with many of the same questions faced by WILPF women in Philadelphia. They struggled to determine the exact purpose of interracial committees and the exact relationship between the work for social justice and the work for peace. They labored under trying conditions: the unevenness of national WILPF leadership, the persistence of local racism, the economic impact of the Great Depression, and the instability of world politics. Even when they shared similar struggles, they designed distinct approaches to the interracial peace project. In this way these three branches illuminate the fluidity of formats adopted by interracial

193

committees and the importance of local context to the shape of each. Baltimore and Washington, DC, shared a strong reliance on the leadership offered by women involved in institutions of higher education. Cleveland and Washington, DC, worked hard to provide programs that addressed both the international issues facing the world and local and national racial justice concerns. Baltimore stood alone in its decision to work primarily to tackle racism in public institutions. All three branches accepted the challenge to put into practice the WILPF's stated commitment to the twin issues of peace and freedom.

Cleveland

Addie Hunton bestowed enormous praise on the work accomplished by the women and men of the Cleveland WILPF. For Hunton, Cleveland represented a branch graced with strong African American and white participation and leadership. In the details of its program, Hunton found a commitment to uniting the range of issues facing the world and the citizens of Cleveland. Their programs stretched from global disarmament and corporate intrusion in Liberia to segregated housing and poverty in Cleveland. The committee's work also extended from the informal and social to the more pragmatic. In Hunton's estimation, the efforts of Cleveland and like-minded committees represented a "fuller understanding of the program of the League."[2] With these remarks, Hunton returned to her underlying concern that in order for the WILPF to be an effective organization and for the interracial committees to serve competently they needed to consistently knit together the work for peace and freedom. The mistreatment of black citizens and the amassing of military arms, for instance, needed to be understood as linked injustices. Through endeavoring together in "understanding and harmony," Hunton believed that Cleveland WILPF members sought to not only disarm the weapons of war, but also to disarm the weapons of Jim Crow racism.[3]

How to end racism and segregation and establish racial harmony was a debated topic in progressive political circles in the 1930s. In the fashion of the Philadelphia committee, Cleveland offered a liberal approach that showcased the values and accomplishments of its middle-class members.

They promoted the art of the Harlem Renaissance, encouraged members to break racial barriers through their personal associations, and contested the city's practice of segregation in housing.

Spirited exchange over the issue of segregated institutions occurred throughout Cleveland's African American communities. With economic tensions high in the 1930s and public institutions segregated in the city "by custom not law," African Americans adopted numerous strategies to secure access to education, housing, and medical care and to contest racial discrimination.[4] Cleveland's racial landscape had changed dramatically from 1870 through the 1930s as the city experienced an overall population expansion. European immigration extended Cleveland's population from 92,000 to more than 550,000 in the years between 1870 and 1910.[5] In the 1920s and 1930s more than twenty-five million African Americans left the South and migrated north to cities like Cleveland, Detroit, Pittsburgh, and New York. Pre–World War I, eighty-five hundred blacks lived in Cleveland. By 1931 the number increased to eighty-four thousand with 90 percent of the population living in the segregated Central Area and 80 percent receiving some form of assistance because of the economic hardships of migration and the Great Depression.[6]

Working-class African Americans participated in labor strikes, pickets, the Communist Party, and black nationalism as ways to protest the failing economy and persistent segregation. Thousands in Cleveland turned out for Marcus Garvey's parades and speeches during the first half of the 1920s. In 1920 UNIA claimed fifteen thousand Clevelanders as members.[7] In 1931 the eight Unemployed Councils run by the local Communist Party organized pickets and strikes to sound an alarm over the racism of the city's economy. The creation in 1935 of the Future Outlook League (FOL) symbolized the ongoing radicalism of Cleveland's underemployed and unemployed black community. By 1938 the FOL enlisted ten thousand members and featured participation and strong leadership from women including Maude White. Despite police brutality and tear gas, a picket by 2,550 Cleveland FOL members against a store that would not hire black employees successfully changed the hiring policies of the store and other businesses. These "Don't Buy Where You Can't Work" campaigns emerged as women used their consumer power to challenge Jim Crow.[8]

In contrast to the forms of public protests advanced by women like Maude White, Cleveland WILPFers adhered to a more discreet approach. They aligned themselves with a range of middle-class models of protest. These included the accommodationist politics of Jane Edna Harris's Phillis Wheatley Association, the legalist interracial approach of the NAACP and Urban League, and the cultural interracialism of the Karamu Theatre. From 1930 to 1935 Clevelanders who attended WILPF events ventured to create a "sprit of understanding." WILPFers reinforced the middle-class sensibilities, political allegiances, and tastes of many of the city's prominent residents at the same time that they promoted a radical political analysis that linked the practice of racial segregation in their city to the practice of economic colonialism and global militarization.[9]

Programs featured in Cleveland's inaugural year exemplified the middle-class approach the committee favored. The first year showcased both crowd-drawing speeches by national leaders and more intimate gatherings designed to challenge local Jim Crow practices and foster goodwill. Speeches by Cleveland-born and African-inspired artist Paul Bough Travis, Howard University president Dr. Mordecai Johnson, Dr. W. E. B. Du Bois, national educational innovator and immigrant rights advocate Alonzo Grace, and national peace activist Frederick Libby linked the racial unrest experienced in Cleveland to the mistreatment of colonial subjects abroad. Cleveland WILPF's programming explicitly suggested that the inability to move about freely in Cleveland linked the black residents of the city with colonial subjects experiencing restricted mobility and citizenship around the world in places like Haiti, Egypt, India, and Algeria. Even if the form of the Cleveland events was subdued in comparison to the boycotts of the FOL, the message of the interracial committee's program—that American Jim Crow practices were akin to colonialism—carried radical potential.

Confronting Jim Crow

In January of 1932, eighty people attended a WILPF-sponsored lecture entitled "Doctors in Literature." Held in a branch library, the lecture featured Dr. Charles H. Garvin. Dr. Garvin was the first African American surgeon in the city and the first black physician commissioned in the US Army during World War I. In Cleveland, Garvin helped build a hospital staffed solely by black physicians. He also had a national reputation for protesting the racism prevalent in the treatment of tuberculosis. Not only did Dr. Garvin contest the color line in medicine, he also fought against racial housing covenants when he built a house for his family on Wade Park Avenue, in one of Cleveland's white neighborhoods. Even though his new home was twice firebombed, he refused to be intimidated. Even when faced with violence and frequent threats to his family, he moved his family into the home and made it their permanent residence.[10] In February, a smaller group of forty people gathered in the home of an African American couple, Charles H. Jackson and his wife, for an evening of music and poetry. As in the past, the entertainment lineup paired an African American and an Anglo-American artist and reflected the refined middle-class politics of respectability. Internationally acclaimed African American soprano Cleota Collins Lacey performed spirituals and white poet Hazel Collister Hutchison read from some of her work.[11]

Teas and musicales held in the homes of black middle-class members who lived in white neighborhoods challenged the often violent Jim Crow politics of Cleveland. In 1931, Dr. and Mrs. R. T. Wise defied Cleveland's racist housing practices when they purchased their home in a "restricted district." Although 80 percent of the city's black residents lived in the segregated Central District, many of the rising professional class attempted to move into white-dominated neighborhoods. The primarily white crowd of eighty people who gathered in the Wise's new home for tea, speeches on peace, and music understood that their central purpose was to protest the racist mistreatment of their hosts and to spread goodwill. The guests were entertained by a black pianist and a white violinist, and they reportedly "wandered through [the] beautiful home" and "showed no signs of antagonism." Along with music, David Pearce, a white journalist and high school principal, delivered a talk entitled "Peace Without Freedom and Peace with Freedom." Understood to be "a man of very liberal views," Pearce's presence and speech criticized the harsh racism practiced by many members of the city's white powerful professional class and offered an alternative model of community based on cosmopolitan ideals of mutuality. Addie Hunton remarked that she hoped that the "intelligent understanding" modeled during the Wise event would become the hallmark of the WILPF's interracial proceedings.[12] This Sunday tea merged the local concerns of Clevelanders with internationalists' desires to create a world that existed beyond the borders of nation-states and Jim Crow covenants. The goodwill and respectability emanating from the eighty guests of Dr. and Mrs. Wise marked, according to Hunton and others, an important step in removing the man-made boundaries of race and embracing the twin goals of peace and freedom.

Phillis Wheatley Association and Karamu House Theatre

House parties offered just one way to challenge the race politics of Cleveland. Support of Cleveland's Phillis Wheatley Association and Karamu House Theatre also engaged WILPF members in reshaping the politics of the city in the early 1930s. The Phillis Wheatley Association and the Karamu House Theatre both aimed to alleviate the social conditions faced by black city residents and both relied in part upon the resources of white citizens to accomplish their goals. The Wheatley Association adopted the accommodationist sensibilities of Booker T. Washington in its efforts to provide desperately needed social services to poor and working-class African American girls and women. The Karamu House, a theater project launched by white philanthropists, trained black actors and featured the plays of Harlem Renaissance playwrights. With mixed theater audiences, the Karamu House simultaneously developed black pride and introduced white audience members to a range of black struggles and perspectives. The WILPF's endorsement of these two projects enhanced its connections with the city's black middle class while engaging the organization in the complexity of Cleveland's racial politics.

In 1905 Jane Edna Hunter migrated to Cleveland from South Carolina. She had nursing credentials but was unable to find work in any of the local hospitals or white homes because of her race. When she turned to Cleveland's YWCA for assistance she was turned down because she was black. Hunter, in the spirit of so many other race women, turned her misfortune and mistreatment into an opportunity to advance the race.

Determined to pave an easier path to employment and fair treatment for other young black women who found themselves with few resources, Hunter established the Phillis Wheatley association in 1913. The association served as an all-purpose social service and job training center for working-class black women. It was also a residence hall. Facing a high and unrelenting demand for services and affordable and clean housing, Hunter methodically planned to expand the association's facilities. And in 1927 a new eleven-story building opened.[13]

Designed to meet the needs of Cleveland's black working class and poor women, the Phillis Wheatley Association worried some black Clevelanders. Some feared that the establishment of race-segregated institutions like the Phillis Wheatley Association suggested that black citizens sanctioned racial segregation. Black support of the association, these critics concluded, was a step backward in the struggle for racial integration. Their fears materialized as prominent white citizens came forward to finance the building of Hunter's new eleven-story facility and to control the membership of the association's board of directors. The white financers of Hunter's project hoped that the construction of this new building would protect the "racial purity" of their own neighborhoods, social service agencies, and recreational facilities.[14] People who supported Hunter's efforts, but who were not motivated by racist or segregationist intent, faced a conflict. Which did more harm, accepting the financial largess of segregationist whites in order to provide social services to struggling African Americans living in segregated cities, or standing on principle even if it limited the ability to amass the financial resources necessary to provide desperately needed schooling, vocational training, and medical services?

The segregationist intent of the white financers of the association was clear. A significant number of the white supporters of Hunter's project also served on the board of the city's YWCA. To them the creation of the Phillis Wheatley Association provided the assurance that the YWCA would remain a facility solely for the membership of white women. Some white donors also leveraged their financial power to attempt to stop members of the black middle class from moving into white neighborhoods. When a black undertaker purchased a home in Shaker Heights, white Phillis Wheatley Association donors threatened to withhold pledges from Hunter's project unless the undertaker withdrew his purchase. The NAACP responded to these threats with a resolution directing black citizens of Cleveland to refuse the financial support of white Clevelanders if it meant accepting residential segregation.[15] In the midst of this controversy, the new Phillis Wheatley Association building opened. In 1928, Booker T. Washington associate R. R. Moton gave the dedication speech during the opening ceremony. Even with the controversy among black Clevelanders over the politics of the association, Hunter's Cleveland association served as a prototype for the establishment of other Phillis Wheatley Associations throughout the country.[16]

In February of 1931, the Cleveland WILPF patronized the Phillis Wheatley Association with a program featuring Fredrick Libby, the executive secretary of the National Council for the Prevention of War. The forty people attending the dinner were entertained by local musical talent and were updated on the status of international efforts to control the arms race. By using the center the WILPF announced its support of local black women reformers like Hunter. Hosting Libby's talk at the Phillis Wheatley Association also exemplified the potential contradictions involved in designing interracial peace programs.

As the interracial group of guests arrived at the venue for the six o'clock dinner, Myrtle Wiggins entertained them with "Negro" spirituals as they awaited the keynote event. Fredrick Libby, the night's speaker, founded the National Convention for the Prevention of War (NCPW) in 1921. As a powerful clearinghouse of antiwar organizations, the NCPW at its apex maintained a staff of eighteen people, had more than thirty organizational affiliates, and published a monthly newsletter that reached twenty thousand members. Jeannette Rankin, a suffragette and the first woman elected to US Congress, served as the NCPW's first lobbyist.[17] In the winter of 1931, Libby hoped to rouse his Cleveland crowd to quicken their pace of support for the Geneva Disarmament Campaign and ancillary efforts to make the League of Nations and World Court effective institutions. In his speech he painted in gruesome detail the impact new arsenals of poisonous gas and bombs would have on American youth if a new world war commenced. To prevent the maiming of American youth at the hands of arms profiteers, Libby rallied his audience to support the Geneva petition and to strengthen the power of international institutions to arbitrate arms agreements. Addie Hunton called Libby's event a "Red-Letter Day" for the Cleveland group. People stayed for several hours to discuss Libby's findings, buy his literature, and generate signatures for the international peace mandate.[18]

The social and political dynamics surrounding the Libby event make evident that even as Libby, the NCPW, and the WILPF popularized a utopian vision of a global community united in harmony and equality, they were caught up in the real day-to-day practices of the unequal distribution of power. How was one practically to transcend the borders of nation-states or the racial covenants of Jim Crow Cleveland? By holding an interracial event in a racially controversial facility like the Phillis Wheatley Association, did the WILPF reify or dilute the racial boundaries of Cleveland? The presence of the interracial audience gathered to hear Libby may on the one hand have served to contest the association's segregationist financers' vision of racial purity and separateness. In this regard, Libby's vision of a global citizenry united against the destructive potential of power-hungry nations may have been cultivated by the interracial unity practiced by those attending his talk. Yet, when the trinity of race, class, and gender is considered the picture becomes muddier. Those attending the Libby event would have been served dinner by the poor and working-class young black women trained by Hunter in the domestic arts. Although Libby urged those dining at the Phillis Wheatley Association to stand against the arms race in order to save the world's youth from the dangers of military warfare, critics of accommodationist vocational projects like the Phillis Wheatley Association doubted that such projects saved poor black women, many of whom were recent migrants, from a life of racial poverty and dead-end domestic service.[19]

Cleveland's Karamu Theatre avoided the particular controversy surrounding the Phillis Wheatley Association and provided an opportunity for the local WILPF to support the black arts and promote peace work. A month after the Libby dinner, peace-minded interracialists attended a benefit play by the Gilpin Players at the Karamu Theatre. This event again brought together an interracial audience in an effort to strengthen the networks working for peace and the formation of antiracist understanding. Through supporting the Karamu Theatre the Cleveland WILPF aided the black cultural arts movement, a vital feature of 1920s and 1930s black resistance politics. The Karamu Theatre started as the Playhouse Settlement. The white husband and wife team of Rowena and Russell Jelliffe provided the initial stability to turn the playhouse into one of the powerhouse amateur theaters of the Harlem Renaissance outside of New York City.[20] In 1926, the theater moved from a settlement house schoolroom when the actors converted a former saloon into the newly named Karamu House, an African appellation for community and enjoyment. Producing six plays a year, the volunteer actors hailed from a "vertical slice of Negro society, ranging from hucksters and maids to doctors and teachers."[21] The varied class backgrounds of the actors stood in contrast to the intraracial class tensions of the Wheatley Association. In harmony with the cultural agenda of the New Negro, the Gilpin Players and Karamu House looked to "express the thoughts and feelings of the Negro" to their audiences.[22] In March of 1933 the Gilpin Players featured the work of Andrew Burris. Born in Arkansas at the turn of the century, Andrew Burris moved to Harlem in the 1920s. Making his livelihood as a librarian, Burris joined the ranks of the New Negro artists, writing novels and plays as well as homage to Charles Chestnut and Paul Laurence Dunbar. One of his unpublished plays, *You're No Man*, portrayed the turmoil of a black soldier castrated during World War I.[23]

The Burris play featured as the WILPF fund-raiser did not address issues of war or peace. It did examine debates within segments of black society over religion and moral values. The weeklong performance of Andrew Burris's play *You Mus' Be Bo'n Ag'in* delivered a critical account of the religious revival politics of an Arkansas Southern black community at the turn of the century. Those attending the final performance of the play, a fund-raiser for the Interracial Committee of the Cleveland WILPF, joined the ongoing debate among the New Negro over the value of portraying rural black life versus the "sophisticated" life of the middle-class talented tenth. Some feared that dialect-thick plays about Southern life reinforced white stereotypes and did little to convince white America of black intellectual sophistication and preparedness for citizenship.[24]

In *You Mus' Be Bo'n Ag'in,* a comedy/drama, Burris turned his audience's attention to religious revivals in Southern black culture and debates over morality. The play's protagonist, Clem Coleman, has to negotiate the ridicule launched at him by his small-town Baptist community for not marrying Eliza, the mother of his two children. Eliza and Clem, unmarried, live together with their children as a committed and supportive family. Still, Coleman initially consents to the pressure to be "born again" and recants his supposed ungodly behavior. Yet in the end, playwright Burris turns the audience's attention away from Coleman and to the hypocrisy and judgment of the Baptist congregation. Burris concludes that the Baptists' real objective is to commandeer Clem Coleman's money, not to save his soul and make him wed Eliza. The benefit performance of Andrew Burris's play added one hundred dollars to the Emily Greene Balch fund for international programming. The play also provided WILPF members with an opportunity to partake in the ever-evolving creative work of and cultural debates in the Harlem Renaissance as Burris's play exhibited the tensions within the movement over the folk and the urbane.

The benefit play at the Karamu House and the benefit lecture by Frederick Libby at the Phillis Wheatley House illustrated the Cleveland WILPF's concern with uniting the issue of disarmament with the desire to address race politics in Cleveland and the United States. These two benefit programs helped underwrite the expensive transcontinental disarmament car caravan sweeping through cites like Cleveland. The money also enabled the WILPF to continue its campaign to pressure the US on Liberia and to support federal campaigns to pass antilynching legislation. By supporting projects that were interracial in nature and that sometimes pushed back at the structures of Jim Crow, Clevelanders encouraged the proposition that the work for world peace must start close to home.

Race, Internationalism, and Sino-Japanese Relations

Rising tensions in the early 1930s between China and Japan presented the WILPF and black internationalists with a racially complex and transnational dilemma. Japan's invasion of Manchuria in September of 1931 invoked differing responses from white and black internationalists. For the WILPF, the invasion by Japan was another urgent signal of the need to restrict the arms trade. And it could not have been timelier; the WILPF disarmament caravan was scheduled to arrive in Washington, DC, in a few months time and the Geneva disarmament talks were scheduled to open in January.[25] Editors of key black newspapers observed that their readers felt as deeply about the unfolding Manchurian crisis and the rise of Gandhi's resistance to British imperialism as they did about the continued downturn in the national economy.[26] Many leading black internationalists, including WILPF supporter W. E. B. Du Bois, championed Japan's territorial moves against China. The international WILPF, on the other hand, deplored Japanese aggression and instructed its national sections to pressure their governments to resist aiding Japan.

To many African Americans, Japan's 1905 defeat of Russian aggression represented a striking victory for people of color and "encouraged black Americans to believe that the long era of white domination was ending."[27] With its victory over Russia, Japan became the "leader of the nonwhite assault on colonialism."[28] Prominent African Americans' racialized support of Japan in its 1905 victory over imperialist Russia clouded many black leaders' ability to critique Japan's imperialist moves against China in the 1930s, at least before the 1938 Rape of Nanking. Many black internationalists who championed Japan, including men like Du Bois, intoned that China suffered from an Uncle Tom syndrome. China, they argued, allowed white Western imperial and economic interests too much sway over its country and national sovereignty. In this context, Japan's incursions into China were applauded and seen as "natural and moral."[29] Black internationalists painted Japan as a benevolent Asiatic country merely attempting to save and uplift another Asiatic people (China) from the misdeeds of white power. Through the lens of racial unity, Japan's control of Manchuria denoted a friendly concern for the future of people of color the world over. Many black leaders offered that, relative to the West, Japan deserved to design an "Asiatic Monroe Doctrine."[30]

The WILPF disagreed with the assessment made by many prominent African American's that Japan's militarism was "natural and moral." And they bristled at the idea that promoting regional dominance, even within a context of race pride and anticolonialism, could ever produce peace or freedom. In December of 1931 the Cleveland WILPF interracial committee hosted an event that furnished an opportunity to promote WILPF's position on Japan and to influence the politics of the NAACP on the topic. The daylong event took place at two locations, a recently opened Chinese restaurant and the Chinese Tong Temple. The keynote speaker was Dean William Pickens, the NAACP's field secretary. Cleveland's Chinese population had expanded from the thirty-eight people recorded in the 1890 census to roughly eight hundred Chinese residents by the early 1930s. The city had a number of Chinese merchant associations, restaurants, and business establishments. The interracial committee's event signified an opportunity to support Cleveland's Chinese population and influence the political position of the NAACP.[31]

Pickens's presence in Cleveland represented, then, yet another moment in which local WILPF interracial committees confronted the complexity of nation and race. Under the seemingly innocent interracial committee mantle of goodwill and respectability, the seventy-five people who gathered to share a five-course Chinese meal and listen to Pickens's remarks participated in a keen political move to challenge the use of race as a tenet of foreign policy, even when championed by the racially oppressed. His appearance in Cleveland may not have changed Pickens's politics, but it engaged the WILPF and the NAACP in a debate about transnationalism and race.[32] Leaders of the NAACP held varying views on Japan. Walter White sided with the WILPF's analysis and refused to embrace Japan as a symbol of resistance to white imperialism. On the other hand, the evening's featured speaker William Pickens sided with Du Bois and believed that Japan stood as a vital international symbol of race progress and the power of people of color around the world to determine their own destiny.[33] The Cleveland WILPF was joined by other interracial committees in the project of contesting Japan's actions and shaping black internationalist's thinking on this topic. The Boston WILPF interracial group, for instance, took the recent flare-up in the Sino-Japanese crisis as an opportunity to develop an ongoing study group with the city's chapter of the Urban League. The question that surfaced in the Sino-Japanese crisis was similar to the question that surfaced in relation to Liberia: could the WILPF sanction the use of race as a pretense for nation building or expansion when promoted by the historically racially oppressed? In both cases the WILPF remained steadfast in its disapproval of racialized nationalism even when advocated by racially marginalized groups. The WILPF believed it was its duty to persuade its allies, like the NAACP, to rethink advocating militarism or nationalism even when the cause was the freedom of oppressed people.

Charitable Programs

Charitable programs were in many ways out of step with the national WILPF's political style. Even though most members came of age through the social settlement house movement, they joined the WILPF because it was dedicated to changing political policy rather than engaging in social reform work. Yet as segregated public schools took hold in Cleveland and the Depression deepened its toll on poor black communities, the Cleveland WILPF looked to more immediate ways to help alleviate the impact of racism on black residents. To address segregation and attendant poverty, in 1931 the committee, for instance, hosted a Christmas party for 630 children in one of the poorest public schools. A few months later the committee sponsored a Mother's Party that was attended by more than two hundred women. As a part of the event fifty-six dollars was distributed to the mothers for the purchase of children's shoes. These charitable efforts reflected the Cleveland WILPF's connection with Hunter's Wheatley Association and the growing material crisis befalling so many during the Depression. If world peace was predicated on the end to local suffering, then shoes and holiday gatherings for the poor might be appropriate WILPF work after all. Yet, whereas the interracial committee collected fifty-six dollars for the Mother's Shoe Fund, the committee collected one hundred dollars for their second annual contribution to the Emily Greene Balch Fund for international programming. The Balch money supported the international disarmament caravan and petition drive. The disparity in dollar amounts indicates the committee's reluctance to endorse the charity/maternal form of relief work and its preference for more directly internationalist and disarmament-related work.[34]

Cleveland's Decline

As quickly as the Cleveland interracial committee sprang to life, it also withered away. By the spring of 1933, its programs were dramatically reduced. No longer the highlight of Hunton's annual national board report, Cleveland seemed to suffer from a lack of clarity about its purpose and methods and from a lack of attention from the national WILPF office. In its spring 1933 report, Cleveland concluded that its work with social service and philanthropic projects, like the Phillis Wheatley House and the school charity programs, weakened its mission and purpose. Undertaken initially to "stabilize itself in the community," these community projects detracted from Cleveland's ability to work on international issues. Cleveland's subsequent programming would concentrate on public educational events on topics of international concern. For instance, an interracial gathering at a white school principal's house featured a local minister reporting on his year abroad in the Soviet Union.[35]

Hunton mourned the decline in committees like Cleveland. She placed the blame for the shrinking accomplishments of her early protégés on the limited support provided by the national office for interracial committee work. In the same report that announced the decline in Cleveland, Hunton deemed it "rather essential" that the national board cultivate qualified board members who could advise fledgling interracial committees through visits and consistent assistance. Hunton herself had planned a trip with stops in Chicago, Milwaukee, and Minneapolis to nurture interracial committees, but a severe injury and hospitalization forced Hunton to cancel her trips. The dearth of national WILPF leaders trained in interracial work meant that the direct attention that might benefit committees like Cleveland had to wait until Hunton's health improved.[36]

Cleveland represented one model of how an interracial committee might approach the twin issues of racial justice and the building of the social and political foundations necessary to prevent war and militarization. The interracial committees in Washington, DC, and Baltimore approached their work with their own style, in part influenced by their proximity to the South. Many believed that the establishment of interracial committees in these two cities represented significant progress because of their geographic location. According to Hunton, their ability to "function in a very normal way" signaled movement by the WILPF against the culture and politics of Jim Crow.[37] Although their location as border states/communities complicated race relations, their proximity to the WILPF national office in Washington, DC, gave them the national support Cleveland lacked. The Washington, DC, committee united African American female educators and reformers located at Howard University with white WILPFers. Dorothy Detzer, WILPF's legislative secretary and leading white member committed to race relations, served as a key inspiration for the group, as did Addie Hunton, who had a long history with many of the Howard University women.

The variations in focus and style between Washington and Baltimore in comparison to Cleveland illustrate the fluid and changeable nature of the WILPF interracial projects. The Washington, DC, committee convened in 1930 and set an agenda that included study of international politics, networking among leading African American and white women's associations, and challenging racism within the peace movement. The lynching of George Armwood in Prince Anne, Maryland, in the fall of 1933 set the Baltimore committee in motion. From that point on, the committee moved to address the persistence of lynching and segregated educational and social service facilities in Baltimore and surrounding municipalities. With the theme "justice for all, education for ourselves against prejudice and tolerance,"[38] Baltimore became the prototype of future interracial committees. Its work became increasingly single-minded and dedicated to overturning racial segregation. It was less interested in expanding the peace movement's membership among African Americans. Washington, DC, on the other hand, attempted to maintain the dual agenda of promoting good race relations and linking the work for peace with the work of racial harmony.

Washington, DC: Creating an Esprit de Corps

The Washington, DC, WILPF interracial committee began in 1930 "over teacups." Female educators and reformers from the district convened in each other's homes as they set out to create an interracial "esprit de corps."[39] Their early social gatherings engendered a powerful salon of women who challenged the racial limits of white women reformers and advanced a multivalent agenda of peace and freedom. Through concerted effort they enhanced African American participation in the international Emergency Peace Campaign and prompted the WILPF to push for integration on all fronts. They fought to integrate US congressional dining rooms along with the organizational structure of the WILPF. The committee also hosted major public conferences that examined the relationship of race to foreign policy in the mid-1930s. In sum, the actions of the Washington IEC illustrate the discrete ways in which race mattered to and influenced the WILPF and the nation during the reign of Jim Crow.

Howard University and College Women's Associations

Women in the Washington, DC, committee were free to determine the shape and content of their programs, but they also took into account the advice and direction offered by Addie Hunton. In her April 1932 list of suggestions for interracial work, Hunton encouraged committees to work more closely with college women's clubs and sororities. Washington made the resources offered by Howard University the centerpiece of its program and leadership. Howard's Dean of Students, Lucy Diggs Slowe, provided the durable link between the intellectual and grassroots resources of African American women educators and the campaigns to secure disarmament, to end economic imperialism, and to establish racial equality. Slowe, born in 1885, attended the segregated Colored High School in Baltimore. Later she attended Columbia University, receiving a master's in English in 1915. After serving as a principal in Washington, DC, she was hired at Howard University in 1922 to serve as its first African American female dean. A champion tennis player and contralto singer, Slowe would be dean until her untimely death in 1937. Slowe brought to the Washington WILPF superb standing in the arena of higher education and connections to esteemed writers, activists, and scholars.[40] The Washington WILPF interracial committee listed eighteen African American and white women as committee members, but it was Lucy Diggs Slowe,

Mary Church Terrell, Bertha McNeil, and Dorothy Detzer who provided the vision and resources that inspired the committee's accomplishments.

The committee's programming in the winter of 1931 and spring of 1932 illustrated the importance of black women's leadership to the education of the WILPF. Teas hosted by the committee functioned as mini-seminars on the evolving politics of interracial sentiment in Washington, DC, and the nation at large. Slowe's residence served as the centerpiece of meetings promoting interracial education. At one such meeting, African American playwright and Dunbar High School teacher Mary Burrill and Howard economics professor Abram Harris helped Slowe outline for three white WILPF members the "phases of interracial attitudes."[41] Burrill, a writer of protest plays and a teacher, wrote two plays that marked her as a significant contributor to the New Negro art scene and a central figure in examining both women's issues and the intersections of race, war, and citizenship. Published in 1919, Burrill's play They Sit in Darkness featured a poor Southern black woman named Melinda who died in childbirth, leaving behind a husband and four other children. The play aimed to both humanize the difficulties faced by women like Melinda and to advocate for the legalization of birth control. Burrill's other 1919 play, Aftermath, was published in Crystal and Max Eastman's radical left journal, the Liberator. This play told the story of a young black veteran who had just returned from fighting in the segregated US Army in France. Upon his return home he learned that his father had been lynched. The protagonist responds to the white mob's killing of his father with anger and seeks violent revenge. Harris, a Marxist economist, wrote for the Crisis in his younger years and introduced Du Bois to many leading socialist and communist thinkers.[42]

Mary E. Cromwell, a mathematics professor at Dunbar High School, hosted an interracial tea in November of 1931. Cromwell was also the first secretary of the National Association of College Women, a club founded by African American women educators, including Howard's Slowe. The tea at Cromwell's house featured leaders of the Philadelphia WILPF interracial committee who shared lessons from their two years of interracial activity. Soon after the tea, the Washington committee devised a series of educational programs focused on international developments and on supporting the Geneva disarmament campaign. One of the first steps involved utilizing Cromwell's leadership in the National Association of College Women to gather sixty pro-disarmament signatures from members of African American college alumnae clubs in four different cities. The signatures would be among the millions delivered to the Geneva Disarmament Conference in February of 1932.[43]

Gender and "The World Today" Symposium

After its inaugural year, the Washington, DC, committee assembled leading African American and white internationalists in symposiums addressing international developments. Regrettably the symposiums lessened the public presence of African American women internationalists even while they deepened the WILPF's ties with African American male intellectuals. The March 11, 1933, symposium entitled "The World Today" revealed the strong interracial alliance amassed to tackle the quickly unraveling world. By March of 1933, the failure of the Geneva Disarmament Conference was apparent to all, Japan had moved through more of China, and Hitler was expanding his power. Although the last of the US troops had left Nicaragua, US economic interests in Liberia expanded. The 150 people who attended the interracial committee's symposium heard from an array of scholars who hoped to provide some insight about the world situation and directions for strategic intervention. The event included six sessions led by scholars from Howard University, American University, the Brookings Institute, the Foreign Policy Association, and the WILPF. The president of the Washington WILPF chaired the morning session and Slowe convened the afternoon program.

The day began with remarks from African American historian Rayford Logan and ended with an address by Dorothy Detzer. Their comments provided perfect bookends to the event as they both invoked the specter of transnational mobility and identity. Logan, through his speech "The Movements of Peoples Across the Earth," presented a transnational context for the audience. He reviewed how practices of nationalism, economic expansion, and colonialism had forced the migration and displacement of peoples and resources. Detzer, in "Our Responsibility as World Citizens," offered pragmatic ways for citizens to use democratic means to enact legislation that could trump nationalist impulses. Whereas Logan evoked the involuntary realignment of peoples that produced shifting racial consciousness, Detzer called for a voluntary summoning of a global collective will that could undo the structural inequalities Logan historicized.

The remaining presentations kept the conference grounded in the details of contemporary global politics. They delineated the role of race and nationalism in conflict and trumpeted the salve of internationalism. American University economist John H. Gray delivered an extensive economic analysis of the financial systems and business exploits that bound global communities to each other and inflamed military intervention. Over a luncheon chaired by Slowe, Dr. Wilhelm Solzbacher of Germany described the impact Germany's fascism was having on the country's youth both as victims and perpetrators. In the afternoon, William T. Slone of the Foreign Policy Association discussed the implications of Japan's escalating military aggression against China in Manchuria. Next, Dr. Charles H. Wesley, chair of the department of history at Howard University, reviewed the Firestone Corporation's economic aggression in Liberia and its implications for the history of racial oppression and liberation. Dr. Wesley was the third African American to have received a PhD in history from Harvard University.[44] Finally, Frank Tannenbaum, of the Brookings Institute, examined contemporary politics in Latin America.[45]

The March 11 symposium underscored the continued solidification of working strategic alliances that had begun in the early 1920s between WILPF leaders and liberal black intellectuals. One outcome of these strategic relationships was the ability of the WILPF's Detzer and the NAACP's Walter White to secure a meeting in the summer of 1934 with Acting Secretary of State William Phillips. The purpose of the meeting was to sound the alarm over US policy in Liberia. On July 31, 1934, after months of letters and meetings between the WILPF and the NAACP, a delegation of ten people met with Phillips. The meeting stands not only as a representation of the WILPF's influence, but also as an example of the kind of role organized black womanhood played in advancing the liberal response to US foreign policy. Although historians place importance on the participation of Du Bois, Mordecai Johnson (president of

Howard University), and Rayford Logan of the Association for the Study of Negro Life and History in the delegation, leading black women also were present at the meeting with Phillips. They accounted for three of the ten participants. They included Addie Dickerson, WILPF member and president of the ICWDR; Washingtonian Nannie Helen Burroughs, representing the NACW; and Addie Hunton. These black female delegates announced to the State Department that black women paid serious attention to international politics and were poised to galvanize their associations to contest US economic imperialism. The delegation also signaled to the State Department and White House the strengthening of liberal interracial alliances poised to expose the missteps of the government and publically to pronounce the government's actions as racist. As Du Bois concluded in his July 1933 *Foreign Affairs* article, Liberia's "chief crime is to be black and poor in a rich, white world; and in precisely that portion of the world where color is ruthlessly exploited as a foundation of American and European wealth."[46]

The Washington, DC, interracial committee like other committees made Liberia a central issue. In addition to "The World Today" symposium and the meeting with the State Department, the committee held other community meetings on the topic. One of those meetings featured the WILPF's Anna Melissa Graves, who, along with Emily Greene Balch, played a significant role in uncovering the politics of the Liberian situation. In Dorothy Detzer's August 1933 Branch Letter she urged all WILPF branches to utilize their local black churches, clubs, and political associations as an avenue for publicizing the Liberian situation. Chicago's Zonia Baber noted with pride meetings held in her city about Liberia. Baber addressed Chicago's Douglass League of Women Voters on the developments in Liberia. After her address the League passed a resolution of "sincere gratitude" to the WILPF and a note of special appreciation for Detzer's leadership on the issue. Baber's work with local black organizations on Liberia made it easier for her to return to the same organizations for support for the WILPF's national campaign to secure congressional hearings to investigate the profiteering of the munitions industry.[47]

The 1933 "World Today" symposium and the meeting with the State Department demonstrated the vitality of the interracial peace coalition.

These events also revealed the vexed position of black women working in the arena of international politics. Their organizational experience continued to be essential to the building of coalitions and the pragmatics of local, national, and international conference planning. Yet, in many mixed-gender events the contributions of black women appeared primarily in the form of the practical. For instance, aside from informal remarks from a female guest from India, Dorothy Detzer was the only woman to present a prepared speech to "The World Today" conference. In many ways, these gender dynamics echoed the dynamics surrounding the 1927 Pan-African Congress. African American women performed the invisible, yet essential, work of building networks and keeping people and resources flowing and united. They performed the bridge work that brought black internationalists and their allies together. Rayford Logan and Charles Wesley addressed the 1927 Pan-African Congress and the 1933 "World Today" conference. In both cases, their public remarks would not have been possible without the organizational finesse and fortitude of women like Lucy Diggs Slowe and Addie Hunton.

Addressing Segregation and Lynching

The racial unity modeled during the March 11 "World Today" conference stood in stark contrast to the practice of segregation in the US Congress building and the resurgence of lynching marked by the lynching in October 1933 of George Armwood. The campaigns to pass federal antilynching legislation and the debates within black and interracial organizations about the best political strategies in the face of continued economic hardship and renewed violence would preoccupy the national WILPF, produce tensions in the Washington IEC, and launch a new IEC in Baltimore.

The practice of segregation continued to plague the nation and the WILPF. Two incidents in Washington reveal the uneven response in the WILPF to segregation. When it appeared in the most public of institutions, like US Congress, the WILPF responded forcefully and directly. By contrast, when segregation insinuated itself into the social and programmatic practices of the WILPF, many members and leaders claimed limited understanding of the problem. This uneven response to segregation troubled antiracist members of the WILPF. The organization's leadership on national campaigns to end lynching pleased women like Hunton and Slowe. Yet, the organization's evasiveness about the racial tensions within its own membership ultimately caused Hunton to end her association with the organization. If the cause of war was the misuse of power, the cure required a redistribution of resources and power sharing. Hunton concluded that the WILPF knew little about the cause and cure of racial discrimination in the private sphere of female associations. Two instances reveal the variation in the WILPF's treatment of the segregation that plagued the nation. The first involves Oscar De Priest, the only African American member of the US House of Representatives. The second involves a series of conversations between Addie Hunton and Dorothy Detzer in 1935 about the persistent undervaluation of WILPF's interracial committees.

In the US House of Representatives' building, two public restaurants and a private members-only restaurant existed. Of the two public restaurants, one unofficially served only white visitors and the other, located in the basement and next to the kitchen, served black visitors. The members-only dining room did not bar Oscar De Priest when he dined alone, but bristled when he hosted interracial groups of diners. These policies of segregation erupted on January 23, 1934, when De Priest's secretary, Morris Lewis, and Lewis's son were forcibly removed from the public restaurant. North Carolina representative Lindsay C. Warren ordered their removal. Their mistreatment sparked a three-month wave of sit-ins, protests, and lobbying efforts, involving, among others, WILPF members and students, faculty, and staff from Howard University.[48]

The protests occurred simultaneously with the hearings in the Capitol pushing for the passage of the Costigan-Wagner Bill that would make lynching a federal crime. WILPF's lobbyist, Dorothy Detzer, teamed up with Walter White of the NAACP and Addie Hunton to devise a strategy on the antilynching bill. During the hearings, WILPF national president Hannah Clothier Hull provided testimony in favor of its passage. During the hearings for the Costigan-Wagner Bill, four African American women were forcibly removed from a dining facility. The week following their removal, mixed racial groups dined in protest, including members of the WILPF, the Socialist Party, and the Quakers.[49] When a female African American social worker was ordered removed from a Senate building dining facility, faculty and students from Howard protested and tried to dine in the US House of Representatives building. Detzer and her assistant, Dorothy Cook, who was directing some of the protests, received coverage of their work in the *Baltimore Afro-American*. In a March 1934 article entitled "Interracial Group of Women Lunch in Senate Café," the reporter detailed how "both liberal white and colored groups have been hammering daily at the door of prejudice." In particular, Detzer, Cook, and a female reporter from the *Baltimore Afro-American* took seats together in the café and awaited service. After a back-and-forth confrontation with the manager in which Detzer stated "that I have been coming here for nine years and I have never been refused before," Detzer's interracial party received service. This was just a temporary victory. That same week, a year to the month after Charles H. Wesley addressed the Washington WILPF "World Today" symposium, Wesley was forcibly removed from a congressional dining room. As he attempted to dine with three white educators and researchers, Wesley was approached by the dining staff and asked to state his citizenship and race. When he responded that he "was colored," he was denied service. In response to Wesley's mistreatment, thirty Howard undergraduates marched on the dining rooms. De Priest succeeded in getting a House Special Commission assigned to investigate these segregated practices, but the committee voted to uphold them. President Franklin Roosevelt did not intervene and the dining rooms remained segregated until the late 1940s.[50]

Questioning Racial Awareness in the WILPF

The WILPF's principled action on the antilynching bill and against the practice of segregation in the US Congress dining facility was not enough to convince Addie Hunton that the organization did not allow passive segregation and racism within its own walls. For those who cared to pay attention, Addie Hunton's frustration with the pace of change in the WILPF was obvious by the fall of 1934. One person who listened and shared Hunton's concern was WILPF executive secretary Dorothy Detzer.

In her role as executive secretary and key point person on legislative strategy, Detzer showed keen understanding of the contours of racism in the nation, the world, and the WILPF. Her dedication to racial justice and her skill as a political strategist garnered support from many national black political leaders. Detzer provided the strategic and intellectual backbone on key legislative issues, like Liberia and lynching, that were central to the political agenda of black leaders and that exposed the racist practices of US domestic and international politics. Her own deep frustration with the inconsistencies and passive racism within the WILPF provided Addie Hunton with reassurance that some of the white leaders of the organization understood and endorsed Hunton's views and concerns.

A letter Hunton wrote Detzer in January of 1935 reflects the warm friendship and mutual respect that had been building between the two of them. It also reflected Hunton's frustration with the WILPF. In the letter Hunton wrote to Detzer that, "I know of no person of your race for whom I have greater esteem, whose sincerity I believe in more than you. In fact, I am rather too much in love with you at times when you are so courageous."[51] On the same day, January 8, Detzer received a letter from Walter White. White began his letter with the salutation "My Dear Dorothy," and then praised her for her astute and detailed work helping him orchestrate the upcoming hearings on the Costigan-Wagner Bill. White noted that he looked forward to their continued work on the bill and the relationship between the NAACP and the WILPF.[52] In her letter to Detzer, Hunton concluded on a less positive note. She confirmed Detzer's fears that Hunton had tired of the WILPF. Hunton confessed to Detzer, "It is true that for a year or so I have felt less and less sure of the fact that the organization was really ready for an interracial program." Hunton did not close the door completely; she asked Detzer to secure a half hour for discussion at the next national board meeting on the future of the interracial project.[53]

Three days after receiving Hunton's letter, Detzer composed a letter to all branch chairs, legislative chairs, and interracial committee chairs. This letter symbolized the emergence of a change in the national WILPF's approach to the problem of racism. Detzer's letter differed from the usual legislative alerts she had composed. As people expected, Detzer's two-page letter provided them with vital legislative details on the ongoing battle to win passage of the Costigan-Wagner antilynching bill. She listed the current head count of those House and Senate members who supported the bill and she highlighted specific members to target for lobbying. She also presented talking points for passage of the bill, reminding them that lynching was a "tool of terror" used to intimidate black citizens from pursuing economic advancement and enfranchisement. But what was different was that in addition to this traditional legislative update she addressed the racial climate within the WILPF. She began by stating that legislation could not "touch the roots of race prejudice in America."[54] She then directed WILPF leaders to dedicate themselves 100 percent to ending racism, wherever it existed. The dismantling of racism, Detzer directed, required that each member confront its vestiges within their own lives and within their own familial, social, and political communities. Detzer added that for interracial work to be successful, the committees and their members must be completely and thoroughly integrated within the structure of the WILPF. For the next year, Detzer kept up her pressure to direct branches to work on the twin goals of passing antilynching legislation and changing the remedial quality of racial awareness within the organization.

In the same month as Detzer's branch letter, the Washington, DC, interracial committee hosted an impromptu but very important meeting with a select group of interracial activists. Addie Hunton was in the city to attend Carrie Chapman Catt's Cause and Cure of War Conference. Even though Hunton was feeling extremely pessimistic about the WILPF, she met up with friends, including Lucy Diggs Slowe, and they determined to have a luncheon to strategize on the WILPF's internal problem with racism. Slowe hosted the discussion at Howard University. The group included leaders of WILPF interracial committees from throughout the country and other non-WILPF officials. From Washington Slowe was joined by three other members, including Georgia Bond, the mother of the future civil rights leader Julian Bond. Mildred Scott Olmsted and Evelyn Dickerson from Philadelphia attended, as did WILPF representatives from Baltimore and Detroit. Zonia Baber of Chicago with whom Hunton had traveled to Haiti a decade earlier was also present. Mary Rossi, representing the World Office of the YWCA in Geneva, and a member of the New Jersey Federal Council of Churches were the non-WILPF attendees.

Perhaps the most important effect of the meeting was a sense of solidar-
ity among the women gathered at the luncheon hosted by Slowe. Hunton
reported that the women engaged in a "very full and frank discussion of
our problems, methods of work and need for new interest." Zonia Baber
noted that in Chicago black women served on numerous committees, not
just the interracial committee. Baber called, as she had in previous years,
for other branches to also integrate its members.[55]

In her May 1935 WILPF interracial committee annual report, the one
in which she discussed the luncheon hosted by Slowe, Hunton acknowledged that the slow pace of development on the interracial front had
made her feel as if she were trying to "make bricks without straw."[56] She
lamented the continued lack of financial support for the national interracial committee, the haphazard endorsement of it from the majority of
national board members, and the reluctance to accept African American women as equal members. She did share some good news. African
American women were now serving as state board members in Pennsylvania, Illinois, Massachusetts, New Jersey, and the District of Columbia.
Additionally, she applauded her own primarily single-handed work to
continue to extend support of the peace movement within black women's
organizations. Hunton recounted that her attendance and speech during
the Annual Ball of her sorority, Alpha Kappa Alpha (founded in 1908 for
college-trained black women), resulted in the sorority forming a "strong
national peace committee." In addition, the 168 delegates pledged to
stimulate support for peace in their local chapters. Yet her own successes
only pointed to the fact that much of her work was done alone. Whereas
aspects of her assessment of the IECs and the Slowe luncheon seemed
to give her some renewed hope, Hunton concluded the report on a stern
note. She listed in detail five areas of improvement the national WILPF
should attend to. These included many of her regular requests: financial
support, more consultation with the interracial chair about the best manner of approaching interracial work, and integration of the committees
and their members into the full working of the organization. The last line
of her report stated that "twelve million people cannot be ignored."[57]

The inability of the WILPF to effectively and consistently unite the
work for peace and the work for freedom made women like Hunton

question the usefulness of the WILPF. In what would be her final report as national interracial committee chair, Hunton concluded that many black Americans still did not grasp "the deeper implications" of the peace movement and that it had not "won their first and deepest loyalties." This reluctance, Hunton explained, arose because "with the struggle for mere existence and against an unjust oppression in an overwhelming civilization" many lacked the luxury to work for a peace that seemed so detached from their own suffering.[58]

Hunton's departure signaled more than her own frustrations. It also signaled a growing consensus among many black Americans that the time had come to reinvest in black organizations and move away from the politics of gradualism. Hunton's resignation did not spell the end of the national interracial committee or the work being done in Washington, DC. Bertha McNeil, a resident of the district, took over for Hunton and worked with the WILPF for the next twenty-five years. Under McNeill's watch the new national interracial committee (soon to be renamed the Minorities Committee) attended to issues that directly affected the conditions of African Americans in the United States, like racism in housing, education, and the labor force. It also joined the growing movement to demand civil rights. The shift in the national committee did not necessarily indicate a widespread improvement in the white racial consciousness of the average WILPF member. It did, however, mark the shifting strategy in black political thought and continued incisive leadership by strategic white women like Detzer, Olmsted, and Balch. Polite interracialism lost favor as the language of rights and justice gained momentum.

Baltimore

The Baltimore WILPF inaugurated an interracial committee that functioned quite differently from the committees in Cleveland and Washington, DC. It offered its own interpretation of the purpose and mission of the interracial project of the WILPF. The brutal lynching of George Armwood in Princess Anne, Maryland, on October 18, 1933, and the vibrant economic boycott movement led by black high school and college students influenced the alliances and politics of Baltimore WILPF women.

Baltimore abided much less by Mildred Scott Olmsted's original motivation for the committee—the formation of an African American peace constituency. Women in Baltimore set out instead to join those struggling to lessen the structural inequalities faced by black citizens in the areas of education, juvenile justice, housing, and mob violence. The prevalence of the word *justice* in the language of the Baltimore committee and the near absence of phrases like *goodwill* and *friendship* situated the Baltimore committee, at least discursively, more firmly in the more radicalized politics that emerged out of the economic hardships and persistence of lynching endured by many blacks in the early 1930s. Events in the fall of 1933 would have a significant impact on the Baltimore women. In the span of a few months, racial violence beset the Eastern Shore and new labor justice campaigns and organizations emerged. Timing made a big difference. Cleveland's committee was closing down in 1933 as Baltimore's emerged in the midst of the radicalizing politics produced by the enduring Depression. As the economic toll of the Great Depression mounted and the programs of the first New Deal raised hopes but offered little in way of actual relief for black Americans, the call for justice and equality took shape.

In 1930, Baltimore had the fourth largest black population in the nation. And by the fall of 1933, many black Baltimoreans, fed up with the racist hiring practices of white-owned businesses in black neighborhoods, took issues into their own hands and began a Buy Where You Can Work campaign and boycott. Similar boycotts appeared in thirty-five cities across the country by 1935. Labor unrest coupled with the frustration over racist hiring practices stimulated the development of two new organizations. One was the People's Unemployment League (PUL). The second organization, the Citywide Young People's Forum, emerged out of the Buy Where You Can Work boycott that would grip the city through June of 1934. Young women participated in the boycott and forum in remarkable numbers and stood out as some of the most influential leaders.

The Citywide Forum was started by a small group of black college and high school students who were frustrated with the impact of the city's segregationist education and employment practices on their prospects for achievement. Their Friday night meetings in which they discussed the political and social issues they faced and how to change them turned into a vibrant venue attracting upwards of a thousand people. The Young People's Forum generated the majority of the leadership and willpower that sustained the Buy Where You Can Work campaign. Ten of its fifteen board members were women. One young woman in particular, Juanita Jackson, would translate this experience into a commanding lifelong career as a civil rights activist. WILPF's Mildred Scott Olmsted was impressed by the energy and popularity of the Citywide Forum and by the leadership skills of Jackson. When it was time for Juanita Jackson to go to college, she was closed out of the University of Maryland because of her race. She did receive admission to the University of Pennsylvania. While at the University of Pennsylvania Jackson heard Olmsted give a speech on the peace movement, and she invited Olmsted to address one of the Citywide Forum's Friday night events. Olmsted was so moved by the evening's turnout and energy she attempted—unsuccessfully—to persuade the young Jackson to work for the WILPF.[59] Jackson maintained interest in the WILPF, but her first loyalty was the fight for equal rights.

Other youthful and militant energy emerged in the PUL, founded in Baltimore in January of 1933. In the early 1930s, five thousand white garment workers went on strike for better wages and three thousand of the city's longshoremen also rattled the city with strikes over wages and work conditions. In this atmosphere, the PUL quickly gained popular support and recorded an initial membership of six thousand. Organized initially by young white socialists, its membership base expanded to include 25 percent representation from African Americans. With the slogan, "Black and White, Unite and Fight" the PUL worked to make the New Deal "more equitable and responsive" to the needs of everyone. Many of the Baltimore WILPF's members were also supporters and leaders of the PUL.[60]

Proof that the Baltimore WILPF embraced the range of political protest taking place in the early 1930s exists in the publicity and speaker's bureau brochure published by the Maryland branch in July of 1934. Three of the speakers served as members of the executive committee of the PUL, three were on the board of the Baltimore Urban League, one was a member of the Interracial Commission of the Baltimore Federation of Churches, and one was a state organizer for the Socialist Party. Dr. Francis M. Wood, an African American man and director of the city's black schools, also served as a Maryland WILPF branch official spokesperson. Additionally, Dr. Mary Williams, the chairperson of the Maryland WILPF branch, listed among her credentials her membership on the executive committee of the Maryland Anti-Lynching Federation. Further, the roster of topics the speakers were prepared to address indicated the branch's commitment to a racial justice agenda. Three of the suggested talks were: Justice for the Maryland Negro, Negro Accomplishments in Baltimore, and Anti-Lynching Legislation. The remaining topics ranged from the demilitarization of the Mexican border to US policy in the Pacific.[61]

Responding to the Lynching of George Armwood

The lynching of twenty-eight-year-old George Armwood on the evening of October 18, 1933, in Somerset County, Maryland, reflected the ongoing racial terror blacks on the Eastern Shore of Maryland faced. In 1931, Matthew Williams, also of the Eastern Shore, was lynched before a crowd estimated at five hundred to one thousand people. Large crowds also gathered in the fall of 1933 to watch and participate in the killing of Armwood. And both men were lynched on the lawn of their local courthouse. Somerset County, Maryland, where Armwood was murdered, recorded the largest number of lynchings in the state. Whereas racial discrimination occurred in other parts of Maryland, the situation for the Eastern Shore's black citizens resembled more that of Virginia than the city of Baltimore. African Americans made up 15 percent of the population and found far fewer job and educational prospects than did black citizens in many other parts of the state.[62]

Armwood was arrested for snatching the purse of Mary Denston, an eighty-two-year-old local resident. When Mary Denston resisted the purse snatching, Armwood ran. Armwood was apprehended later in the day at the farm of his employer, John Richardson. Some believe that Armwood's employer plotted the purse snatching as it was well known that Denston frequently carried large sums of cash. In any case, the twenty-eight-year-old Armwood was arrested at Richardson's farm and badly beaten before being transported to the jail where the lynch mobs had already gathered.

Fearful for Armwood's safety, Maryland Governor Albert Ritchie intervened and insisted that Armwood be taken to a Baltimore jail for his own protection. Armwood was taken to Baltimore, but only for one night. Armwood was returned to Princess Anne the following day and placed in the local jail. Mobs again formed. The crowd of men and women stormed the jail, dragged Armwood outside, stabbed him, cut off his ear, dragged him through the town, hung him from a tree, and set him on fire. His burnt body was left in a local lumberyard for all to see. Young black children reported having to walk by Armwood's charred and mutilated body the next day as they made their way to school.[63]

One of the first forms of public protest of the lynching of George Armwood was the organizing of a meeting with the Maryland governor. WILPF's Dr. Mary W. Williams joined the interracial delegation convened to confront Governor Albert C. Ritchie on the Friday following the Armwood lynching. The meeting, as the delegation must have suspected, turned out to be a very tense one. First, the group arrived unannounced at the governor's office at three o'clock in the afternoon. The governor sent the group away, agreeing to meet with them later in the day at four-thirty. By the time of the reconvened meeting, the streets outside of the Union Trust Building and the halls leading to the meeting room were lined with uniformed and plainclothes police officers. There were many reasons for the tension and high security. The Scottsboro Boys' trial was in the news. And two years previous to Armwood's killing, Matthew Williams had been lynched on the Eastern Shore. Most alarming to city officials was the presence of Bernard Ades as a member of the interracial delegation. Ades was an avowed communist and a lawyer with the International Labor Defense (ILD). Not only was the ILD leading the campaign to save the Scottsboro Boys, but Ades was the defense lawyer for Euel Lee, a black man accused of killing the white family he worked for. Found guilty of the crime, Lee was being held in a Baltimore jail and was to be executed in Baltimore on October 28, five days after the meeting with the governor and ten days after the lynching of Armwood. The police and governor's office feared that the Armwood meeting would turn into an all-out demonstration instigated by the ILD. The delegation had harsh words for the governor, but a demonstration did not occur.[64]

In addition to Mr. Ades the delegation included representatives from the Socialist Party; Dr. Broadus Mitchell, a professor at Johns Hopkins University; the president of the local NAACP; members of the Urban League; Juanita Jackson of the Citywide Young People's Forum; local pastors; and the WILPF. The *Baltimore Afro-American* reported that the group voiced strong opinions, including "branding" the governor an "accomplice" to the lynching of Armwood for his failure to provide more protection to Armwood once he had been arrested. The central political demand of the group was for the governor to use "his good graces and influence" to secure the passage of a state antilynching bill, as had recently been accomplished in West Virginia. Describing the Armwood lynching as "the symptom of a disease that demanded immediate surgical treatment," the group pressured the governor to act aggressively and swiftly. Baltimore WILPF's Mary W. Williams endorsed the call for the governor to use his "legal and moral power" to usher through the state legislature an antilynching bill "that has teeth in it."[65]

The Armwood murder and the meeting with the governor spurred on activists like Mary W. Williams to work against mob rule and to look more seriously at the situation faced by blacks in the city, state, and nation. It was only fitting that Mary W. Williams, as Maryland WILPF legislative chair, should serve as a member of the board of the Maryland Anti-Lynching Federation. The federation aimed to lobby Governor Ritchie to make good on a state law that would make lynching a crime. Other WILPF women joined Williams in keeping the pressure on the governor and the state judiciary. Elizabeth Merritt and Bertha King represented the WILPF, along with Williams, at organizing meetings held in Baltimore. King traveled to Annapolis to lobby members of the state judiciary committee that was considering an antilynching bill. To add further pressure on the state legislature, the Maryland branch sent letters to each assembly member urging them to take a stand against the heinous crime. Mary Church Terrell spoke at a Federal Council of Churches meeting in Washington, DC, two months after Armwood's brutal death. She warned that the continuation of lynching and the accompanying lack of action on the behalf of lay and religious leaders left a bad impression on black youth. She advised those gathered, "I could not go forth from this conference unless I said that the attitude of the Christian Church toward lynching and the injustices perpetrated against the colored people is such that colored youth are wondering whether they can put any faith in it at all."[66] Terrell's remarks and the ongoing pressure from national and state WILPF members did not meet with success. Williams, as legislative chair, penned articles for the white-owned *Baltimore Sun* and *Baltimore Sunday Sun* pressing the need for a state bill. The *Baltimore Sun* also printed Dorothy Detzer's letter to President Roosevelt appealing to him to ensure that federal antilynching legislation passed through the Congress and reached his desk for a swift signature. Yet, the proposed Maryland antilynching bill failed by one vote to be voted out of the judiciary committee. The Armwood lynching and the Claude Neal lynching two years previous kept pressure on US Congress to use the power of the government to send a stern message against racist violence. In the wake of the Armwood killing, six members of the Maryland branch traveled to the nation's capital to attend hearings on the proposed federal law, the Costigan-Wagner Bill. This bill and future bills introduced up to 1938 would be filibustered by Southern congressional members. The NAACP's James Weldon Johnson, looking back on the tireless antilynching campaigns waged by the NAACP and others, remarked that although legislation never passed the campaigns, efforts by women like Williams "dented the national consciousness."[67]

Race and Educational Justice

As many now note, the Great Depression was a watershed period for the development of the civil rights movement and for the cultivation of white allies. This was indeed true in regard to the battles in greater Baltimore to chip away at the racially disparate educational structures and experiences offered white and black residents. From 1934 to 1940 the Baltimore interracial committee provided support to efforts to equalize teacher pay and to gain more black control over black educational institutions. The emphasis in these cases was not necessarily to dismantle the segregated school system, but nonetheless the goal was to make black education more equitable. In the 1930s the statutory minimum wage for white teachers was 1,250 dollars and for black teachers it was only 765 dollars. Beyond the obvious separate but not equal injustice of this state-sanctioned pay scale, the fight for equality in pay and status was important for the stability and prosperity of Maryland's black citizens. Black Baltimoreans argued that without equal pay and status they would not be able to secure and keep good-quality black teachers. Additionally, because teaching was one of the few professional jobs open to blacks, the suppression of black teachers' and administrators' pay stymied efforts to grow a stronger black middle class in the city. Legal efforts to equalize teacher pay began in 1934 when the NAACP brought a lawsuit. The Baltimore WILPF gave its support to the legal campaign initiated by the organization. According to Addie Hunton's observations, the Baltimore WILPF's work in support of the NAACP received "fine comments" from the black educators in Baltimore that Hunton was acquainted with. In 1939 the US District Court found in favor of the NAACP, stating that pay differentials based on race were unconstitutional. A few years later, in 1941, the Maryland legislature finally ruled to allocate the funds necessary to monetarily equalize black and white teachers' pay. These developments and the legal work of the then-young lawyer Thurgood Marshall helped pave the way for the landmark 1954 *Brown v. Board of Education* Supreme Court ruling.[68]

Equal pay or not, students still attended racially segregated schools. And black parents wanted control over those schools as one way to ease the damage of school segregation. Starting at the turn of the century, parents waged battles to win the right to shape and monitor their children's education. One early Baltimore victory was won in 1901 when the white managers of the Colored High School and Training School (later renamed the Frederick Douglass High School) agreed to only hire black teachers. The next two demands were harder to win—designating a black educator as supervisor of the black schools and seating a black member on the city's school board. Finally, in 1925 Francis M. Wood was selected as the first black supervisor of black schools and in 1927 he was promoted to director. In the 1930s Mr. Wood advised the Baltimore WILPF on race and education. In 1934 he served as a featured member of the Maryland WILPF's Speaker's Bureau. Efforts begun in 1899 to place a black educator on the school board met strong resistance. In 1939 and 1940 the Maryland WILPF joined the renewed call to end the practice of racially exclusive school boards. WILPF women participated in public meetings calling for the integration of the white board, they wrote letters and articles advocating integration, and they passed a resolution calling for the placement of a black member on the board. Yet, it would not be until 1944 that the city put an end to the all-white school board.[69]

Race and Juvenile Justice

In 1936 and 1937, the problems faced by black male youth held in a state-funded facility caught the attention of Maryland WILPF women. After participating in two interracial tours of a state-funded youth facility, the Baltimore WILPF championed the fight against racism in child welfare. The findings of their investigation outraged the Baltimore WILPF. As they reported in the branch newsletter, they discovered that the four hundred black male youth were living in unbelievably inhumane conditions. The youth were denied basic access to recreation with only "one ball and bat among four hundred boys." Lack of health care and harsh punishment frequently caused death. The WILPF newsletter alerted its readership that "healthy children entered the institution and died of tuberculosis or were infected with venereal diseases." African American youth sentenced to the state facility not only faced these indignities, but in addition because there "was no real parole system," would endure these detrimental and racist conditions for an undetermined amount of time. Additionally troubling was the observation that whereas state-funded facilities also existed for so-called delinquent white boys, white girls, and African American girls, the facilities for African American boys were the only ones not to receive public review and oversight.[70]

Armed with this troubling information, the interracial committee adopted a range of approaches. One approach included consulting with national and local leaders in the area of child welfare. Nannie Helen Burroughs, who frequently addressed WILPF events up and down the Eastern coast, provided her insight, support, and energy to the Baltimore group's efforts. As the founder of the National Training School for Women and Girls, Burroughs approached the issues of youth, education, and employment with great concern, expertise, and influence. The Baltimore branch featured Nannie Burroughs in the beginning of 1936 for a meeting on child welfare held in the Friends Meeting House. Burroughs was accompanied by Anna Ward, a white social worker who had worked for the Baltimore Emergency Relief Commission. The two women educated those gathered about the general issues facing the nation's children and the particular issues faced by Baltimore's black youth. In her remarks Burroughs "pleaded for civic, educational, and social justice for the colored child."[71]

The Baltimore WILPF heard Burroughs's plea and called together a meeting of forty people at the office of the Council of Social Agencies to establish the Citizens' Committee for Colored Boys. Through public hearings and pressure on the governor, the committee secured the enactment of legislation that placed the Cheltenham facility for black male youth under state oversight effective June 1937. In addition, new personnel were hired and new practices were implemented. Although pleased with the speed with which the legislature acted, the citizens' committee accepted these initial promises of improvement with caution. In a report to the state WILPF branch, the citizens' committee apprised the women that "we realize that the problem of the care of negro boys in Maryland is not solved by any means, but we do feel that a great forward step is being taken."[72]

Race and the New Deal

Labor and Employment

Many African Americans approached the first New Deal with a high level of warranted skepticism. It remained unclear if equitable assistance would be allocated for black relief and how New Deal programs would affect the Jim Crow culture of the nation. The degree of black disillusionment could be witnessed by the fact that before 1935 many African Americans referred to the National Recovery Act (NRA) as the "Negro Run Around" and the "Negro Removal Act."[73] The race politics of the New Deal, along with the overall horrendous state of working Americans and the unemployed, prompted many activists to engage in new coalitions, alliances, and projects. In 1933 and 1934 Maryland WILPF's chairwoman, Esther J. Crooks, who was a professor of romance languages at Goucher

College, used her leadership position to bring the WILPF into the fold of the spiraling efforts to make the New Deal accountable to the racially oppressed. Her work on behalf of the WILPF in the areas of relief for farmers and laborers, women's employment needs, and public housing placed the Maryland WILPF with those across the country calling for attention to the needs of black citizens who were experiencing the worst of the nation's economic collapse. Part of this work meant supporting the efforts of the Socialist Party and others who made inroads fostering interracial coalitions. In 1933 the Socialist Party called a Continental Congress of Workers and Farmers in Washington, DC. In the shadow of this meeting similar smaller regional meetings took place. In August of 1933 the Maryland WILPF helped to organize and Crooks attended a Maryland Congress of Workers and Farmers meeting held in Hagerstown. Two months earlier, in June of 1933, the WILPF cosponsored a meeting at the Westminster Church featuring ACLU founder and Socialist Party figurehead Norman Thomas. Crooks received useful support in the area of workers rights from Naomi Riches. Riches, a Goucher College assistant professor of history, was an active socialist member of the PUL, and served on the Maryland WILPF's publicity and speaker's bureau committee. The struggles of Southern sharecroppers would increasingly become of concern to the national WILPF. In 1935 Dorothy Detzer turned her office over to the Southern Tenant Farmers Union who had brought an interracial group of sharecroppers to the Capitol to lobby Congress. In May of 1936 WILPF's Lois Jameson, who went to Arkansas to investigate conditions faced by farm workers, reported that what she found was "incipient fascism."[74]

Women faced particular employment relief concerns under the unfolding programs of the New Deal. In Baltimore, as in other cities, women complained about gender discrimination in the work relief programs made available to them. Because many of the employment projects in Baltimore were "pick and shovel" programs, they were designed to put men to work. Yet, 25 percent of the households in Baltimore relief rolls were headed by women. One way in which women's employment needs were addressed in Baltimore was through establishing training programs in domestic work and creating three large-scale women's sewing rooms. The sewing rooms employed nine hundred women who earned wages sewing clothing for the poor. Both of these projects not only limited women's employment options based on gender norms, but they also furthered the Jim Crow culture of women's work. In the case of the sewing rooms, for instance, one was designed for black workers and two for white workers.[75]

In May of 1934 Crooks organized a conference on household employment. The arena of domestic work was fraught with racial tensions. Domestic work, historically, was both one of the only forms of employment open to black women and one of the most overlooked forms of employment when it came to state and federal regulation. The working conditions for black women employed in domestic work deteriorated with the Depression. First, there was the fact that fewer and fewer households could afford to hire domestic help; so many women simply lost their employment. Additionally, black women who were employed found the conditions of their workdays crumbling as they faced longer hours, decreased wages, and worsening employer attitudes. As one woman reported, "they seem to think colored women have no feeling of tiredness."[76] New Deal training programs in Baltimore and other locales designed to professionalize domestic workers also came under scrutiny because of the differential treatment and services received by white women and by black women. For instance, it was reported that unlike white women, black women who went through New Deal–sponsored professional domestic training programs and turned down a job offer were quickly cut from the relief rolls. White women, on the other hand, were not penalized for turning down a job that did not meet their standards or expectations. In perhaps the most important measure—wages—discrimination persisted. White workers on average who had completed professional training received six dollars a week in pay whereas black workers with equal credentials received three dollars. Crooks's conference on household employment helped contribute to the ongoing pressure to make sure that the issues of women, in particular black women, were taken seriously as the nation and city experimented with devising a recovery plan that could move all people out of poverty and into economic health.[77]

Housing and the New Deal

During the Great Depression and New Deal, housing issues also ranked high among the concerns facing black citizens and for good reason. Segregated and poor-quality housing negatively affected the infant mortality and overall health status of poor and working-class black residents. In 1927 Baltimore ranked as the city with the highest infant mortality rate of the ten largest cities in the nation. Black infant mortality was twice that of white. Lack of access to good housing, medical care, and employment were all considered contributing factors to this crisis. In 1928 the Interracial Commission of Maryland began encouraging legislators to enact state housing codes and to develop better-quality housing as one step to improve the health and maternal standards of black residents. As one survey determined: "practically no housing of any kind designed for colored use has been created in Baltimore since antebellum times." The establishment in 1934 by the New Deal administration of agencies like the Federal Housing Authority and the Public Works Administration Housing Division brought hope to many across the country that relief was on the way. Unfortunately, Baltimoreans faced intransigent state and local officials who were unwilling to use these measures for the benefit of black residents.[78]

Baltimore's anti–New Deal mayor and pressure from real estate interests meant that Baltimore activists had to organize and work diligently in order to pressure recalcitrant local officials to capitalize on the housing improvement opportunities offered by the Roosevelt administration. Changed with "slum clearance," by 1937 New Deal authorities had already torn down dilapidated housing and erected fifty-one new housing projects in various cities nationwide, but not in Baltimore. In 1937 thirty-two various organizations, including the PUL, the Baltimore Urban League, and *Baltimore Afro-American* editor Carol Murphy, came together under the auspices of the newly formed Baltimore Citizen Housing Committees to wage a campaign to mandate that the city tap New Deal resources for the building of improved public housing for the poor and working poor. Maryland WILPF's recent president Esther J. Crooks, who was also a member of the board of the Baltimore Urban League, assisted with this

campaign. One strategy of the campaign was a program of citizen education. If Baltimore residents were knowledgeable about successful public
housing developments established or under way in other locales, they
could more effectively pressure the city to take positive action. With this
goal in mind, Crooks traveled during the winter of 1936 and the spring
of 1937, investigating race and public housing efforts in Newport News,
Virginia, and Louisville, Kentucky. Her findings contributed to citizen
education and the political campaign in Baltimore to move the city to join
the New Deal public housing endeavors. Finally, in the fall of 1939 the first
new public housing units for black residents, the Edgar Allen Poe apart-
ments, were built.[79]

Under the motto "Justice for all, education for ourselves against prejudice and intolerance," Baltimore WILPF's interracial committee coalesced
around anti-lynching legislation, school reform, labor justice, and the fair
treatment of black juveniles.[80] Laissez-faire goodwill, they believed, did
little to put a stop to racism or the practice of lynching. White women,
many of whom were on the faculty at Baltimore's Goucher College, constituted the majority of the committee's leaders. In fact, initially little
effort was made to recruit black women to the committee or the Baltimore
branch itself. Black educator Vivian Cook did join the committee, and she
became a lifelong member of the WILPF, serving on numerous national
organizational committees.[81] Not all of the work of the Baltimore committee departed from the forms of activities witnessed in Cleveland and Philadelphia. In 1933 the committee sponsored a lecture on Liberia featuring
Dorothy Detzer and the city editor from the *Baltimore Afro-American*. In
May 1936, the committee promoted an exhibit of Harlem Renaissance art
and held a piano recital by a young African American man. And another
meeting dedicated itself to a lecture on African folklore. Timing was
everything. The Baltimore IEC came into existence as the Cleveland committee ceased to have a presence. Baltimore's influences were different
from Cleveland's. It evolved first and foremost as a part of the burgeoning
developments that fused labor issues, racial justice, and liberal reform.
The language of justice and rights took precedence in the mid-1930s to late
1930s as the historical turn of events looked ahead to new methods and
new demands.

From Interracial Understanding to Social Justice

Baltimore's work to stop lynching and improve the conditions of black youth reflected Bertha McNeill's instructions to the WILPF to "bring nearer the social justice in America, so important to world peace."[82] No longer "noble women" who gathered over teacups, McNeill's ideal member now rolled up her sleeves and ventured to enact measurable change in her local community. From the beginning of her leadership on the interracial front, McNeill advocated direct involvement over talk and tea. McNeill rejoiced in her 1937 report that "talkfests have been supplanted by field work of the most practical nature."[83] She warmly greeted the move from extensive study and cautious deliberation on the status of race relations and world affairs to community reform and strategic intervention.

Bertha McNeill, born two decades after Addie Hunton, would echo the core values of earlier clubwomen while also venturing into a more radical analysis of economic inequality and a less patient attitude toward concepts like goodwill. A graduate of the Gregory Normal Institute in Wilmington, North Carolina, McNeill attended Columbia University and received a master's degree in English from Catholic University. She joined the WILPF in 1934 and remained a prominent member until her death in 1979. During those years she served as the chair of the Interracial Committee, taking over for Addie Hunton. In 1940 the committee was renamed the Minorities Committee. McNeill believed strongly in workers' rights. She was a member of the Women's Trade Union League and the League for Industrial Democracy. During the McCarthy era red scare, she chaired the WILPF committee designed to address the proliferating smear campaigns targeted against the WILPF. In 1954, she became the chair of the Washington, DC, WILPF and during her four decades as a member she represented the WILPF at four international congresses.[84]

Many changes occurred within the WILPF and the world during McNeill's years as chair of the WILPF Interracial and Minorities committees. Concomitant with US entry into World War II, the US peace movement crumbled. The rise in patriotism and nationalism after the Japanese bombing of Pearl Harbor and the suspicion with which pacifists were regarded resulted in WILPF membership declining in numbers by 50 percent. At the same time, the WILPF's work on minority rights issues moved forward, in sync with civil rights developments in the nation more broadly.

McNeill found reason for optimism early on in her WILPF career. Not only did the approach of the Baltimore WILPF encourage her to believe that WILPF women could leave talk behind and work on pragmatic issues aimed to overturn racial oppression, but she also reported signs that more space was opening for black leadership in the organization. In her March 31, 1936, progress report, she noted that at least seven state branches had "colored women" on their state boards. McNeill's approach to the interracial project honored the battles waged by Addie Hunton to integrate the WILPF and reflected the growth of a liberal, action-oriented civil rights movement in cities and communities across the country. McNeill directed WILPFers to work on issues faced by sharecroppers, to expand the representation of African Americans on the national Emergency Peace Campaign, and to work on all "civic, political, and social welfare issues" of interest to African Americans.[85] McNeill received backing for her call for a concentrated focus on race relations from Mildred Scott Olmsted. In her May 2, 1937, national board report, Olmsted called upon the organization to step up its work to end racism. She told WILPF leaders that "we have made progress along the lines of two of our principal objectives: Peace between nations and between classes. I feel the time has come when we should lay much greater stress than formerly done upon the problem between races."[86]

WILPF members in Cleveland, Washington, DC, and Baltimore did not need Olmsted to convince them that the time had come for the WILPF to take seriously the eradication of racism. They each had worked diligently to design a relationship between the manifold concepts of peace and freedom. The local politics and culture in each city influenced the tone of the work of local interracial projects. Cleveland used the politics of respectability to contest racist housing patterns and to promote the culture of the New Negro movement. Washington, DC, relied upon the intellectual fortitude and organizational resources of African American educators and foreign policy experts to draw attention to the connections between domestic racism and economic imperialism. Baltimore pushed to the sidelines traditionally defined peace work—disarmament and US foreign policy—for a more concentrated campaign to uproot the invasive structures of racial inequality. Baltimore decided that achieving *right local relations* must be the first order of business.

Baltimore's achievements and Addie Hunton's departure from the WILPF marked a complex turning point in the organization. Hunton's resentment at being asked "to make bricks without straw" reflected the WILPF's inability to fully attend to the guidance Hunton and others had offered the WILPF for more than a decade. Yet Hunton's work would have a lasting effect, even though the spread of well-intentioned interracial committees in the mid-1930s did not occur at the pace Hunton desired and the issues demanded. Still, as McNeill's 1940 Minorities Committee report proves, the building blocks constructed by Hunton, in alliance with women like Olmsted and Detzer, readied the organization to continue to contribute to the burgeoning civil rights movement. In the shadow of World War II, McNeill reported a strong rise in the number of minorities committees, with new groups developing in places like Seattle and Santa Barbara and Minnesota, and growth in anchor interracial committees in places like Philadelphia, Baltimore, and Detroit. In communities across the country WILPF members advocated for the rights of sharecroppers, the need to end segregated housing and education and to support interracial couples, and the need to confront anti-Semitism. The discrimination faced by Japanese Americans, Chinese Americans, and Mexican Americans also occasioned increased attention by WILPF women. Additionally, McNeill noted that the WILPF was cooperating with other organizations to consider a plan to push for a national civil rights bill. In 1944, the US WILPF's three-day annual meeting would dedicate one entire day to the impact of racism on American society. This was a marked improvement from the frustration Hunton experienced when she tried to secure a mere hour of conversation on interracial matters during board meetings. Clearly, by the 1940s, the WILPF had entered another chapter in its efforts to understand the inextricable link between racism and war and between peace and freedom. The struggle of the many women engaged in the interracial projects of the interwar era had set the stage for the WILPF to participate in the civil rights struggle that took shape in the 1940s and

1950s. In other words, the work of peace women during the interwar years helped prepare the groundwork for the radical transformation of American racial politics that resulted from the classic civil rights movement. Their efforts provide us today with the mandate to continue to unmask the links between racial injustice and militarization.[87]

Conclusion

> In individual and personal relations, as well as in political and
> international relations, we must apply the principles which underlie
> consent, and, still better, cooperation and struggle of the fruitful and
> invigorating type . . . We have made but the merest beginnings in
> the highest of human arts, that of living and working together on the
> plane of consent and cooperation without coercion.
>
> —EMILY GREENE BALCH, 1919

> Always there is a race relations question in the atmosphere . . . Since
> there can be no world peace without right local and national relations,
> we believe that this may after all be one of our chief concerns.
>
> —ADDIE HUNTON, 1932

MIDDLE-CLASS REFORM-MINDED African American and white women
held much in common during the interwar years. Foremost, they shared
a deep belief in the vital importance of women's contributions to the
future development of the nation and the world. As women who came
of age during the Progressive Era and the Woman's Era, they believed
that through public education and active political participation women
could change society. Women like Balch and Hunton encouraged the
understanding that the route to peace lay in women's ability to rehabilitate all forms of relationships from the most personal and intimate to the
institutional and international. They believed that the social hierarchies
of race, gender, and nation harbored the conditions for war and that these
divisions needed to be replaced with new forms of relating based upon
mutuality, cooperation, and respect. They turned to the WILPF as a practical forum for exploring the possibility of living out these ideals. As such,

peace women's postwar interracial engagement became a testing ground for the belief that eliminating racism and encouraging interdependence were central to the production of peace.

The US WILPF came of age in an era rife with racial tensions at home and abroad. From the postwar race riots and rise in lynching, to the denial of freedom to colonial subjects and the generation of Pan-African consciousness, to the US occupation of Haiti, race infused the spaces black and white women traversed in their work as peacemakers. The early mission statements of the international and US WILPF indicated the organization's awareness of the complex dynamics of race and articulated the link between racism and war. A 1922 resolution by the US section proposed that because "race prejudice creates distrust, suspicion, antagonism, and hatred towards the people of other nations," it "encourage[d] the war spirit." The antidote to the war spirit was to "collectively" and "individually" uproot racism and in its place foster an "international spirit" and habits of cooperation and coexistence.[1] As such, the WILPF's hallmark ideals, its community-based internationalism and drive to replace national allegiances with allegiances based in the acknowledgment of a common humanity, were rooted in part in its response to early twentieth-century American racism.

Race was, of course, always present in the fabric of the women's peace movement. As this study has shown, to think about the trajectories of race in women's social movements we need to take into consideration the different dimensions of race and racism at work at any historical moment. As Michael Omi and Howard Winant encourage, we need to think about "race as a phenomenon."[2] It is expressed, practiced, contested, and transformed within myriad interactions and spaces that include but are not limited to the personal, the institutional, the cultural, the ideological, and the political. And of course race does not stand alone; it is expressed, experienced, understood, and regulated in concert with other sociohistorical categories, most important for this study the categories of gender and class. From early contemplation about the significance of the racial underpinnings of World War I to the consideration of the racial politics of the movement itself, race gave shape to the women's peace movement in complex ways.

As racial modernists, peace women advanced the attack on the ideology of scientific racism that dominated much of early twentieth-century thought and public policy. They did this work from various vantage points. Through curricular reform, the teaching of world-mindedness in schools, and the promotion of JILs, the WILPF hoped to inspire the nation's youth to believe in a common humanity and walk away from the nativism and American exceptionalism that dominated American society. As social settlement house leaders and critics of anti-immigrant legislation and forced assimilation, peace women contested the argument that immigrants of Eastern European or Asian origin were racially different, possessed dangerous "racial qualities," and represented a threat to the "racial" stability of the nation. The WILPF's protest of the crime of lynching and the attendant lack of will by US Congress to pass anti-lynching legislation can also be understood as part of the WILPF's agenda as Progressive Era liberals. Race as a marker of fitness for citizenship and sovereignty also came under scrutiny by peace women in the early twentieth century. This appears most prominently in two areas, African American participation in World War I and US intervention in Haiti and Liberia. As we see through the lives of Addie Hunton, Alice Dunbar-Nelson, and Jessie Fauset, African American wartime participation became a battleground over the very question of race, gender, and citizenship. The circumscribing of black women's wartime participation at home and in France served as a catalyst for the rise of black feminist critiques of the intertwined race and gender politics of warfare and nationalism. The maligning of the contributions of black soldiers gave rise to a reverse gaze as women like Hunton, Dunbar-Nelson, and Fauset questioned the fitness of white America and white manhood in particular.

The organizational culture of the WILPF was influenced by the complex racial legacies of white women's associations and the abolitionist and woman's suffrage movement. Likewise, the Progressive Era model of interracial politics ushered in by the NAACP, the power of middle-class black women's clubs, and the political and aesthetic sensibility of the Harlem Renaissance and the New Negro informed the WILPF's work during the interwar years. As this study illustrates, women participated in interracial peace projects for a variety of reasons. Class, perhaps as much as the disturbances wrought by World War I, set a foundation upon which women endeavored to work interracially. Class became the bridge discourse across which African American and white women engaged in peace work. Their noble womanhood not only united them, it set them apart from other class-defined interracial political projects of the era, namely, the more radical approach of interracial labor unionists and socialists. For many black women interracial peace projects were an extension of an overall strategy for dismantling American racism. Securing more white allies advanced the goals of black reformers. Sometimes the drive within the WILPF for interracial peace work was a very practical one, as in the desire to expand black membership and leadership in order to enhance the chances of success in the grassroots movement to secure disarmament. It could have also been motivated by a deeply felt philosophical compunction to prove that conflict and race hatred were not natural human qualities. The appeal of interracial politics waxed and waned during the interwar years as the increased negative impact of the Great Depression encouraged many black liberals, like Addie Hunton, to grow impatient with and suspicious of the slow pace of interracial organizing. Likewise, many white leaders in the WILPF, like Dorothy Detzer, engaged in and were encouraged by the interracial labor radicalism emerging around issues like sharecroppers and domestic workers' rights.

Local studies of women's interracial peace programs reveal a number of important points. They remind us that the form and priorities of branch-level WILPF interracial projects were as much set by the local personalities, politics, and interests of women who took up the challenge as they were by the wishes of national leaders like Hunton, Olmsted, and Detzer. The variety in the types of programs offered and the political issues examined remind us that local context matters. The work of women in places like Cleveland, Baltimore, Philadelphia, and Washington, DC, underscores that the interracial projects of the WILPF were dynamic and variable. They took form not only in response to international and national developments and pressures, but also in the context of local politics. Some local communities engaged in charity work, whereas others eschewed this form of work for involvement in campaigns to contest race restrictions in housing and education. For some, working for the success of the disarmament campaigns motivated their interracial agenda, for others disarmament did not merit much attention.

Peace women's ventures in interracial unity were at times fraught with tensions and problems. The slow pace with which the concerns raised by black women like Addie Hunton were addressed indicated the organization's ambivalence about the significance of the project. Likewise, the inability of powerful white women like Dorothy Detzer and Mildred Scott Olmsted to deepen the appeal of the interracial project among more local WILPF branches underscored the lower priority many WILPF women gave to racial justice projects. Questions circulated about the core intention of the interracial project: was it a form of racial segregation or was it an effort to practice cross-racial unity? At the same time, the persistence with which some women like Detzer, Olmsted, Reynolds, and Hunton, for instance, pursued interracial women's community building even in the face of resistance to it from within the WILPF, indicates that for them it symbolized a meaningful avenue through which the twin goals of peace and freedom could be merged and practiced. Through interracial peace work, WILPF women attempted to fulfill Hunton's direction that to secure peace one must also secure "right local relations." When black and white women came together at luncheons and garden parties, in the homes of black members who had moved into hostile white neighborhoods, and at mass peace meetings organized to contest US policies in Liberia and Haiti and the escalation of the arms race, they hoped to exemplify through their unity the new world order of peace and togetherness.

The history of the racial politics of the WILPF is notable for a number of reasons. Most importantly, it documents that women's interwar-era interracial peace work helped ready the ground for the "long civil rights movement."[3] As historians increasingly acknowledge, signs of the civil rights movement could be detected decades before the 1954 *Brown. v. Board of Education* Supreme Court case, which for many has marked the beginning of the classic period of the movement.[4] One of the early indicators can be found in the work of the WILPF during the first three decades of the twentieth century. The effort of women in interracial committees, the internal struggle in the WILPF over its own organizational racism, and the organization's steadfast protest of racism-laden US domestic and international policy constitute some of the intricate ways in which the WILPF engaged with the politics of the Jim Crow era. These early efforts signaled the contributions of the peace movement to the nascent fight for racial justice and primed the WILPF to contribute to the classic period of the civil rights movement. In addition, the story of the WILPF expands our understanding of the kinds of political and social conditions that have caused unity and division between African American and white women and reminds us that class mattered as women negotiated the racial divide of the 1920s and 1930s. War mattered as well. The racism and destruction of World War I transformed—in distinct ways—the consciousness and political strategies of middle-class African American and white women, compelling some to work for a peace rooted in racial justice. Still in existence and still endeavoring to break the world of its addiction to racism and war, the WILPF provides a compelling case study for all interested in examining the politics of race in US women's movements.[5]

The WILPF worked diligently to challenge injustice and to secure practical reform. We can see this in its efforts to influence the shape and meaning of the League of Nations, its campaigns to expose the politics of the profit-driven arms industry, its alliances with groups trying to secure the passage of anti-lynching legislation, and its protest over US intervention in Haiti. Central to the WILPF's interwar-era alarm over war and racism was its distress over the endurance of nationalism. And so perhaps what matters the most to us today as we face a world still deeply wedded to mentalities of violence, racism, and chauvinistic nationalism is the WILPF's belief in the general principles of cosmopolitanism. To return to the words of Emily Greene Balch and Addie Hunton, if we are to succeed in our campaign for peace and racial justice, we need to learn a new art of living—one that takes root in our personal lives, in civil society, and in governments, one that honors and grounds us in the rich and shifting particularities of our local communities and acknowledges and fosters a sense of belonging and connectedness that is planetary and transnational.

Notes

Bibliography

Index

Notes

Preface

1. Emily S. Rosenberg, *Financial Missionaries to the World: The Politics and Culture of Dollar Diplomacy, 1900–1930* (Durham, NC: Duke Univ. Press, 2003); Mary Renda, *Taking Haiti: Military Occupation and the Culture of US Imperialism, 1915–1940* (Durham: Univ. of North Carolina Press, 2001).

2. Mercedes Randall, *Improper Bostonian: Emily Greene Balch, Nobel Peace Prize Laureate, 1946* (New York: Twayne Publishers, 1964), 303.

3. For literature on cosmopolitanism and women's internationalism see: Kwame Anthony Appiah, *Cosmopolitanism: Ethics in a World of Strangers* (New York: W. W. Norton, 2006); Leila Rupp, *Worlds of Women: The Making of an International Women's Movement* (Princeton, NJ: Princeton Univ. Press, 1997); Jane Addams, *Democracy and Social Ethics* (New York: Macmillan, 1902); Jane Addams, *Newer Ideals of Peace* (New York: Macmillan, 1907); Sondra Herman, *Eleven Against the War: Studies in American Internationalist Thought, 1898–1921* (Palo Alto, CA: Stanford Univ. Press, 1969); Charlene Haddock Seigfried, *Pragmatism and Feminism* (Chicago: Univ. of Chicago Press, 1996).

Introduction: Race and the Politics of Peace and Freedom

1. For this history, see Harriet Hyman Alonso, *Peace as a Women's Issue: A History of the US Movements for World Peace and Women's Rights* (Syracuse: Syracuse Univ. Press, 1993), 20–55; Robert David Johnson, *The Peace Progressives and American Foreign Relations* (Cambridge, MA: Harvard Univ. Press, 1995); and Valerie Ziegler, *The Advocates of Peace in Antebellum America* (Bloomington: Indiana Univ. Press, 1992).

2. Emily Greene Balch, Jane Addams, and Alice Hamilton, eds., *Women at The Hague: The International Congress of Women and Its Results* (New York: Macmillan, 1915), 150.

3. David Levering Lewis, *W. E. B. Du Bois: Biography of a Race, 1868–1919* (New York: Henry Holt and Company, 1993), 576.

4. Brent Edwards, *The Practice of Diaspora: Literature, Translation, and the Rise of Black Internationalism* (Cambridge, MA: Harvard Univ. Press, 2003).

247

5. Alonso, *Peace as a Women's Issue*, 56–58.

6. Ibid., 56–84.

7. Nancy Cott, *The Grounding of Modern Feminism* (New Haven, CT: Yale Univ. Press, 1987), 246. See also Susan Zeiger, "Finding a Cure for War: Women's Politics and the Peace Movement in the 1920s," *Journal of Social History* (Fall 1990): 69–86.

8. For the history of the WPU, see Harriet Hyman Alonso, *The Women's Peace Union and the Outlawry of War, 1921–1942* (Knoxville: Univ. of Tennessee Press, 1989).

9. Carrie Foster, *The Women and the Warriors: The United States Section of the Women's International League for Peace and Freedom, 1915–1946* (Syracuse: Syracuse Univ. Press, 1995), 8.

10. The women's associations in the NCCCW included the AAUW, the General Federation of Women's Clubs, the YWCA, the National Woman's Christian Temperance League, and the National Women's Trade Union League. Alonso, *Peace as a Women's Issue*, 106–7.

11. Frances H. Early, *A World Without War: How US Feminists and Pacifists Resisted World War I* (Syracuse: Syracuse Univ. Press, 1997); Kathleen Kennedy, *Disloyal Mothers and Scurrilous Citizens: Women and Subversion During World War I* (Bloomington: Indiana Univ. Press, 1992).

12. Early, *World Without War*, xxi.

13. For more history of the international sections of WILPF, see Gertrude Bussey and Margaret Tims, *Pioneers for Peace: Women's International League for Peace and Freedom, 1915–1945* (1965; repr., Oxford: Alden Press, 1980); Rupp, *Worlds of Women*.

14. Alonso, *Peace as a Women's Issue*, 90.

15. For the international membership of the WILPF and the international women's movement more generally, see Rupp, *Worlds of Women*, 63–81.

16. Bussey and Tims, *Pioneers for Peace*, 34.

17. Rupp, *Worlds of Women*, 34.

18. Addams, *Newer Ideals*, 19.

19. Ibid., 14.

20. For more on the community internationalist perspective, see Marilyn Fischer, Carol Nackenoff, and Wendy Chmielewski, eds., *Jane Addams and the Practice of Democracy* (Chicago: Univ. of Illinois Press, 2009); Herman, *Eleven Against the War*.

21. C. A. Foster, *Women and the Warriors*, 6.

22. Balch, "Journey and Impressions," in *Women at The Hague: The International Congress of Women and Its Results*, ed. Emily Greene Balch, Jane Addams, and Alice Hamilton, 15 (New York: Macmillan Company, 1915).

23. Balch, Addams, and Hamilton, *Women at The Hague*, 150–54.

24. For this perspective, see Alonso, *Peace as a Women's Issue*, and Rupp, *Worlds of Women*.

25. Balch, Addams, and Hamilton, *Women at The Hague*, 136.

26. Addams, "Women and Internationalism," in *Women at The Hague*, 128.

27. Ibid., 128.

28. Ibid., 139.

29. For a general discussion of the ideological frameworks and strategy of the US peace movement, see Charles Chatfield, *The American Peace Movement: Ideals and Activism* (New York: Twayne Publishing, 1992). For shifting public sentiment toward the peace movement, see Lawrence Wittner, *Rebels Against War: The American Peace Movement, 1933–1983* (Philadelphia: Temple Univ. Press, 1984), 5–12.

30. Alonso, *Peace as a Women's Issue,* 69.

31. C. A. Foster, *Women and the Warriors,* 93.

32. Ibid., 91–92.

33. For this history, see Marjorie Spruill Wheeler, *New Women of the New South: The Leaders of the Woman Suffrage Movement in the Southern States* (New York: Oxford Univ. Press, 1993); Rosalyn Terborg-Penn, "Discontented Black Feminists: Prelude and Postscript to the Passage of the Nineteenth Amendment," in *Decades of Discontent: The Women's Movement, 1920–1940,* ed. Lois Scharf and Joan M. Jensen (Westport, CT: Greenwood Press, 1983), 261–78.

34. For women's response to the Spanish-American War, see Kristin Hoganson, "'As Badly Off as the Filipinos': US Women's Suffragists and the Imperial Issue at the Turn of the Twentieth Century," *Journal of Women's History* 13 (Summer 2001): 9–33.

35. For more on the racial politics of the woman's suffrage movement and the settlement house movement and general interracial work, see Elisabeth Dan Lasch, *Black Neighbors: Race and the Limits of Reform in the American Settlement House Movement, 1890–1945* (Chapel Hill: Univ. of North Carolina Press, 1993); Jacqueline Ann Rouse, *Lugenia Burns Hope: Black Southern Reformer* (Athens: Univ. of Georgia Press, 1989); Paul E. Baker, *Negro–White Adjustment: An Investigation and Analysis of Methods in the Interracial Movement in the United States* (New York: Association Press, 1934); Rosalyn Terborg-Penn, *African American Women in the Struggle for the Vote, 1850–1920* (Bloomington: Indiana Univ. Press, 1998); Peggy Pascoe, *Relations of Rescue: The Search for Female Moral Authority in the American West, 1874–1939* (New York: Oxford Univ. Press, 1990).

36. For information on the CIC, in particular women's participation, see Jacquelyn Dowd Hall, *Revolt Against Chivalry: Jessie Daniel Ames and the Women's Campaign Against Lynching* (New York: Columbia Univ. Press, 1993).

37. For a history of women's interracial work, see Joyce Blackwell, *No Peace Without Freedom: Race and the Women's International League for Peace and Freedom, 1915–1970* (Carbondale: Southern Illinois Univ. Press, 2004); Glenda Gilmore, *Gender and Jim Crow: Women and the Politics of White Supremacy in North Carolina, 1896–1920* (Chapel Hill: Univ. of North Carolina Press, 1996); Hall, *Revolt Against Chivalry;* Susan Lynn, *Progressive Women in Conservative Times: Racial Justice, Peace, and Feminism, 1945 to the 1960s* (New Brunswick, NJ: Rutgers Univ. Press, 1992); Nancy Marie Robertson, *Christian Sisterhood, Race Relations, and the YWCA, 1906–46* (Chicago: Univ. of Illinois Press, 2007).

38. For the general history and psychology of Jim Crow and the racial violence of the time period, see Herbert Shapiro, *White Violence and Black Response: From Reconstruction to*

Montgomery (Amherst: Univ. of Massachusetts Press, 1988); C. Vann Woodward, *The Strange Career of Jim Crow* (New York: Oxford Univ. Press, 1966).

39. Adele Logan Alexander, "Introduction," in *Two Colored Women with the American Expeditionary Forces,* by Addie W. Hunton and Kathryn M. Johnson (1920; repr., New York: G. K. Hall and Company, 1997), xxvi.

40. Barbara Foley, *Spectres of 1919: Class and Nation in the Making of the New Negro* (Chicago: Univ. of Illinois Press, 2003), 31.

41. For a general history of interwar year black politics, see Aug. Meir, Elliott Rudwick, and Francis L. Broderick, *Black Protest Thought in the Twentieth Century* (Indianapolis: Bobbs-Merrill Educational Publishers, 1971).

42. For founding officers of the NAACP, see Charles Flint Kellogg, *NAACP: A History of the National Association for the Advancement of Colored People* (Baltimore: The Johns Hopkins Univ. Press, 1967), 30.

43. For Jane Addams's early connections with W. E. B. Du Bois, see Lewis, *W. E. B. Du Bois,* 377–78, 369–70. For Addams's general work on race issues and connections with black leaders, see Regene Silver, "Jane Addams: Peace, Justice, Gender: 1860–1918" (PhD diss., Univ. of Pennsylvania, 1990).

44. Anna Julia Cooper, *A Voice from the South: By a Black Woman of the South* (1892; repr., New York: Oxford Univ. Press, 1988).

45. For general history of African American women and self-organizing, see Deborah Gray White, *Too Heavy a Load: Black Women in Defense of Themselves* (New York: W. W. Norton and Company, 1999); Paula Giddings, *When and Where I Enter: The Impact of Black Women on Race and Sex in America* (New York: William Morrow, 1984); Dorothy Salem, *To Better Our World: Black Women in Organized Reform 1890–1920,* (New York: Carlson Publishing, 1990).

46. For information on the ICWDR, see Cynthia Neverdon-Morton, *Afro-American Women of the South and the Advancement of the Race, 1895–1925* (Knoxville: Univ. of Tennessee Press, 1989), 198–202; White, *Too Heavy a Load,* 134–48.

47. Rupp, *Worlds of Women,* 31.

48. In Balch, Addams, and Hamilton, *Women at The Hague,* 143.

49. Leonora O'Reilly to her mother, Apr. 14, 1915, reel 102, Leonora O'Reilly Papers, Schlesinger Library.

50. Mary Church Terrell, *A Colored Woman in a White World* (Washington, DC: Ransdell Incorporated Publishers, 1940), 332–35.

51. Ibid., 332.

52. Resolution passed at the 1919 Zurich Congress as reported in the Notes of the Annual Meeting, reel 5, US WILPF Papers, SCPC.

53. C. A. Foster, *Women and the Warriors,* 158.

54. Executive Committee Minutes, June 27, 1921; Executive Committee Minutes, Nov. 21, 1921, reel 5, US WILPF Papers, SCPC.

55. Mary Church Terrell to Jane Addams, Mar. 18, 1921, Mary Church Terrell (MCT) Papers, Library of Congress.

56. Amy Woods to Lucy Biddle Lewis, Mar. 28, 1923, reel 40, folder 33, US WILPF Papers, SCPC.

57. Lucy Biddle Lewis to Amy Woods, Mar. 26, 1923, reel 40, folder 33, US WILPF Papers, SCPC.

58. See minutes of the WILPF executive committee, Nov. 12, 1921, Dec. 10, 1921, Jan. 11, 1922, Feb. 23, 1922, and Apr. 29, 1922, reel 5, US WILPF Papers, SCPC.

59. Lewis to Woods, Mar. 26, 1933, reel 40, folder 33, US WILPF Papers, SCPC.

60. Hannah Clothier Hull to Mary Church Terrell, Nov, 29, 1922, reel 8, MCT Papers, Library of Congress.

61. C. A. Foster, *Women and the Warriors,* 46–47.

62. For information on the Spider Web Chart and the War Department's campaign against the WILPF, see Joan M. Jensen, "All Pink Sisters: The War Department and the Feminist Movement in the 1920s," in *Decades of Discontent: The Women's Movement, 1920–1940,* ed. Lois Scharf and Joan M. Jensen (Westport, CT: Greenwood Press, 1983), 199–222; Cott, *Grounding of Modern Feminism,* 243–58.

63. 1924 International WILPF Congress Program, May 1–7, Washington, DC, reel D 3, subseries F, Leonora O'Reilly Papers, Schlesinger Library.

64. In *Pax Special,* vol. 1, no. 1, June 1924, DG 45, reel 93, US WILPF Papers, SCPC. For more information on student peace protests in the late 1920s and 1930s, see Eileen Eagan, *Class, Culture, and the Classroom: The Student Peace Movement of the 1930s* (Philadelphia: Temple Univ. Press, 1981).

65. James Weldon Johnson, "The Race Problem and Peace," May 1924, reel 33, box 1, folder 16, US WILPF Papers, SCPC.

66. Ibid.

67. Ibid.

68. Emily Greene Balch, "Racial Contacts and Cohesions: As Factors in the Unconstrained Fabric of a World at Peace," *Survey,* Mar. 6, 1915, 611.

69. US WILPF Executive Committee Minutes, Sept. 12–13, 1924, reel 5, US WILPF Papers, SCPC.

70. Balch, "Racial Contacts and Cohesions," 610–11.

71. Lewis Gannett, *Bulletin* no. 5, May 1923, reel 93, US WILPF Papers, SCPC.

72. Mary Beard, "The Japanese–American Crisis," *Bulletin,* June 1925, reel 93, US WILPF Papers, SCPC. In 1926 during the WILPF International Congress in Dublin, Tano Jodai, a WILPF member from Japan, criticized the militarization of Japan and warned of growing Japanese hostility toward the United States because of US activity in Hawaii and the Philippines. See Bussey and Tims, *Pioneers for Peace,* 55.

73. W. E. B. Du Bois, "Postscript," *Crisis* 41 (Mar. 1932): 93.

74. For discussion of the WILPF's involvement in the disarmament campaigns, see C. A. Foster, *Women and the Warriors*, chaps. 6 and 7; Bussey and Tims, *Pioneers for Peace*, 94–103; Alonso, *Peace as a Women's Issue*, 117–24.

75. Julia West Hamilton to Mrs. Sallie W. Stewart, Oct. 23, 1931, reel 7, NACW Papers.

76. The US Department of State began efforts to explore "commercial conditions in the empire" of Ethiopia in 1903. In the fall of 1927 J. G. White started its survey of Lake Tsana with the support of Ethiopian officials. For this history, see Frank J. Manheim, "The United States and Ethiopia: A Study in American Imperialism," *Journal of Negro History* 17, no. 2 (Apr. 1932): 141–55.

77. For more on WILPF's work in this area, see C. A. Foster, *Women and the Warriors*, 169–71.

78. Dorothy Detzer to Balch and Hull, Aug. 19, 1930, reel 8, Emily Greene Balch Papers, SCPC.

1. African American Women and the Search for Peace and Freedom

1. *National Association Notes*, National Association of Colored Women, Feb. 1935, reel 25, NACW Papers.

2. Addie W. Hunton, Annual Report of the Interracial Extension Committee, May 1932, US WILPF Papers, SCPC.

3. For a similar argument about the historiography of the civil rights movement, see Kathryn Nasstrom, "Down to Now: Memory, Narrative, and Women's Leadership in the Civil Rights Movement in Atlanta, Georgia," *Gender and History* 11, no. 1 (Apr. 1999): 113–44.

4. For a general history of African American women and self-organizing, see White, *Too Heavy a Load*; Giddings, *When and Where I Enter*.

5. W. E. B. Du Bois, *Darkwater: Voices from Within the Veil* (New York: AMS Press, 1920), 179.

6. Ibid., 181.

7. For the masculinist politics and culture of the New Negro era and its effect on black women's organizing strategies and political discourse, see White, *Too Heavy a Load*, 110–41; Kevin Gaines, *Uplifting the Race: Black Leadership, Politics, and Culture in the Twentieth Century* (Chapel Hill: Univ. of North Carolina Press, 1996), particularly chapter 8, "The Everyday Struggles and Contradictions of Uplift Ideology in the Life and Writings of Alice Dunbar-Nelson." An increasing amount of scholarship considers the life and writing of W. E. B. Du Bois as a way to understand how gender and power worked during the New Negro era. For this scholarship, see Hazel V. Carby, *Race Men* (Cambridge, MA: Harvard Univ. Press, 1998), in particular chapter 1; Joy James, "The Profeminist Politics of W. E. B. Du Bois," in *W. E. B. Du Bois on Race and Culture: Philosophy, Politics, and Poetics*, ed. Bernard W. Bell, Emily Grosholz, and James Stewart (New York: Routledge, 1996), 141–60.

8. James, "The Profeminist Politics," 156–57.

9. In 1917 sculptor Meta Vaux Warrick Fuller received second place in a Woman's Peace Party competition for her work *Peace Halting the Ruthlessness of War;* see Elsa Honig Fine, *The African American Artist: A Search for Identity* (New York: Holt, Rinehart, and Winston, 1973), 75. Laura Wheeler Waring later produced a peace painting as a benefit for the WILPF.

10. For black men's military contributions, see Garna L. Christen, *Black Soldiers in Jim Crow Texas, 1899–1917* (College Station: Texas A&M Univ. Press, 1995); Gerald W. Patton, *War and Race: The Black Officer in the American Military: 1915–41* (Westport, CT: Greenwood Press, 1981). For a cogent discussion of the complex representational power of the black soldier, see William Gatewood, *"Smoked Yankees" and the Struggle for Empire: Letters from Negro Soldiers, 1898–1902* (Urbana: Univ. of Illinois Press, 1971).

11. Patton, *War and Race,* 103–13.

12. Shapiro, *White Violence,* 106–11.

13. W. E. B. Du Bois, "Returning Soldiers," *Crisis* 18 (May 1919): 14.

14. Karen S. Adler, "'Always Leading Our Men in Service and Sacrifice': Amy Jacques Garvey, Feminist Black Nationalism," *Gender and Society* 6, no. 3 (Sept. 1992): 346–75.

15. W. E. B. Du Bois, "Pan-Africa and New Racial Philosophy," *Crisis* 40 (Nov. 1933): 247.

16. For scholarship on the gender politics of the Garvey movement, see Beryl Satter, "Marcus Garvey, Father Divine and the Gender Politics of Race Difference and Race Neutrality," *American Quarterly* 48, no. 1 (Mar. 1996): 43–76; Barbara Bair, "True Women, Real Men: Gender, Ideology and Social Role in the Garvey Movement," in *Gendered Domains: Rethinking Public and Private in Women's History,* ed. Dorothy O. Helly and Susan M. Revereby (Ithaca, NY: [Cornell Univ. Press, 1992), 165–66; Adler, "'Always Leading Our Men in Service,'" 346–75.

17. Hunton's letters from 1921 to 1933 report that her work often compromised her health, requiring hospital stays of three days to three weeks; see Addie Hunton to Mary White Ovington, Mar. 25, 1921, reel 16, NAACP Papers; Addie Hunton, "NAACP Field Report," Summer 1923, reel 16, NAACP Papers; Addie Hunton to Walter White, June 3, 1933, reel 16, NAACP Papers.

18. For biographical information on Addie Hunton, see Gretchen E. MacLachlan, "Addie Waits Hunton," in *Black Women in America: An Historical Encyclopedia,* ed. Darlene Clark Hine, 556–57 (Brooklyn: Carlson, 1993). Also see Addie Hunton's biography of her husband, Addie W. Hunton, *William Alphaues Hunton: A Pioneer Prophet of Young Men* (New York: Association Press, 1938). Hunton promoted the NACW and black women's espousal of social motherhood to the readership of the *Crisis.* See Addie W. Hunton, "The National Association of Colored Women," *Crisis* 2 (May 1911): 17–18; Addie W. Hunton, "Women's Clubs Caring for the Children," *Crisis* 2 (June 1911): 78–79. For the Amenia Conference, see Herbert Aptheker, ed., *A Documentary History of the Negro People in the United States: 1910–1932* (Secaucus, NJ: Citadel Press, 1973), 32–36.

19. For biographical information on Kathryn Johnson, see Thea Arnold, "Kathryn Magnolia Johnson (1878–1955)," in *Black Women in America,* ed. Darlene Clark Hine (New

York: Carlson, 1993), 644–45. In 1920 Johnson, twelve years younger than Hunton, became one of the first field organizers for the NAACP. She was later fired, reportedly for her bluntness and belief that the NAACP should be led completely by black officers and staff.

20. Hunton and Johnson, *Two Colored Women*, 32.

21. Hunton and Johnson, *Two Colored Women*, 24.

22. Alice Dunbar-Nelson reported that three hundred black women served as Red Cross nurses during the war by passing as white. See Alice Dunbar-Nelson, "Negro Women in War Work," in *Scott's Official History of the American Negro in the World War*, ed. Emmett J. Scott, (Chicago: Homewood Press, 1919), 374–97. One month before the end of the war the services of two dozen black nurses were used in three US Army bases, in comparison to the twenty-one thousand white nurses enlisted; see Darlene Clarke Hine and Kathleen Thompson, *A Shining Thread of Hope: The History of Black Women in America* (New York: Broadway Books, 1998), 225. For more on the history of black women and nursing, see Darlene Clark Hine, *Black Women in White: Racial Conflict and Cooperation in the Nursing Profession, 1890–1950* (Bloomington: Indiana Univ. Press, 1989).

23. Hunton and Johnson, *Two Colored Women*, 33. For race and motherhood, see Patricia Hill Collins, "Producing the Mothers of the Nation: Race, Class and Contemporary US Population Politics," in *Women, Citizenship and Difference*, ed. Nira Yuval-Davis and Pnina Werbner (London: Zed Books, 1999), 188–29. Another example of the denial of black female citizenship through the denial of black motherhood occurred in 1930 when US Congress designated funds for the transportation of "Gold Star Mothers" to Europe to visit the American cemeteries in which their sons were buried. Black women were excluded from this initial voyage. After much protest, arrangements were made for black women to travel to Europe on "second rate vessels." In David Levering Lewis, *When Harlem Was in Vogue* (New York: Knopf, 1981), 255.

24. Hunton and Johnson, *Two Colored Women*, 32.

25. Ibid., 31.

26. Zeiger, *In Uncle Sam's Service: Women Workers with the American Expeditionary Force, 1917–1919* (Ithaca, NY: Cornell Univ. Press, 2000), 57.

27. On the citizen soldier, see Jean Bethke Elshtain, *Women and War* (New York: Basic Books, 1987); R. Claire Snyder, *Citizen-Soldiers and Manly Warriors: Military Service and Gender in the Civic Republic Tradition* (New York: Rowman and Littlefield, 1999).

28. Hunton and Johnson, *Two Colored Women*, 236. The literature on political motherhood is extensive; see Annelise Orleck, Alexis Jetter, and Diana Taylor, eds., *The Politics of Motherhood: Activist Voices from Left to Right* (Hanover: Univ. Press of New England, 1997); Kennedy, *Disloyal Mothers*; Susan Zeiger, *In Uncle Sam's Service*.

29. Hunton and Johnson, *Two Colored Women*, 236.

30. Hunton, "Negro Womanhood Defended," *The Voice of the Negro* 7 (July 1904): 280.

31. Hunton and Johnson, *Two Colored Women*, 156–57.

32. Ibid., 234–38.

33. For an insightful discussion of Wells's analysis of lynching see Gail Bederman, *Manliness and Civilization: A Cultural History of Gender and Race in the United States, 1880–1917* (Chicago: Univ. of Chicago Press, 1995).

34. Hunton and Johnson, *Two Colored Women,* 235.

35. Ibid., 9–10.

36. See Rosalyn Terborg-Penn, "African American Women's Networks in the Anti-Lynching Crusade," in *Gender, Class, Race and Reform in the Progressive Era,* ed. Noralee Frankel and Nancy S. Dye (Lexington: Univ. Press of Kentucky, 1991), 151–60; Suzanne Lebsock, "Woman Suffrage and White Supremacy: A Virginia Case Study," in *Visible Women: New Essays on American Activism,* ed. Nancy A. Hewitt and Suzanne Lebsock (Chicago: Univ. of Illinois Press, 1993), 62–100.

37. Shapiro, *White Violence,* 114–18.

38. "Reception for Mrs. A. W. Hunton, Given to Her by the Ladies of Brooklyn on Her Return from the Western Front," *Crisis* 19, no. 3 (Jan. 1920): 121; "American Delegation at the International Congress of Women for Permanent Peace in Zurich, Switzerland," *Crisis* 19, no. 2 (Dec. 1919): 67.

39. Addie Hunton, "Remarks of Mrs. Addie W. Hunton," Thirteenth Annual Conference, June 20, 1922, reel 9, NAACP Papers.

40. "Demands Full Citizenship for Colored Women," Press Release of the NAACP, June 21, 1922, reel 8, NAACP Papers.

41. Ibid.

42. Addie Hunton to Mary White Ovington, Mar. 25, 1921, reel 16, NAACP Papers.

43. Cott, *Grounding of Modern Feminism,* 69–71; Addie Hunton to Mary White Ovington, Mar., 25, 1921, reel 16, NAACP Papers. For more on the racial politics of women's suffrage, see Louise Michele Newman, *White Women's Rights: The Racial Origins of Feminism in the United States* (New York: Oxford Univ. Press, 1999); and Terborg-Penn, African *American Women in the Struggle.* In response to the NWP mistreatment of black women's concerns, one NWP advisory board member resigned and Florence Kelly reported that she "felt chagrin" that the "convention welshed on the Negro question," Cott, *Grounding of Modern Feminism,* 71.

44. Maclachlan, "Addie Waits Hunton," 597.

45. For Hunton's prewar belief in idealism, see "Votes for Women: A Symposium," *Crisis* (Aug. 1915), reprinted in Aptheker, *Documentary History,* 111.

46. Addie Hunton, Report of Addie Hunton, Oct. 6–Nov. 8, 1922, and Jan. 3–Feb. 7, 1923, reel 16, NAACP Papers.

47. Addie Hunton, Report of Addie Hunton, Oct. 6–Nov. 8, 1922, reel 16, NAACP Papers.

48. Salem, *To Better Our World,* 231–35.

49. Terborg-Penn, "African American Women's Networks," 157–58.

50. Addie Hunton, Field Report, 1923, reel 16, NAACP Papers.

51. Addie Hunton to NAACP Board of Directors, Jan. 14, 1924, reel 16, NAACP Papers; Addie Hunton to Mary White Ovington, Mar. 25, 1921; Addie Hunton to James Weldon Johnson, Apr. 18, 1924, reel 16, NAACP Papers.

52. Adele Logan Alexander, "Introduction," in Hunton and Johnson, *Two Colored Women*, xxii. Two other black clubwomen attended the Pan-African Congress as nondelegates, Mary Talbert and Ida Gibbs Hunt. Talbert and Hunt also attended the International Council of Women for Permanent Peace meeting in Zurich.

53. Alexander, "Introduction," xxii; "The Pan-African Congress: The Story of a Growing Movement," *Crisis* 34, no. 8 (Oct. 1927): 263–64; NAACP National Board Minutes, Nov. 8, 1926, reel 1, NAACP Papers; publicity flyer, unsigned, "About the Fourth Pan-African Congress," in Aptheker, *Documentary History*, 545–46.

54. See "Resolutions of the Pan-African Congress," in Aptheker, *Documentary History*, 250–52.

55. *Bulletin* 1, no. 3 (Oct. 1920), reel 93, US WILPF Papers. In preparation for the trip Emily Greene Balch requested that steps be taken to make sure that the black delegates received first-class accommodations on the ship to Haiti; National Board Minutes, Nov. 11, 1925, reel 5, US WILPF Papers. Lucy Biddle Lewis reported that she raised three hundred dollars toward the cost of Hunton's and Atwood's participation in the Haiti mission; National Board Report, Feb. 7, 1926, reel 5, US WILPF Papers. Charlotte Atwood was among the Haiti team members to address the WILPF 1926 Annual Meeting in Washington, DC, about the trip; *Newsletter*, Apr. 1926, roll 93 US WILPF Papers; "The Pan-African Congresses: The Story of a Growing Movement," *Crisis* 34, no. 8 (Oct. 1927): 263.

56. Emily Greene Balch, ed., *Occupied Haiti* (New York: The Writers Publishing Company, 1927), 113–21.

57. Addie Hunton to James Weldon Johnson, Mar. 6, 1926, reel 16, NAACP Papers.

58. Addie Hunton, "Speech Made by Mrs. Addie Hunton at the Twenty-third Annual Conference of the National Association for the Advancement of Colored People, Washington, DC, May 17–22," reel 9, NAACP Papers.

59. Ibid.

60. Alice Ruth Moore, *Violets and Other Tales* (Boston: The Monthly Review Press, 1895); Alice Dunbar-Nelson, *The Goodness of St. Rocque and Other Tales* (New York: Dodd, Mead, and Company, 1899).

61. Gloria Hull, *Color, Sex and Poetry: Three Women Writers of the Harlem Renaissance* (Bloomington: Indiana Univ. Press, 1987), 83–88.

62. Ibid., 35–36, 67–70, 91–94.

63. On the debate over the nature of black support of the war, see William Jordan, "'The Damnable Dilemma': African-American Accommodation and Protest During World War I," *Journal of American History* 8 (Mar. 1995): 1562–83; Mark Ellis, "W. E. B. Du Bois and the Formation of Black Opinion in World War I: A Commentary on 'The Damnable Dilemma,'" *Journal of American History* 81, no. 4 (Mar. 1995): 1584–90. For discussion of surveillance of

black militants and the black press during and after the war, see Theodore Kornweibel, Jr., *"Seeing Red": Federal Campaigns Against Black Militancy: 1919–1925* (Bloomington: Indiana Univ. Press, 1998).

64. Pageants were a literary device popularized by suffragettes and used often by female educators. Two other African American women who turned to pageants to explore the meaning of the war were Mary P. Burrill in her 1919 play *Aftermath* and May Miller in her 1930 play *Strangers in the Dust*. Both plays can be found in Kathy Perkins, *Black Female Playwrights: An Anthology of Plays Before 1950* (Bloomington: Indiana Univ. Press, 1989).

65. Claire M. Tylee, "Womanist Propaganda, African-American Great War Experience, and Cultural Strategies of the Harlem Renaissance: Plays by Alice Dunbar-Nelson and Mary P. Burrill," *Women's Studies International Forum* 20 (1997): 153–63.

66. Alice Dunbar-Nelson, *"Mine Eyes Have Seen,"* Crisis 15, no. 6 (Apr. 1918): 271–75.

67. Ibid.

68. W. E. B. Du Bois, "Close Ranks," *Crisis* 16 (July 1918): 111.

69. Hull, *Color, Sex and Poetry,* 67.

70. Dunbar-Nelson, "Negro Women."

71. Salem, *To Better Our World,* 204.

72. Ibid., 384.

73. Dunbar-Nelson, "Negro Women," 379. Dunbar-Nelson desired to go overseas as a YMCA worker with the American Expeditionary Forces or as a journalist. Her request to the *Philadelphia Public Ledger* to be assigned as a war correspondent was turned down. Dunbar-Nelson reports that three hundred black women served in the Red Cross in France by passing for white. As Dunbar-Nelson notes in her Scott report, numerous leaders in the black women's club and education movements served with the committee including Anna Julia Cooper, Mary McLeod Bethune, and Mary Church Terrell; see Dunbar-Nelson, "Negro Women," 384–85. For Anna Julia Cooper's account of her work, see "Sketches from a Teacher's Notebook: Loss of Speech Through Isolation," in *The Voice of Anna Julia Cooper,* ed. Charles Lemert and Esme Bhan (New York: Rowman and Littlefield, 1998), 224–29. Terrell, *Colored Woman,* 318–50.

74. Dunbar-Nelson, "Negro Women," 374.

75. Ibid., 376.

76. William J. Breen, "Black Women and the Great War: Mobilization and Reform in the South," *Journal of Southern History* 44, no. 3 (Aug. 1978): 425–26.

77. Terrell, *Colored Woman,* 320, 328, 392.

78. Dunbar-Nelson, "Negro Women," 392.

79. Ibid., 391–92.

80. Evelyn Brooks Higginbotham, *Righteous Discontent: The Women's Movement in the Black Baptist Church, 1880–1920* (Cambridge: Howard Univ. Press, 1993), 225.

81. Ibid., 225–26.

82. Alice Dunbar-Nelson, "I Sit and Sew," reprinted in *The Works of Alice Dunbar-Nelson: Volume 2,* ed. Gloria Hull, 84 (New York: Oxford Univ. Press, 1988).

83. Ibid.

84. Dunbar-Nelson, "Negro Women," 697.

85. Ibid., 387.

86. Ibid., 376. As Dunbar-Nelson wrote: "As is usually the case when any problem presents itself to the nation at large, the Negro faces a double problem."

87. Hull, *Color, Sex and Poetry*, 68; Rosalyn Terborg-Penn, "African American Women's Networks in the Anti-Lynching Crusade," in *Gender, Class, Race and Reform in the Progressive Era*, ed. Noralee Frankel and Nancy S. Dye (Lexington: Univ. Press of Kentucky, 1991), 154. For more on black women's influence in party politics, see Evelyn Brooks Higginbotham, "'In Politics to Stay': Black Women Leaders and Party Politics in the 1920s," in *Women, Politics, and Change*, ed. Louise A. Tilly and Patricia Gurin, (New York: Russell Sage Foundation, 1979), 199–220. Dunbar-Nelson's political work had its negative personal repercussions. In 1920 she was fired from Howard High School for her work with the Republican Party. From 1920 to 1922 Dunbar-Nelson and her husband published the *Wilmington Advocate*, highly supported by Republican money. In 1922 the pulling away of Republican support forced the folding of the paper and Robert moved to Washington, DC, to become editor of the *Washington Eagle*, the national newspaper of the Improved Benevolent and Protective Order of the Elks of the World.

88. Terborg-Penn, "African American Women's Networks," 154.

89. Ibid.

90. The NAACP delegation included a number of men and women who had served during the war: Emmett J. Scott, R. R. Moton, Mary Church Terrell, Nannie H. Burroughs, and Mary B. Talbert. Dunbar-Nelson recorded that the committee used pressure politics in its effort to persuade the president to do the right thing, reminding him that "the eyes of the colored people will be focused upon . . . you." Yet, as she recorded, this threat received from Harding only a promise of further study—"Bang! went the door of hope." See Aptheker, *Documentary History*, 332–35; Gloria Hull, *Give Us Each Day: The Diary of Alice Dunbar-Nelson* (New York: W. W. Norton, 1984), 85. For more on the Houston riots, see Shapiro, *White Violence*, 106–11.

91. For clubwoman Mary Waring's support of the war, see Wanda A. Hendricks, *Gender, Race, and Politics in the Midwest: Black Clubwomen in Illinois* (Bloomington: Indiana Univ. Press, 1998), 124–27. In 1935, as president of the NACW, Waring spoke in favor of the disarmament movement.

92. Hannah Clothier Hull to Alice Dunbar-Nelson, Oct. 7, 1925, reel 1, Hannah Clothier Hull Papers.

93. Alice Dunbar-Nelson to Mildred Scott Olmsted, Aug. 6, 1928, folder, Interracial Committee, US WILPF Papers, SCPC.

94. Hull, *Give Us Each Day*, 341.

95. Hull, "Introduction," in *Works of Alice Dunbar-Nelson*, liii.

96. Dunbar-Nelson, in Hull, *Works of Alice Dunbar-Nelson*, 138.

97. Hull, *Color, Sex and Poetry*, 92.

98. Dunbar-Nelson, in Hull, *Works of Alice Dunbar-Nelson*, 147.

99. Ibid., 176.

100. Ibid., 205–6.

101. Hull, *Color, Sex and Poetry*, 92.

102. Dunbar-Nelson, in Hull, *Works of Alice Dunbar-Nelson*, 208.

103. Hull, *Give Us Each Day*, 434.

104. *Crisis* 39 (Jan. 1932): 445.

105. Alice Dunbar-Nelson, "Harlem John Henry Views the Airmada," *Crisis* 39 (Jan. 1932): 458, 473.

106. Ibid.

107. Dunbar-Nelson, Sept. 28, 1928, "As in a Looking Glass," in Hull, *Works of Alice Dunbar-Nelson*, 232.

108. For biographical information on Jessie Fauset, see Carolyn Wedin Sylvander, *Jessie Redmon Fauset, Black American Writer* (New York: Whitson Publishing Company, 1981). Although there is an increasing amount of literary criticism focused on Fauset's novels very little of it interrogates her nonfiction writing for the *Crisis* or her writing in relationship to issues of national identity and Pan-African consciousness. The one text that begins this exploration is Carol Allen, *Black Women Intellectuals, Strategies of Nation, Family, and Neighborhood in the Works of Pauline Hopkins, Jessie Fauset, and Marita Bonner* (New York: Garland Publishing, 1998). Fauset's novels include *There Is Confusion* (New York: Boni and Liveright, 1924); *Plum Bun* (New York: Stokes, 1929); *The Chinaberry Tree: A Novel of American Life* (New York: Stokes, 1931); and *Comedy American Style* (New York: Stokes, 1933); see Sylvander, *Jessie Redmon Fauset*, 28.

109. Jessie Fauset's "Some Notes on Color" is reprinted in Aptheker, *Documentary History*, 354–58.

110. Sylvander, *Jessie Redmon Fauset*, 58–63.

111. Jessie Fauset, "Tracing Shadows," *Crisis* 10 (Sept. 1915): 247–55.

112. See Jessie Fauset, "Pastures New," *Crisis* (Sept. 1920), reprinted in *The Chinaberry Tree and Selected Writings* (Boston: Northeastern Univ. Press, 1995), 355–60.

113. Sylvander, *Jessie Redmon Fauset*, 57–61, 114–19.

114. Jessie Fauset, "Nationalism and Egypt," *Crisis* 19, no. 6 (Apr. 1920): 316.

115. Ibid.

116. For a biographical account of Egyptian women's protest, see Huda Shaarawi, *Harem Years: The Memoirs of an Egyptian Feminist: 1879–1924*, ed. Margot Badran (New York: Feminist Press, 1986).

117. Jessie Fauset, "Impressions of the Second Pan-African Congress, *Crisis* 23 (Nov. 1921): 12–14.

118. Ibid., 13–15.

119. Ibid., 15.

120. Sylvander, *Jessie Redmon Fauset*, 67–68.

121. Ibid.

122. Fauset, "Dark Algiers, the White," *Crisis* (Apr. 1925): 255.

123. Ibid., 257.

124. Ibid., 256.

125. Fauset, *There Is Confusion*, 232.

126. Allen, *Black Women Intellectuals*, 57.

127. Fauset, "Impressions," 12.

128. Ibid., 13.

129. Fauset, "Some Notes on Color," in Aptheker, *Documentary History*, 355–56.

130. Sylvander, *Jessie Redmon Fauset*, 65.

2. Race and the Social Thought of White Women in the WILPF

1. John Higham, *Strangers in the Land: Patterns of American Nativism: 1860–1925* (New Brunswick, NJ: Rutgers Univ. Press, 1992), 144.

2. For scientific racism, see Thomas Gossett, *Race: The History of an Idea in America* (New York: Schocken Books, 1970); Elazar Barkan, *The Retreat of Scientific Racism: Changing Concepts of Race in Britain and the United States Between the World Wars* (Cambridge: Cambridge Univ. Press, 1992).

3. Madison Grant, *The Passing of the Great White Race or the Racial Bias of European History* (New York: Charles Scribner's Sons, 1916); Lothrop Stoddard, *Clashing Tides of Color* (New York: Charles Scribner's Sons, 1935); for more on Edward Alsworth Ross, see Gossett, *Race*, 168–72.

4. Gossett, *Race*, 329.

5. Ibid., 335–38. For more scholarship on masculinity, race, and civilization, see Bederman, *Manliness and Civilization*.

6. Pascoe, *Relations of Rescue*, 53.

7. On the signifying power of race, see Evelyn Brooks Higginbotham, "African-American Women's History and the Metalanguage of Race," *Signs* 17, no. 2 (1992): 251–74; Toni Morrison, *Playing in the Dark: Whiteness and the Literary Imagination* (New York: Vintage Books, 1992).

8. Herman, *Eleven Against the War*, ix.

9. Pascoe, *Relations of Rescue*, 48.

10. Paul Gilroy, *Against Race: Imagining Political Culture Beyond the Color Line* (Cambridge, MA: Harvard Univ. Press, 2000), 70.

11. Newman, *White Women's Rights*, 19–20.

12. For more on the development of cultural pluralism in the 1920s, see Horace Kallen, *Culture and Democracy in the United States: Studies in Group Psychology of the American People* (New York: Boni and Liveright, 1924).

13. For this view of Rachel Davis Dubois's contributions to education reform, see Nicholas V. Montalto, *A History of the Intercultural Education Movement: 1924–1941* (New York: Garland Press, 1984); Diana Selig, *Americans All: The Cultural Gifts Movement* (Cambridge, MA: Harvard Univ. Press, 2008), 69.

14. Suzanne Desan, "Crowds, Community, and Ritual in the Work of E. P. Thompson and Natalie Davis," in *The New Cultural History*, ed. Lynn Hunt (Berkeley: Univ. of California Press, 1989), 55.

15. For these and other cases of segregation and liberal efforts to correct them, see P. E. Baker, *Negro–White Adjustment*; and Selig, *Americans All*, 76–77.

16. Selig, *Americans All*, 2–10.

17. For more on education in the 1920s, see Kallen, *Culture and Democracy*; Jonathan Zimmerman, "'Each "Race" Could Have Its Heroes Sung': Ethnicity and the History Wars in the 1920s," *Journal of American History* 87 (June 2000): 92–112; Carter G. Woodson, "Celebration of Negro History Week," *Journal of Negro History* 12, no. 2 (1927): 108–9; Charles S. Johnson, *The Negro in American Civilization: A Study of Negro Life and Race Relations in the Light of Social Research* (New York: Henry Holt and Company, 1930).

18. Selig, *Americans All*, 9.

19. Resolutions of the 1919 WILPF International Congress in Zurich, reel 5, US WILPF Papers, SCPC.

20. Rachel Davis Dubois, *All This and Something More: Pioneering in Intercultural Education* (Bryn Mawr, PA: Dorrance and Company, 1984), 5–6, 14–16, 23, 28.

21. Dubois, *All This and Something More*, 41.

22. Ibid., 34–38.

23. For discussion of her time in the WILPF, see Dubois, *All This and Something More*.

24. Annual Report of the National Secretary, May 8, 1924, reel 5, US WILPF Papers. Dubois also served as the acting executive secretary of the WILPF during the summer of 1922.

25. Rachel Davis Dubois, *Education in World-Mindedness: A Series of Assembly Programs Given by Students at Woodbury High School, Woodbury, New Jersey, 1927–1928* (Philadelphia: American Friends Service Committee, 1928); Rachel Davis Dubois, *The Contributions of Racial Elements to American Life* (Philadelphia: Women's International League for Peace and Freedom, 1930). *Education in World-Mindedness* received even wider circulation when it was repackaged for use by African American women's clubs. Distributed by the WILPF with the assistance of Alice Dunbar-Nelson and the AIPC, the remodeled educational program kept the same general principles as the high school program but added more focus on contemporary international political issues, such as politics in Haiti. The program also presented reading lists more suitable for an adult audience.

26. Ibid., 376.

27. Ibid.

28. Rachel Davis Dubois, *A School and Community Project in Developing Sympathetic Attitudes Toward Other Races and Nations* (New York: Service Bureau for Education in Human Relations, 1934), 7.

29. Montalto, *History,* 248.

30. Bruno Lasker, *Race Attitudes in Children* (New York: Henry Holt and Co., 1929), 334.

31. Dubois, *School and Community;* Selig, *Americans All,* 79.

32. Dubois, *School and Community,* 30–31.

33. Ibid.

34. Dubois, *Education in World-Mindedness,* 5.

35. Christine Rauchfuss Gray, "Introduction," in *Plays and Pageants from the Life of the Negro,* ed. Willis Richardson (Univ. Press of Mississippi, 1993), xxvii.

36. Dubois, *Education in World-Mindedness,* 6.

37. Ibid., 10.

38. Ibid.

39. Ibid., 11.

40. For another discussion of the centrality of white female moral authority to the project of the women's peace movement, see Erika A. Kuhlman, *Petticoats and White Feathers: Gender Conformity, Race, the Progressive Peace Movement, and the Debate Over War, 1895–1919* (Westport, CT: Greenwood Press, 1997).

41. Because Dubois was tenured the Board of Education's efforts to fire her did not go very far. About the same time the Board of Education attempted to fire Dubois, two teachers at the Teachers College of West Chester, Pennsylvania, were fired. Dubois, *All This and Something More,* 53–55; Selig, *Americans All,* 75–76.

42. Selig, *Americans All,* 99–100, 107.

43. Rachel Davis Dubois, *Build Together Americans: Adventures in Intercultural Education for Secondary School* (New York: Hinds, Hayden, and Eldredge, Inc., 1945); Rachel Davis Dubois and Emma Schweppe, eds., *The Jews in American Life* (New York: Thomas Nelson and Sons, 1935).

44. For biographical information on Rachel Dubois, see Dubois, *All This and Something More;* Montalto, *History;* Selig, *Americans All.*

45. Lasker, *Race Attitudes,* 343.

46. Ibid., 186, 224.

47. Selig, *Americans All,* 89.

48. Ibid., 16.

49. Emily Greene Balch, "What It Means to Be an American," in *Beyond Nationalism: The Social Thought of Emily Greene Balch,* ed. Mercedes Randall (New York: Twayne Publishers, Inc., 1972), 39.

50. Peggy Pascoe, "Miscegenation Law, Court Cases, and Ideologies of 'Race' in Twentieth-Century America," in *Sex, Love, Race: Crossing Boundaries in North American History,* ed. Martha Hodes (New York: New York Univ. Press, 1999), 466.

51. For more on Balch's social thought, see Linda K. Schott, *Reconstructing Women's Thoughts: The Women's International League for Peace and Freedom Before World War II* (Stanford, CA: Stanford Univ. Press, 1997); Mercedes Randall, *Beyond Nationalism: The Social Thought of Emily Greene Balch* (New York: Twayne Publishers, 1972); and Harriet Hyman Alonso, "Nobel Peace Laureates, Jane Addams and Emily Greene Balch: Two Women of the Women's International League for Peace and Freedom," *Journal of Women's History* 7 (Summer 1995): 6–27. For the influence of spirituality on Balch, see Catherine A. Faver, "Feminist Spirituality and Social Reform: Examples from the Early Twentieth Century," *Women's Studies Quarterly* 21, no. 1–2 (1993): 101.

52. Victoria Bissell Brown, introduction to *Twenty Years at Hull House*, by Jane Addams (1920; repr., Boston: Bedford/St. Martin, 1999), 23.

53. Randall, *Improper Bostonian*, 39. Much of Balch's social thought cohered with the school of American Pragmatism most frequently associated with John Dewey, a close associate of Balch. For discussions of American Pragmatism's relationship to internationalism, see Paul A. Carter, *Another Part of the 20s* (New York: Columbia Univ. Press, 1977); Kerwin Lee Klein, *Frontiers of Historical Imagination: Narrating the European Conquest of Native America, 1890–1990* (Berkeley: Univ. of California Press, 1997), 99–113.

54. Balch, quoted in Faver, "Feminist Spirituality," 101.

55. Randall, *Improper Bostonian*, 86.

56. Balch joined the faculty of Wellesley in 1896 and taught there until 1919 when the board of trustees refused to renew her contract because of her "unpatriotic" radicalism during the war. At Wellesley, Balch taught some of the first courses in sociology along with economics and the history of socialism while serving as chair of the economics and sociology departments. Other Wellesley faculty included Vida Scudder, a suffragist and member of the Socialist Party; Ellen Hayes, a suffragist known for using the *Communist Manifesto* in her lectures on astronomy; and Katharine Corman, an economist who helped found the Consumer League. For more on Balch's years at Wellesley, see Randall, *Improper Bostonian*, 105–6.

57. Emily Greene Balch, *Our Slavic Fellow Citizens* (New York: Charities Publication Committee, 1910).

58. Carl Kelsey, "Book Review," *Annals of the American Academy of Political and Social Science*, 1911, 233.

59. Robert D. Cross, "How Historians Have Looked at Immigrants to the United States," *International Migration Review* 7, no. 1 (Spring 1973): 9.

60. Robert W. Dimand, "Economists and the Shadow of 'The Other' before 1914," *American Journal of Economics and Sociology* (July 2005): 10.

61. Higham, *Strangers in the Land*, 159, 18662. Grant, *Passing*, chap. 7.

63. For this history, see Mae M Ngai, "The Architecture of Race in American Immigration Law: A Re-Examination of the Immigration Act of 1924," *Journal of American History* 86, no. 1 (June 1999): 67–92; Higham, *Strangers in the Land*; Gossett, *Race*. For the history

of the Chinese Exclusion Act, see Andrew Gyory, *Closing the Gate: Race, Politics, and the Chinese Exclusion Act* (Chapel Hill: Univ. of North Carolina Press, 1998); Erika Lee, *At America's Gate: Chinese Immigration During the Exclusion Era* (Chapel Hill: Univ. of North Carolina Press, 2007).

64. Randall, *Improper Bostonian*, 120.

65. Ibid.

66. Thomas C. Leonard, "More Merciful and Not Less Effective," Eugenics and American Economics in the Progressive Era," *History of Political Economy* 35, no. 4 (2003): 697.

67. Edward Alsworth Ross, "Racial Consequences of Immigration," *Century Magazine* 87 (Feb. 1914): 615–22, reprinted in Jane Addams, *Twenty Years at Hull House* (1910; repr., Boston: Bedford/St. Martin's, 1999), 239–40.

68. Balch, *Our Slavic Fellow Citizens*, 405–6.

69. Ibid.

70. Ibid., 419.

71. Balch, "What It Means," 37.

72. Ibid., 39.

73. Ibid., 36.

74. Ibid., 37.

75. "Jane Addams Condemns Race Prejudice in Film," *New York Evening Post*, Mar. 13, 1915. For more on Jane Addams's position on lynching, see Maurice Hamington, "Public Pragmatism: Jane Addams and Ida B. Wells on Lynching," *Journal of Speculative Philosophy* 19, no. 2 (2005): 167–74.

76. Ibid., 38.

77. Ibid., 37.

78. Ibid., 38.

79. Emily Greene Balch, "Racial Contacts and Cohesions: As Factors in the Unconstrained Fabric of a World at Peace," *Survey*, Mar. 6, 1915, 611.

80. Balch, "What It Means," 38.

81. Ibid., 39.

82. Ibid., 38.

83. Renda, *Taking Haiti*, 301.

84. Ibid., 301–2.

85. Alonso, *Peace as a Women's Issue*, 72; Jane Addams, *Peace and Bread in War Time* (New York: Macmillan, 1922), 54–57.

86. Schott, *Reconstructing Women's Thoughts*, 147.

87. 1924 International WILPF Congress Program, May 1–7, Washington, DC, reel D 3, subseries F, Leonora O'Reilly Papers, Schlesinger Library.

88. Balch, *Occupied Haiti*, viii.

89. Ibid., 115–16.

90. Ibid., 7.

91. Donald Bogle, *Toms, Coons, Mulattoes, Mammies and Bucks: An Interpretive History of Blacks in American Film* (New York: Viking Press, 1973).

92. Balch, *Occupied Haiti*, 7.

93. Ibid., 12.

94. Ibid., 119.

95. Ibid., 116.

96. For more on US activity in Haiti and US anti-imperialism activism, see Robert David Johnson, *The Peace Progressives and American Foreign Relations* (Cambridge, MA: Harvard Univ. Press, 1995); Renda, *Taking Haiti*, 268.

97. Balch, "Memorandum on Haiti," in Randall, *Beyond Nationalism*, 152.

98. Ibid., 37.

99. Ibid., 309.

100. Newman, *White Women's Rights*, 19.

101. Du Bois, "Pan-Africa," 247.

102. My analysis of Graves has been influenced by the following texts: Nupur Chaudhuri and Margaret Strobel, eds., *Western Women and Imperialism: Complicity and Resistance* (Bloomington: Indiana Univ. Press, 1992); Rupp, *Worlds of Women*; Reina Lewis, *Gendering Orientalism: Race, Femininity, and Representation* (London: Routledge, 1996); Edward Said, *Orientalism* (New York: Pantheon, 1978); Vron Ware, *Beyond the Pale: White Women, Racism and History* (London: Verso, 1992); Alison Blunt, *Travel, Gender, and Imperialism: Mary Kingsley and West Africa* (New York: Guilford Press, 1994); Laura E. Donaldson, *Decolonizing Feminisms: Race, Gender, and Empire Building* (Chapel Hill: Univ. of North Carolina Press, 1992); Mary Louise Pratt, *Imperial Eyes: Travel Writing and Transculturation* (London: Routledge, 1992); Newman, *White Women's Rights*.

103. Annual Report of the National Secretary, Presented at the Annual Meeting, May 8, 1924, reel 5, US WILPF Papers, SCPC. For Graves's efforts to encourage women in Peru to join the WILPF, see Alonso, *Peace as a Women's Issue*, 114. For the development of Pan-American feminist peace alliances, see Francesca Miller, *Latin American Women and the Search for Social Justice* (Hanover: Univ. of New England Press, 1991); Ascuncion Lavrin, *Women, Feminism and Social Change in Argentine, Chile and Uruguay, 1890–1940* (Lincoln: Univ. of Nebraska Press, 1995).

104. In all, Graves published four volumes of her letters and one book on the history of Africa. Those books included: *Benvenuto Cellini Had No Prejudice Against Bronze: Letters from West Africa* (Baltimore: Waverly Press, 1943); *Both Deeper than and above the Melee, Letters from Europeans* (Baltimore: Waverly Press, 1945); *But the Twain Do Meet: Letters from the Near East* (privately published, 1941); and *The Far East Is Not Very Far: Letters from Liu Yuan-Lung and Wang Shou-Ming* (Baltimore: Waverly Press, 1942). Excerpts from *Benvenuto Cellini* were reprinted in 1961 under the new title *Africa: The Wonder and the Glory* as a part of the educational Afrocentric Black Classic Press series of texts for young readers.

105. Anna Melissa Graves, June 1922 or 1923(?), reel 39, file 15, US WILPF Papers, SCPC.

106. Flora Shaw became the first colonial writer for the *London Times,* traveling to the British possessions and authoring from 1890 to 1900 more than five hundred articles in support of the British Empire. For more on Flora Shaw, see Helen Callawy and Dorothy O. Helly, "Crusader for Empire: Flora Shaw/Lady Lugard," in *Western Women and Imperialism: Complicity and Resistance,* ed. Nupur Chaudhuri and Margaret Strobel (Bloomington: Indiana Univ. Press, 1992), 79–97.

107. Graves, *Far East,* v.

108. Ibid.

109. Ibid.

110. Ibid., xix.

111. Ibid., x.

112. Said, *Orientalism.*

113. Graves, *Far East,* xi.

114. Ibid., xx.

115. Ibid., 16.

116. Ibid., xii.

117. Ibid.

118. Graves, *Benvenuto Cellini,* 18.

119. Ibid., 42.

120. Ibid., 39.

121. For these two perspectives, see C. A. Foster, *Women and the Warriors,* 170–78; Elizabeth L. Normandy, "African-Americans and US Policy Towards Liberia, 1929–1935," *Liberian Studies Journal* 18 (1993): 203–30; I. K. Sundiata, *Black Scandal: America and the Liberian Labor Crisis: 1929–1936* (Philadelphia: Institute for the Study of Human Issues, 1980), 107–25.

122. Sundiata, *Black Scandal,* 107.

123. Anna Melissa Graves to Emily Greene Balch, Jan. 1931, reel 8, Emily Greene Balch Papers, SCPC. For discussion of the US WILPF's role in the Liberian crisis, see C. A. Foster, *Women and the Warriors,* 169–78; Sundiata, *Black Scandal,* 107–25.

124. For a general history of Liberia and the crisis of the 1920s and 1930s, see Sundiata, *Black Scandal.* For more on Liberia, see Katherine Harris, *African and American Values: Liberia and West Africa* (New York: Univ. Press of America, 1985); Charles S. Johnson, *Bitter Canaan: The Story of the Negro Republic* (1930; repr. New Brunswick, NJ: Transaction Books, 1987).

125. Sundiata, *Black Scandal,* 11–32.

126. Ibid., 46. Also see Du Bois, "Pan-Africa," 247; and W. E. B. Du Bois, "Liberia, the League and the United States," *Foreign Affairs* 11, no. 4 (July 1933): 682–95.

127. The work of the WILPF to assist with the Liberian crisis was strongly applauded by many leaders in the NAACP. For this perspective, see Roger Baldwin to Walter White, Dec. 18, 1933, NAACP Papers I, C329, folder, Latin America, Haiti, Library of Congress.

128. For information on WILPF's role in the Liberia campaign, see Dorothy Detzer, *Appointment on the Hill* (New York: Henry Holt and Company, 1948); and I. K. Sundiata,

Brothers and Sisters: Black Zion, Black Slavery, 1914–1940 Durham: Duke Univ. Press, 2004), 140–210.

129. Detzer, *Appointment*, 114–37.

130. After spending time in Liberia, Graves traveled to ten black colleges in the United States, including Howard, Hampton, Shaw Univ., and Charlotte Hawkin Brown's Palmer Memorial Institute, presenting her perspective on the Liberian situation; see Anna Melissa Graves to Emily Greene Balch, Mar. 20, 1931, reel 8, Emily Greene Balch Papers, SCPC. While at Spelman Graves reports helping W. E. B. Du Bois prepare his 1933 Foreign Affairs article, "Liberia and the League of Nations."

131. Graves to Balch, Jan. 1931, reel 8, Emily Greene Balch Papers, SCPC.

132. Ibid.

133. Ibid.

134. Sundiata, *Black Scandal*, 107.

135. Emily Greene Balch to James Grafton Rogers, Mar. 16, 1932, reel 9, Emily Greene Balch Papers, SCPC.

136. Balch, "Economic Imperialism with Special Reference to the United States," *Pax International* 2, no. 1 (Nov. 1926), in Randall, *Beyond Nationalism*, 142.

137. Emily Greene Balch, Report on Liberia, June 14, 1934, reel 9, Emily Greene Balch Papers, SCPC.

138. Ibid.

139. Anna Melissa Graves to Emily Greene Balch, July 13, 1934, reel 9, Emily Greene Balch Papers, SCPC.

140. W. M. Morais was an "educated native" strongly opposed to the Americo-Liberians. He represented the native population during the League of Nations meetings. Barclay was the Americo-Liberian president of Liberia at the time.

141. Graves to Balch, July 13, 1934, reel 9, Emily Greene Balch Papers, SCPC.

142. Ibid.

143. Balch, Report on Liberia, June 4, 1934, reel 9, Emily Greene Balch Papers, SCPC. For a treatment of the variety of black perspectives on Liberia, see Sundiata, *Black Scandal*, 81–125.

144. Graves writes to Balch that she wants to finish her book so that she can "prove the negligibility of the differences between people of so-called different races and nations." Graves to Balch, Jan. 1931, reel 8, Emily Green Balch Papers, SCPC.

145. Graves to Balch, Mar. 3, 1934, reel 9, Emily Greene Balch Papers, SCPC.

146. Balch, Report on Liberia, June 4, 1934, reel 9, Emily Greene Balch Papers, SCPC.

147. Newman, *White Women's Rights*.

3. Philadelphia: Forging a National Model of Interracial Peace Work

1. Evelyn Reynolds, "Dear Friends Letter," Nov. 1, 1929, DG 43, series B3, box 13, US WILPF Papers, SCPC.

2. Penn. IEC minutes, Feb. 6, 1930, DG 43, series B3, box 34, US WILPF Papers, SCPC.

3. For the "politics of respectability," see Higginbotham, *Righteous Discontent;* Anne Meis Knupfer, *Toward a Tenderer Humanity and a Nobler Womanhood: African American Women's Clubs in Turn-of-the-Century Chicago* (New York: New York Univ. Press, 1997). In Glenda Gilmore's treatment of the intersection of race, class, and gender she shows how notions of black manhood and womanhood were constructed and manipulated for both black and white advantage. Southern whites used the ideology of "Best Man" to limit enfranchisement and control black behavior, whereas middle-class African Americans demanded that class serve as a marker of manhood and womanhood, hoping for recognition by white society of the differentness of black middle class. In return whites would receive the assurance from the black middle class that they would control black behavior; see Gilmore, *Gender and Jim Crow*, 62, 75.

4. Eileen Boris, "The Power of Motherhood: Black and White Activist Women Redefine the 'Political,'" reprinted in Mary Norton and Ruth Alexander, eds., *Major Problems in American Women's History* (Lexington, MA: D. C. Heath and Company, 1996); Hazel V. Carby, "Policing the Black Woman's Body in an Urban Context," *Critical Inquiry* 18 (Summer 1992). 738–56; Hunton, "Negro Womanhood Defended," 282.

5. Carby, "Policing," 739.

6. Nina Miller, "Femininity, Publicity, and the Class Division of Cultural Labor: Jessie Redmon Fauset's 'There Is Confusion,'" *African American Review* 30 (Summer 1996): 205.

7. For class tensions in Philadelphia resulting from urban migration, see Charles T. Banner-Haley, *To Do Good and To Do Well: Middle Class Blacks and the Depression, Philadelphia, 1929–1941* (New York: Garland Publishing, 1993); E. Franklin Frazier, *The Black Bourgeois* (New York: Free Press, 1957); Alice Dunbar-Nelson, "Woman's Most Serious Problem," in Hull, *Works of Alice-Dunbar Nelson,* 287–92. For the historical and sociological context of African American women's struggle with the politics and culture of "controlling images" of black womanhood, see White, *Too Heavy a Load;* Giddings, *When and Where I Enter;* Patricia Hill Collins, *Black Feminist Thought: Knowledge, Consciousness, and the Politics of Empowerment* (Boston: Unwin Hyman, 1990); Cooper, *A Voice from the South.* For the politics of masculinity in the New Negro movement and its effect on black women social reformers, see Gaines, *Uplifting the Race;* White, *Too Heavy a Load;* Adler, "'Always Leading Our Men,'" 346–75. For the Harlem Renaissance, see D. L. Lewis, *When Harlem Was in Vogue;* Alain Locke, ed., *The New Negro: An Interpretation* (New York: Albert and Charles Boni, 1925). For the treatment of bourgeois black womanhood in the writings of Jessie Fauset, see Hazel V. Carby, *Reconstructing Womanhood: The Emergence of the African American Woman Novelist* (New York: Oxford Univ. Press, 1987); Miller, "Femininity"; Sharon Harley, "Nannie Helen Burroughs: 'The Black Goddess of Liberty': Vindicating the Race: Contributions to African American Intellectual History," *Journal of Negro History* 81 (1996): 67.

8. Olmsted to Bethune, Dec. 29, 1925, DG 43, series B3, box 23, US WILPF Papers, SCPC.

9. WILPF Pennsylvania State Educational Secretary to Reynolds, Mar. 21, 1932, DG 43, series B3, box 40, US WILPF Papers, SCPC; Mary Hoxie Jones, *Swords into Ploughshares: An Account of the American Friends Service Committee, 1917–1937* (New York: The Macmillan Company, 1937), 170.

10. Addie Dickerson, "Mrs. Dickerson Gives Her Impressions of Conference Held by W.I.L. in Prague," *Associated Negro Press*, 1929, DG 43, box 28, folder, Addie Dickerson, US WILPF Papers, SCPC.

11. President's Monthly Message, *National Association Notes*, Jan., 1927, reel 24, NACW Papers.

12. "Miss Burroughs Electrifies a Great Interracial Peace Mass Meeting at the Union Baptist Church," *Christian Review*, Mar. 1930, box 33, Nannie Burroughs Papers, Library of Congress.

13. For intercultural education, see Montalto, *History*.

14. US WILPF National Branch Newsletter, May 1926, reel 93, US WILPF Papers, SCPC.

15. For an earlier formation of goodwill, see Jane Addams's discussion of "new humanitarianism," in Addams, *Newer Ideals*, 23–30.

16. Minutes of "The Committee on Special Peace Work among the Colored," Feb. 18, 1928, DG 43, box 34, folder, Interracial Activity, 1927–1934, US WILPF Papers, SCPC.

17. Ibid.

18. Interracial Committee Annual Report, Apr. 7, 1930, DG 43, box 34, folder, Interracial Activity, 1927–1934, US WILPF Papers, SCPC.

19. For the female talented tenth, see Higginbotham, *Righteous Discontent*.

20. Benjamin Brawley, *The Negro Genius: A New Appraisal of the Achievement of the American Negro in Literature and the Fine Arts* (New York: Dodd, Mead, and Company, 1937), 265; Eve Lynn, *No Alabaster Box and Other Poems* (Philadelphia: Alpress, 1936). Reynolds's poetry portrays the gamut of black life from street youth and gypsies to the middle-class use of the veil to the desire for pure love. Three hundred and fifty copies of this collection were printed.

21. For biographical information of Evelyn Reynolds, see Vincent Franklin, *The Education of Black Philadelphia: The Social and Educational History of a Minority Community, 1900–1950* (Philadelphia: Univ. of Pennsylvania Press, 1979), 123–25. For the Armstrong Association, see Jesse Thomas Moore Jr., *A Search for Equality: The National Urban League: 1910–1961* (Univ. Park: Pennsylvania State Univ. Press, 1981), 16–18; Charles Ashely Harding III, *Race and Opportunity: Black Philadelphians During the Era of the Great Migration* (Philadelphia: Temple Univ. Press, 1989), 244; Franklin, *Education of Black Philadelphia*, 21–22, 27; Salem, *To Better Our World*, 104. WILPF president Hannah Clothier Hull was on the Board of Managers of the Armstrong Association of Philadelphia the year that Reynolds joined the committee; see Evelyn C. Reynolds to Mrs. Springer, Feb. 1, 1929, DG 43, series B 3, box 40, folder, Reynolds, US WILPF Papers, SCPC.

22. Franklin, *Education of Black Philadelphia*, 123–25. Reynolds, like many other black politicians and voters, became a Democrat in 1936.

23. Elizabeth Lindsay Davis, *Lifting as They Climb: The National Association of Colored Women* (Washington, DC: National Association of Colored Women, 1933), 205.

24. Ibid., 206.

25. Addie Hunton was honorary president of the ICWDR and Nannie Helen Burroughs was the chair of the executive committee.

26. Biographical information on Addie Dickerson taken from Davis, *Lifting as They Climb*; Josephine Keene, *Directory of Negro Business and Professional Women of Philadelphia and Vicinity* (Philadelphia, 1939). Biographical information on G. Edward Dickerson from Harding, *Race and Opportunity*, 527, 549.27. Dunbar-Nelson served simultaneously with the AIPC of the American Friends Service Committee and as a representative of the WILPF Pennsylvania IEC on numerous occasions. The AIPC disbanded in Apr. 1931; for this history, see M. H. Jones, *Swords into Ploughshares*, 170–71, 331–34.

28. Biographical information on Alice Dunbar-Nelson taken from Gloria Hull, *Give Us Each Day: The Diary of Alice Dunbar-Nelson* (New York: W. W. Norton, 1984); Hannah Clothier Hull to Alice Dunbar-Nelson, Oct. 3, 1925, reel 1, Hannah Clothier Hull Papers, SCPC; Alice Dunbar-Nelson to Hannah Clothier Hull, Oct. 7, 1925, reel 1, Hannah Clothier Hull Papers, SCPC.

29. For information on Leila Walker Jones, see Davis, *Lifting as They Climb*, 277–78.

30. Philadelphia IEC Minutes, Oct. 18, 1932, DG 43, series B3, box 34, folder, Interracial Activity, 1927–1934, US WILPF Papers, SCPC.

31. Biographical information on Mildred Scott Olmsted taken from Margaret Hope Bacon, *One Woman's Passion for Peace and Freedom: The Life of Mildred Scott Olmsted* (Syracuse: Syracuse Univ. Press, 1993), 3–6, 26–44, 76.

32. *Pax International* 5 (Nov. 1929), reel 93, US WILPF Papers, SCPC.

33. Bacon, *One Woman's Passion*, 82–91, 117–21, 311–12.

34. Ibid., 129–38.

35. MSO to Emily Longstreth, June 8, 1928, DG 43, box 34, folder, Interracial Committee, US WILPF Papers, SCPC.

36. The African American members reported to have attended the first IEC meeting included Dr. Leslie Pinckney Hill, Evelyn Reynolds, Reverend Joseph Henderson of the Pinn Memorial Church, Rose Norwood, Jean Turner of the Philadelphia Health Council, and Nora Waring; MSO to Mary McCurtrie, Feb. 13, 1928, Philadelphia IEC papers, DG 43, series b3, box 34, folder, Interracial Activity, 1927–1934, US WILPF Papers, SCPC; MSO to Rose Norwood, Feb. 14, 1928, DG 43, box 34, folder, Interracial Committee, US WILPF Papers, SCPC. WILPF state chairwoman, Lucy Biddle Lewis, did attend the first two meetings of the committee.

37. MSO to Emily Longstreth, June 8, 1928, DG 43, box 34, folder, Interracial Committee, US WILPF Papers, SCPC.

38. Minutes, The Committee on Special Peace Work Among the Colored, Feb. 18, 1929, DG 43, box 34, folder, Interracial Committee, US WILPF Papers, SCPC; Olmsted to Emily Longstreth, June 6, 1928, DG 43, box 34, folder, Interracial Committee, US WILPF Papers, SCPC.

39. *Philadelphia Tribune*, Feb. 8, 1933.

40. Philadelphia IEC Committee Minutes, June 26, 1928, DG 43, box 34, US WILPF Papers, SCPC.

41. Idabelle Yeiser, "Gas," *Philadelphia Tribune*, Dec. 29, 1932.

42. Zonia Baber to Olmsted, June 14, 1928, reel 42, file 22, US WILPF Papers, SCPC.

43. Ibid.

44. Ibid.

45. From the start black and white women of the Philadelphia IEC rejected the radical interracial politics of the Communist Party as represented by the American Negro Labor Congress; see Hull, *Give Us Each Day*, 253. For more on the Communist Party and interracial labor radicalism, see Robin D. G. Kelley, *Hammer and Hoe: Alabama Communists During the Great Depression* (Chapel Hill: Univ. of North Carolina Press, 1990).

46. Wilbur Thomas to Mary Church Terrell, Nov. 30, 1926, reel 5, MCT Papers, Library of Congress.

47. Olmsted, Dear Member letter, Apr. 28, 1928, DG 53, series b3, box 34, folder, Interracial Activity, 1927–1934, US WILPF Papers, SCPC.

48. For discussion of white women of the Progressive Era as "civilizing forces," see Peggy Pascoe, *Relations of Rescue*; Newman, *White Women's Rights*.

49. Dunbar-Nelson to Mildred Scott Olmsted, Aug. 6, 1928, DG 43, series B3, box 40, US WILPF Papers, SCPC.

50. Ibid.

51. Gilmore, *Gender and Jim Crow*, 48–50.

52. White, *Too Heavy a Load*, 142–75.

53. Ibid., 133–41.

54. For more discussion about the ICWDR, see Neverdon-Morton, *Afro-American Women*, 198–202.

55. "Do Unto Others As You Would They Should Do Unto," *NACW National Notes*, Sept. 1925, NACW Papers.

56. Addie Dickerson, "Mrs. Dickerson Gives Her Impressions of Conference Held by W.I.L. at Prague," for ANP, 1929, DG 43, box 28, series B3, US WILPF Papers, SCPC.

57. Addie Dickerson to Nannie Burroughs, Sept. 1, 1929, box 7, Nannie Burroughs Papers, Library of Congress.

58. Addie Dickerson to Nannie Burroughs, Oct. 14, 1929, box 7, Nannie Burroughs Papers, Library of Congress.

59. Dickerson, "Mrs. Dickerson Gives Her Impressions."

60. Terrell, *Colored Woman*, 331–32. Terrell recalls being the only delegate from "nonwhite" countries positioned as an official delegate to the congress.

61. Terrell, *Colored Woman*, 335.

62. Hull, *Works of Alice Dunbar-Nelson*, 212.

63. Hull, *Give Us Each Day*, 205.

64. Stephanie Shaw, *What a Woman Ought to Be and to Do: Women Workers During the Jim Crow Era* (Chicago: Univ. of Chicago Press, 1996), 135.

65. Hull, *Give Us Each Day*, 232.

66. Ibid.

67. Minutes, Philadelphia IEC, May 29, 1929, and Annual Report, Philadelphia IEC, Apr. 5, 1932, DG 43, series B3, box 34, folder, Interracial Activity, 1927–1934, US WILPF Papers, SCPC.

68. Minutes, IEC, June 2, 1928; Minutes, IEC, June 28, 1928; Minutes, IEC, Sept. 20, 1928; Minutes, IEC, Feb. 21, 1933; Secretary's Report, IEC, Mar. 21, 1933, DG 43, series B3, box 34, folder, Interracial Activity 1927–1934, US WILPF Papers, SCPC.

69. IEC minutes, Jan. 24, 1929.

70. Minutes, IEC, Sept., 20, 1928, DG 43, series B3, box 34, folder, Interracial Activity 1927–1934, US WILPF Papers, SCPC.

71. IEC Minutes, n.d., reel 34, US WILPF Papers, SCPC; IEC Minutes, Nov. 22, 1928, DG 43, series B3, box 34, folder, Interracial Activity 1927–1934, US WILPF Papers, SCPC.

72. For a discussion of the changing role of black churches in Philadelphia, see W. E. B. Du Bois, *The Philadelphia Negro* (Millwood, NY: Krause-Thomson, 1973), 197–220; Robert Gregg, *Sparks from the Anvil of Oppression: Philadelphia's African Methodists and Southern Migrants, 1890–1940* (Philadelphia: Temple Univ. Press, 1993). According to Gregg, by the 1920s the growing urban leisure culture, namely, movie houses and dance theaters, weakened the social role of churches. Further challenges occurred because of the presence of black migrants who threatened church unity. The rise of benevolent and political organizations like the Armstrong Association and the NAACP also challenged the centrality of black churches; see Gregg, *Sparks from the Anvil*, 45–53.

73. For more on the Berean Presbyterian Church and Berean Manual Training and Industrial School, see Gregg, *Sparks from the Anvil*, 58; Du Bois, *Philadelphia Negro*, 197–220. By 1906 the Berean Building and Loan Association was the largest black building and loan association in the city, purchasing 106 homes (Gregg, *Sparks from the Anvil*, 58. For biographical information on Blanche Anderson, see *Who's Who in Colored America* editions from 1933 to 1944; "Sunday Teas," *Philadelphia Tribune*, Dec. 1, 1932.

74. For a similar argument about the gendered dynamics of church organizing, see Higginbotham, *Righteous Discontent*.

75. "The Committee on Special Peace Work Among the Colored," Feb. 18, 1928. Reverend Coleman attends a meeting of the IEC in the fall of 1932, IEC Minutes, Nov. 15, 1932, DG 43, series B3, box 34, folder, Interracial Activity, 1927–1934, US WILPF Papers, SCPC.

76. IEC Minutes, Jan. 24, 1929; IEC Minutes, Nov. 15, 1932; IEC Minutes, Mar. 24, 1928; DG 43, series 43, box 34, folder, Interracial Activity, 1927–1934; Letter from Reynolds and

Mousserone to Ministers, Feb. 14, 1930, DG 43, series B3, box 40, folder, Reynolds, 1929–1933, US WILPF Papers, SCPC.

77. Minutes, IEC, June 2, 1928; Minutes, IEC, June, 28, 1928, DG 43, series 43, box 34, folder, Interracial Activity, 1927–1934, US WILPF Papers, SCPC.

78. IEC Minutes, Mar. 11, 1931, DG 43, series 43, box 34, folder, Interracial Activity, 1927–1934, US WILPF Papers, SCPC.

79. Minutes, IEC, Feb. 6, 1930, DG 43, series 43, box 34, folder, Interracial Activity, 1927–1934, US WILPF Papers, SCPC.

80. Annual Report, IEC Apr. 7-Apr. 27, 1931, DG 43, series 43, box 34, folder, Interracial Activity, 1927–1934, US WILPF Papers, SCPC.

81. Report of the JIL, June 10, 1930-Apr. 20, 1931, Diana Myers, DG 43, series 43, box 34, folder, Interracial Activity, 1927–1934, US WILPF Papers, SCPC.

82. *Philadelphia Tribune,* Dec. 15, 1932.

83. *Philadelphia Tribune,* Feb. 8, 1933.

84. IEC Report to State Convention, Harrisburg, June 9, 1930, DG 43, series B3, box 34, US WILPF Papers, SCPC.

85. Evelyn Reynolds to Peyton, n.d., DG 43, series B3, box 40, folder, Reynolds, US WILPF Papers, SCPC.

86. IEC Minutes, Feb. 6, 1930; IEC minutes, May, 25, 1929; IEC Minutes, Oct. 18, 1929, DG 43, series B3, box 34, folder, Interracial Activity, 1927–1934, US WILPF Papers, SCPC.

87. Philadelphia IEC minutes, Oct. 18, 1929, DG 43, series B3, box 34, folder, Interracial Activity, 1927–1934, US WILPF Papers, SCPC.

88. IEC Minutes, Oct. 18, 1929, DG 43, series B3, box 34, folder, Interracial Activity, 1927–1934, US WILPF Papers, SCPC.

89. Virginia Sears and Blanche Anderson, Tea Invitation, Feb. 30, 1930, DG 43, series B3, box 34, folder, Interracial Activity, 1927–1934, US WILPF Papers, SCPC.

90. Mousserone to Terrell, Nov. 11, 1930, reel 7, MCT Papers, Library of Congress.

91. "Philadelphians Hear Message from Cuba," *Philadelphia Tribune,* Feb. 16, 1933.

92. For biographical information on Lucy Diggs Slowe, see Linda Perkins, "Lucy Diggs Slowe: Champion of the Self-Determination of African-American Women in Higher Education," *Journal of Negro History* 81 (Winter–Autumn 1996): 89–104; Rose Norwood, Luncheon Invitation, Nov. 29, 1929, DG 43, B3, box 13, US WILPF Papers, SCPC.

93. IEC Luncheon Invitation, Nov. 24, 1930, DG 43, B3, box 13, US WILPF Papers, SCPC.

94. "Out of a Job? Why? Do We Want Bullets or Bread?," n.d., DG 43, series B3, box 34, folder, Interracial Activity, 1927–1934, US WILPF Papers, SCPC.

95. Mousserone to Terrell, Dec. 18, 1930 reel 7, MCT Papers, Library of Congress.

96. "Seeks 40,000 Pennies for Peace, Freedom," *Philadelphia Tribune,* Mar. 16, 1933. Idabelle Yeiser's "Peace Corner" columns included: "Your Child," Dec. 15, 1932; "Gas," Dec. 29, 1932; "Cuba—Its Present Situation," Mar. 23, 1933; and "Cuba and the United States," Mar. 30, 1933 (all printed in the *Philadelphia Tribune*).

97. *Philadelphia Tribune*, Dec. 15, 1932.

98. Philadelphia IEC, Dec. 29, 1930, Mrs. Edwin J. Johnson to Editor Public Ledger, DG 43, series B3, box 34, folder, Interracial Activity, 1927–1934, US WILPF Papers, SCPC.

99. Minutes, IEC, Jan. 6, 1933; Minutes IEC, Apr., 11, 1933; Minutes, IEC, June, 7, 1933, DG 43, series B5, box 15, US WILPF Papers, SCPC.

100. IEC Committee Minutes, Apr. 11, 1933, and June 7, 1933, DG 43, series B3, box 34, folder, Interracial Activity, 1927–1934, US WILPF Papers, SCPC. During the June meeting, African American women agreed to pay any leftover bills from the "Movies for Peace" event as well as the cost for Mousserone to attend the State WILPF Convention. Willingness to personally incur these expenses could be a sign of the low finances of the Pennsylvania state branch during the Depression. On the other hand, it could have been another sign of segregation in the organization. If the Pennsylvania WILPF was dedicated to racial integration, providing financial support for a representative of the IEC would be one substantial way to indicate support.

101. Minutes, IEC, May 9, 1928, US WILPF Papers, SCPC; Charlene F. Howard to Mrs. Wilda Robinson Townsend, June 29, 1933, DG 43, series B3, box 34, folder, Interracial Activity, 1927–1934, US WILPF Papers, SCPC.

102. Charlene F. Howard to Mrs. Wilda Robinson Townsend, June 29, 1933; Minutes, IEC July 7, 1933, DG 43, series, B5, box 15, US WILPF Papers, SCPC.

103. Ibid.

104. Philadelphia IEC Minutes, June 1928, DG 43, series B3, box 34, folder, Interracial Activity, 1927–1934, US WILPF Papers, SCPC.

105. Ibid.

106. Mousserone to Mrs. Edwina Johnson, Apr. 4, 1932, DG 43, series B5, box 35, US WILPF Papers, SCPC.

107. Mousserone to Olmsted, Apr. 16, 1934, DG 43, series B5, box 35, US WILPF Papers, SCPC. The state branch's action was in keeping with the national action Dorothy Detzer and Addie Hunton had taken on the Dyer antilynching bill. Mousserone to Edwina Johnson, Apr. 1932, US WILPF Papers, SCPC; Johnson to Mousserone, Nov., 28, 1934, DG 43, series B5, box 35, US WILPF Papers, SCPC.

108. Committee Report, May 9, 1933, DG 43, series B3, box 34, folder, Interracial Activity, 1927–1934, US WILPF Papers, SCPC.

109. Olmsted to Reynolds, Apr. 13, 1933, DG 43, box 28, folder, Reynolds, US WILPF Papers, SCPC.

110. Olmsted to Reynolds, Dec. 11, 1934, DG 43, series B3, box 40, folder, Reynolds, US WILPF Papers, SCPC.

111. Olmsted to Dickerson, Dec. 27, 1934, DG 43, series B3, box 28, folder, Dickerson, US WILPF Papers, SCPC.

112. Dickerson to Olmsted, Jan. 7, 1935, DG 43, series B3, box 28, folder, Dickerson, US WILPF Papers, SCPC.

113. Branch Letter 37, Jan. 11, 1935, reel 93, US WILPF Papers, SCPC.

114. Dickerson, Fauset, and Reynolds to Anderson, Feb. 20, 1935, DG 43, series B3, box 28, folder, Reynolds, US WILPF Papers, SCPC.

115. Addie Hunton to "Dear Co-Worker," Aug. 27, 1932, reel 130.24, US WILPF Papers, SCPC.

116. Dickerson to Hull, Aug. 2, 1934, reel 2, Hannah Clothier Hull Papers, SCPC.

117. Olmsted to Hull, Aug. 14, 1934, reel 2, Hannah Clothier Hull Papers, SCPC.

118. Dickerson to Terrell, Dec. 10, 1934, reel 7, MCT Papers, Library of Congress.

119. Addie Hunton, NAACP Speech, May, 1932, reel 9, group I, series B, box 8, NAACP Papers.

120. White, *Too Heavy a Load*, 149.

121. Ibid., 142–75.

122. Baber to Olmsted, Nov. 16, 1934, reel 69, US WILPF Papers, SCPC; Dorothy Detzer, Branch Letter 7, Jan. 11, 1935, reel 93, US WILPF Papers, SCPC.

123. Baber to Olmsted, Nov. 16, 1934, reel 69, US WILPF Papers, SCPC.

124. Addie Hunton, Report of the Interracial Committee, Year Ending May 1935, reel 93, US WILPF Papers, SCPC.

125. "Mixed Hunger Marches Arrive in Washington" was the title of a photo reporting on the participation of one hundred black women and three hundred white women in this demonstration; see *Philadelphia Tribune*, Dec. 15, 1932. "Reds Go On with Dance Minus Permit," caption of photo in *Philadelphia Tribune*, Feb. 8, 1933.

126. Ray Dixon, "Society Looks on as Pansies Frolic," *Philadelphia Tribune*, Apr. 6, 1933; Ray O. Light, "Organist 'Pansy' Choir Members Say," *Philadelphia Tribune*, Apr. 13, 1933.

127. Dickerson to Mary Church Terrell, May 1935, MCT Papers, Library of Congress.

128. Dickerson to Burroughs, Mar. 4, 1940; Dickerson to Burroughs, May 3, 1940, box 7, Nannie Burroughs Papers, Library of Congress.

129. Mary Waring, "Annual Address," *National Association Notes* 1935, 47, NACW Papers.

130. "Miss Burroughs Electrifies a Great Interracial Peace Meeting at the Union Baptist Church," *Christian Review* (Mar. 1930), box 331, Nannie Burroughs Papers, Library of Congress.

4. Cleveland, Washington, DC, and Baltimore:
Extending the Network of Interracial Peace Work

1. Jacquelyn Dowd Hall, "Long Civil Rights Movement and the Political Uses of the Past," *Journal of American History* 91, no. 4 (Mar. 2005): 1233–63.

2. Addie Hunton, Report of the Interracial Committee, Year Ending May 1931, reel 35, US WILPF Papers, SCPC.

3. Ibid.

4. Kimberley L. Phillips, *AlabamaNorth: African-American Migrants, Community, and Working-Class Activism in Cleveland, 1915–1945* (Chicago: Univ. of Illinois Press, 1999), 168.

5. Ibid., 60.

6. Ibid., 17, 194, 197.

7. Ibid., 186–88.

8. Ibid., 213.

9. Addie Hunton, Report of the Interracial Committee, Year Ending May 1932, reel 35, US WILPF Papers, SCPC.

10. Vanessa Northington Gamble, *Making a Place for Ourselves: The Black Hospital Movement, 1920–1945* (Oxford: Oxford Univ. Press, 1995); Russell H. Davis, *Black Americans in Cleveland: From George Peake to Carl B. Stokes, 1796–1969* (Washington, DC: Associated Publishers, 1972), 225–26; Claudia Marie Calhoon, "Tuberculosis, Race, and the Delivery of Health Care in Harlem, 1922–1939," *Radical History Review* 80 (2001): 101–19.

11. Addie Hunton, National IEC Report, Apr. 1932, reel 35, US WILPF Papers, SCPC.

12. Addie Hunton, National IEC Report, May 1931, reel 35, US WILPF Papers, SCPC.

13. Adrienne Lash Jones, *Jane Edna Hunter: A Case Study of Black Leadership, 1910–1950* (Brooklyn: Carlson Publishing, 1990), 89–94. See also Jane Edna Hunter, *A Nickel and a Prayer* (Cleveland: Elli Kani Publishing, 1940).

14. A. L. Jones, *Jane Edna Hunter*, 86.

15. Ibid.

16. Ibid., 88.

17. Wittner, *Rebels Against War*, 10.

18. Addie Hunton, National IEC Report, May 1931, reel 24, US WILPF Papers, SCPC.

19. For class dynamics of the Phillis Wheatley Association, see Carby, "Policing," 738–55. For relations of rescue, see Pascoe, *Relations of Rescue*.

20. Phillips, 158.

21. Harvey M. Williamson, "The Gilpin Players," *Crisis* 42 (July 1935): 206.

22. Ibid., 214.

23. James V. Hatch and Leo Hamalian, eds., *Lost Plays of the Harlem Renaissance, 1920–1940* (Detroit: Wayne State Univ. Press, 1996), 125–27.

24. For these debates, see Locke, *New Negro*; Nathan Irvin Huggins, *Harlem Renaissance* (New York: Oxford Univ. Press, 1971); Langston Hughes, "The Negro Artist and the Racial Mountain," *The Nation* 122 (1926): 693.

25. Foster, 192–201.

26. Marc Gallicchio, *The African American Encounter with Japan and China: Black Internationalism in Asia, 1895–1945* (Chapel Hill: Univ. of North Carolina Press, 2000), 66–67.

27. Ibid., 3.

28. Ibid., 17.

29. D. L. Lewis, *W. E. B. Du Bois*, 392.

30. Gallicchio, *African American Encounter*, 107.

31. Addie Hunton, National IEC Report, n.d., reel 32, US WILPF Papers, SCPC.

32. Addie Hunton, National IEC Report Year ending Apr. 1932, reel 24, US WILPF Papers, SCPC.

33. Gallicchio, *African American Encounter,* 107.

34. Ibid.

35. Addie Hunton, National IEC Report, May 1933, reel 24, US WILPF Papers, SCPC.

36. Ibid.

37. Addie Hunton, National IEC Report, May 1931, reel 24, US WILPF Papers, SCPC.

38. Addie Hunton, National IEC Report, May 1935, reel 32, US WILPF Papers, SCPC.

39. Addie Hunton, National IEC Report, May 1931, reel 24, US WILPF Papers, SCPC.

40. Linda M. Perkins, "Lucy Diggs Slowe: Champion of the Self-Determination of African-American Women in Higher Education," *Journal of Negro History* 81 (Winter–Autumn 1996): 89–104.

41. Hunton, National Report IEC, Apr. 1932, reel 93, US WILPF Papers, SCPC.

42. D. L. Lewis, *W. E. B. Du Bois,* 263.

43. Hunton, National IEC Report, Apr. 1932, reel 93, US WILPF Papers, SCPC.

44. Robin D. G. Kelley, "But A Local Phase of a World Problem: Black History's Global Vision, 1883–1950," *Journal of American History: A Special Issue* 86, no. 3 (Dec. 1999): 1064.

45. Hunton, National IEC Report, May 1933, reel 93, US WILPF Papers, SCPC.

46. Sundiata, *Black Scandal,* 91; NAACP Memo to file July 31, 1934, LC NAACP I box C335, Fold Liberia 1934, 8990; Walter White to NAACP Board, July 10, 1933, NAACP Papers I, A21; Du Bois, "Liberia," 695.

47. Zonia Baber to Dorothy Detzer, Feb. 17, 1934, reel 57, folder 4, US WILPF Papers, SCPC; Zonia Baber to Dorothy Detzer, Apr. 19, 1934, reel 57, folder 4, US WILPF Papers, SCPC.

48. Elliot M. Rudwick, "Oscar De Priest and the Jim Crow Restaurant in the US House of Representatives," *Journal of Negro Education* 35 (Winter 1966): 79–81.

49. C. A. Foster, *Women and the Warriors,* 163.

50. Florence M. Collins, "Interracial Group of Women Lunch in Senate Café," *Baltimore Afro-American,* Mar. 24, 1934, 3; Rudwick, "Oscar De Priest," 79–81.

51. Addie Hunton to Dorothy Detzer, Jan. 8, 1935, reel 130.60, US WILPF Papers, SCPC.

52. Walter White to Dorothy Detzer, Jan. 8, 1935, reel 130.60, US WILPF Papers, SCPC.

53. Addie Hunton to Dorothy Detzer, Jan. 8, 1935, reel 130.60, US WILPF Papers, SCPC.

54. Dorothy Detzer, Branch Letter No. 7, Jan. 11, 1935, reel 93, US WILPF Papers, SCPC.

55. Addie Hunton, National IEC Report, May 1935, reel 24, US WILPF Papers, SCPC.

56. Ibid.

57. Ibid.

58. Ibid.

59. Andor Skotnes, "Buy Where You Can Work: Boycotting for Jobs in African-American Baltimore, 1933–1934," *Journal of Social History* 27, no. 4 (Summer 1994): 736–51; C. Fraser

Smith, *Here Lies Jim Crow: Civil Rights in Maryland* (Baltimore: The Johns Hopkins Univ. Press, 2008), 84; Olmsted to McNeill, n.d., DG 43, series B3, US WILPF Papers, SCPC.

60. Jo Ann E. Argersinger, *Toward A New Deal in Baltimore: People and Government in the Great Depression* (Chapel Hill: Univ. of North Carolina Press, 1988), 126–40.

61. Esther J. Crooks, "Do You Want a Speaker?" July 1934, DG 43, series B, box 1, folder, Maryland, US WILPF Papers, SCPC.

62. Sherrilyn A. Ifill, *On the Courthouse Lawn: Confronting the Legacy of Lynching in the Twenty-First Century* (Boston: Beacon Press, 2007), 8, 23, 26–33.

63. Ibid., 35–42.

64. Ibid., 50–54.

65. "Interracial Group Raps Governor," *Baltimore Afro-American,* Oct. 28, 1933.

66. "Lynchers are not Christians, Mrs. Terrell Tells Council," *Baltimore Afro-American,* Dec. 16, 1933.

67. Maryland Branch Report Oct. 12, 1933, to Jan. 12, 1934, DG 43, series B, box 1, folder, Maryland, US WILPF Papers, SCPC; Harvard Sitkoff, *A New Deal for Blacks: The Emergence of Civil Rights as a National Issue: The Depression Decade,* 30th anniversary ed. (New York: Oxford Univ. Press, 2009), 223.

68. Hayward Farrar, *Baltimore Afro-Americans, 1892–1950* (London: Greenwood Press, 1998) 32–34; Karen Olson, "Old West Baltimore: Segregation, African-American Culture, and the Struggle for Equality," in *The Baltimore Book: New Views on Local History,* ed. Elizabeth Fee, Linda Shopes, and Linda Zeidman (Philadelphia: Temple Univ. Press, 1991), 64–65; Sitkoff, *New Deal,* 179–83; Bruce Beezer, "Black Teachers' Salaries and the Federal Courts Before Brown v. Board of Education: One Beginning for Equality," *Journal of Negro Education* 55, no. 2 (1986): 200–213; Addie Hunton, Report of Interracial Committee, May 1935, reel 35, US WILPF Papers, SCPC; Richard Kluger, *Simple Justice* (New York: Random House, 1975), 182–94.

69. Farrar, *Baltimore,* 36–37.

70. Newsletter, Maryland Branch, WILPF, Jan. 1937, page 3, DG 43, series B, box 1, folder, Maryland, US WILPF Papers, SCPC.

71. Argersinger, *Toward a New Deal,* 35–40, Bertha McNeill, Annual Report, Apr. 1937, reel 18, folder 2, US WILPF Papers, SCPC.

72. Ibid.

73. Sitkoff, *New Deal,* 42.

74. Donald D. Walsh, "Esther Crooks," *Hispania* 32, no. 4 (1949): 533; Sitkoff, *New Deal,* 128–30, Annual Report of the Maryland Branch, May 1934, DG 43, series B, box 1, US WILPF Papers, SCPC; C. A. Foster, *Women and the Warriors,* 165–67.

75. Argersinger, *Toward a New Deal,* 72.

76. Ibid., 76.

77. Ibid., 72–77; Annual Report of the Maryland Branch, May 1934, DG 43, series B, box 1, folder, Maryland, US WILPF Papers, SCPC.

78. Jesse L. Nicholas, "Conditions in Maryland," in Aptheker, *Documentary History,* 565–69; Argersinger, *Toward a New Deal,* 93.

79. Argersinger, *Toward a New Deal,* 93–101; Rhonda Y. Williams, *The Politics of Public Housing: Black Women's Struggles Against Urban Inequality* (New York: Oxford Univ. Press, 2004), 30–40.

80. Addie Hunton, National IEC Report, May 1935, reel 24, US WILPF Papers, SCPC.

81. Blackwell, *No Peace Without Freedom,* 53.

82. Bertha McNeill, Report of the National Chairman of Interracial Work, 1937, SCPC.

83. Ibid.

84. Melinda Plastas, "Bertha Clay McNeill," in *Notable American Women: A Biographical Dictionary,* ed. Susan Ware, 436–37 (Cambridge, MA: Harvard Univ. Press, 2004).

85. Bertha McNeill, National Board Report Mar. 31, 1936, reel 18, folder 2, US WILPF Papers, SCPC.

86. Mildred Scott Olmsted, Annual Meeting Report, May 2, 1937, reel 9, US WILPF Papers, SCPC.

87. Bertha C. McNeill, National Report of the Minorities Committee, Apr. 27, 1940, reel 24, US WILPF Papers, SCPC.

Conclusion

1. "Race Prejudice" resolution, 1922, reel 5, US WILPF Papers, SCPC.

2. Michael Omi and Howard Winant, *Racial Formation in the United States: From the 1960s to the 1990s* (New York: Routledge, 1994), 138.

3. Hall, "The Long Civil Rights Movement." Also see Patricia Cooper, "The Limits of Persuasion: Race Reformers and the Department Store Campaign in Philadelphia, 1945–1948," *Pennsylvania Magazine of History and Biography* 128, no. 1 (Jan. 2002): 97–126.

4. For this history, see Blackwell, *No Peace Without Freedom,* especially chaps. 6 and 7; "Civil Rights, Test Ban Top Priorities at Annual Meeting," *Four Lights* 23, no. 2 (July 1963); and "WILPF Leaders Join Selma March," *Four Lights* 24, no. 4 (Apr., 1965).

5. For some of the scholarship interested in the racial dynamics of women's movements, see Higginbotham, *Righteous Discontent;* Hall, *Revolt Against Chivalry;* Robertson, *Christian Sisterhood;* Anne M. Valk, *Radical Sisters: Second Wave Feminism and Black Liberation in Washington, DC* (Chicago: Univ. of Illinois Press, 2008); Winifred Breines, *The Trouble Between Us: An Uneasy History of White and Black Women in the Feminist Movement* (New York: Oxford Univ. Press, 2006); Elizabeth Lapovsky Kennedy, "Socialist Feminism: What Difference Did It Make to the History of Women's Studies?" *Feminist Studies* 34, no. 3 (Fall 2008): 497–525.

Bibliography

Manuscript Collections

Library of Congress, Manuscript and Archives Division, Washington, DC
   Nannie Burroughs Papers
   Mary Church Terrell Papers
Schlesinger Library, Radcliffe College, Cambridge, Massachusetts
   Leonora O'Reilly Papers
   Massachusetts WILPF Branch Papers
Swarthmore College Peace Collection (SCPC), Swarthmore College, Swarthmore,
   Pennsylvania
   Emily Greene Balch Papers
   Hannah Clothier Hull Papers
   Bertha McNeil Papers
   Margaret Mosely Papers
   Women's International League for Peace and Freedom, US Section Papers,
      1919–1959, Scholarly Resources Microfilm Edition
   Women's International League for Peace and Freedom, US Section Papers

Microfilmed Collections

National Association for the Advancement of Colored People Papers, microfilmed
   and distributed by Univ. Publications of America, Frederick, Maryland.
National Association of Colored Women Papers, microfilmed and distributed by
   Univ. Publications of America, Bethesda, Maryland.
W. E. B. Du Bois Papers, Library of the Univ. of Massachusetts, Amherst, Univ.
   Publications of America.

Newspapers, Magazines, and Journals

Baltimore Afro-American
Baltimore Sun
Crisis
Four Lights
National Association Notes
Philadelphia Tribune

Secondary Sources

Addams, Jane. *Democracy and Social Ethics.* New York: Macmillan, 1902.
———. *Newer Ideals of Peace.* New York: Macmillan, 1907.
———. *Peace and Bread in Time of War.* New York: Macmillan, 1922.
———. *Twenty Years at Hull House.* 1910; repr., Boston: Bedford/St. Martin's, 1999.
Adler, Karen S. "'Always Leading Our Men in Service and Sacrifice': Amy Jacques Garvey, Feminist Black Nationalism." *Gender and Society* 6, no. 3 (Sept. 1992): 346–75.
Alexander, Adele Logan. Introduction to *Two Colored Women with the American Expeditionary Forces,* by Addie W. Hunton and Kathryn M. Johnson. 1920; repr., New York: G. K. Hall and Company, 1997.
Allen, Carol. *Black Women Intellectuals, Strategies of Nation, Family, and Neighborhood in the Works of Pauline Hopkins, Jessie Fauset, and Marita Bonner.* New York: Garland Publishing, 1998.
Alonso, Harriet Hyman. "Nobel Peace Laureates, Jane Addams and Emily Greene Balch: Two Women of the Women's International League for Peace and Freedom." *Journal of Women's History* 7 (Summer 1995): 6–27.
———. *Peace as a Women's Issue: A History of the US Movement for World Peace and Women's Rights.* Syracuse: Syracuse Univ. Press, 1993.
———. *The Women's Peace Union and the Outlawry of War, 1921–1942.* Knoxville: Univ. of Tennessee Press, 1989.
Anderson, Benedict. *Imagined Communities: Reflections on the Origin and Spread of Nationalism.* Rev. ed. London: Verso, 1991.
Anzaldua, Gloria. *Borderlands/La Frontera: The New Mestiza.* San Francisco: Spinsters/Aunt Lute Press, 1987.
Appiah, Kwame Anthony. *Cosmopolitanism: Ethics in a World of Strangers.* New York: W. W. Norton, 2006.

Aptheker, Herbert, ed. *A Documentary History of the Negro People in the United States: 1910–1932.* Secaucus, NJ: Citadel Press, 1973.

Argersinger, Jo Ann E. *Toward A New Deal in Baltimore: People and Government in the Great Depression.* Chapel Hill: Univ. of North Carolina Press, 1988.

Arnold, Thea. "Kathryn Magnolia Johnson (1878–1955)." In *Black Women in America: An Historical Encyclopedia,* edited by Darlene Clark Hine, 644–45. New York: Carlson, 1993.

Bacon, Margaret Hope. *One Woman's Passion for Peace and Freedom: The Life of Mildred Scott Olmsted.* Syracuse: Syracuse Univ. Press, 1993.

Bair, Barbara. "True Women, Real Men: Gender, Ideology and Social Role in the Garvey Movement." In *Gendered Domains: Rethinking Public and Private in Women's History,* edited by Dorothy O. Helly and Susan M. Revereby, 154–66. Ithaca, NY: Cornell Univ. Press, 1992.

Baker, Houston A., Jr. *Modernism and the Harlem Renaissance.* Chicago: Univ. of Chicago Press, 1987.

Baker, Paul E. *Negro-White Adjustment: An Investigation and Analysis of Methods in the Interracial Movement in the United States.* New York: Association Press, 1934.

Balch, Emily Greene, ed. *Occupied Haiti.* New York: The Writers Publishing Company, 1927.

———. *Our Slavic Fellow Citizens.* New York: Charities Publication Committee, 1910.

———. "Racial Contacts and Cohesions: As Factors in the Unconstrained Fabric of a World at Peace." *Survey,* Mar. 6, 1915, 611.

———. "What It Means to Be an American." In *Beyond Nationalism: The Social Thought of Emily Greene Balch,* edited by Mercedes Randall, 36–39. New York: Twayne Publishers, Inc., 1972.

Balch, Emily Greene, Jane Addams, and Alice Hamilton, eds. *Women at The Hague: The International Congress of Women and its Results.* New York: Macmillan Company, 1915.

Banner-Haley, Charles T. *To Do Good and To Do Well: Middle Class Blacks and the Depression, Philadelphia, 1929–1941.* New York: Garland Publishing, 1993.

Barkan, Elazar. *The Retreat of Scientific Racism: Changing Concepts of Race in Britain and the United States Between the World Wars.* Cambridge: Cambridge Univ. Press, 1992.

Bederman, Gail. *Manliness and Civilization: A Cultural History of Gender and Race in The United States, 1880–1917.* Chicago: Univ. of Chicago Press, 1995.

Beezer, Bruce. "Black Teachers' Salaries and the Federal Courts Before Brown v. Board of Education: One Beginning for Equality." *Journal of Negro Education* 55, no. 2 (1986): 200–213.

Blackwell, Joyce. *No Peace Without Freedom: Race and the Women's International League for Peace and Freedom, 1915–1970.* Carbondale: Southern Illinois Univ. Press, 2004.

Blunt, Alison. *Travel, Gender, and Imperialism: Mary Kingsley and West Africa.* New York: Guilford Press, 1994.

Bogle, Donald. *Toms, Coons, Mulattoes, Mammies and Bucks: An Interpretive History of Blacks in American Film.* New York: Viking Press, 1973.

Brawley, Benjamin. *The Negro Genius: A New Appraisal of the Achievement of the American Negro in Literature and the Fine Arts.* New York: Dodd, Mead, and Company, 1937.

Breen, William J. "Black Women and the Great War: Mobilization and Reform in the South." *Journal of Southern History* 44 (Aug. 1978): 421–40.

Breines, Winifred. *The Trouble Between Us: An Uneasy History of White and Black Women in the Feminist Movement.* New York: Oxford Univ. Press, 2006.

Brown, Victoria Bissell. Introduction to *Twenty Years at Hull House*, by Jane Addams. 1920; repr., Boston: Bedford/St. Martin, 1999).

Bussey, Gertrude, and Margaret Tims. *Pioneers for Peace: the Women's International League for Peace and Freedom, 1915–1965.* London: 1965; repr., Alden Press, 1980.

Calhoon, Claudia Marie. "Tuberculosis, Race, and the Delivery of Health Care in Harlem, 1922–1939." *Radical History Review* 80 (2001): 101–19.

Callawy, Helen, and Dorothy O. Helly. "Crusader for Empire: Flora Shaw/Lady Lugard." In *Western Women and Imperialism: Complicity and Resistance*, edited by Nupur Chaudhuri and Margaret Strobel, 79–97. Bloomington: Indiana Univ. Press, 1992.

Calo, Mary Ann. "African American Art and Critical Discourse between World Wars." *American Quarterly* 51 (Sept. 1999): 580–621.

Carby, Hazel V. "Policing the Black Woman's Body in an Urban Context." *Critical Inquiry* 18 (Summer 1992): 738–56.

———. *Race Men.* Cambridge, MA: Harvard Univ. Press, 1998.

———. *Reconstructing Womanhood: The Emergence of the Afro-American Woman Novelist.* New York: Oxford Univ. Press, 1987.

Carter, Paul A. *Another Part of the 20s.* New York: Columbia Univ. Press, 1977.

Chatfield, Charles. *The American Peace Movement: Ideals and Activism.* New York: Twayne Publishing, 1992.

Chaudhure, Nupur, and Margaret Strobel, eds. *Western Women and Imperialism: Complicity and Resistance.* Bloomington: Indiana Univ. Press, 1992.

Christen, Garna L. *Black Soldiers in Jim Crow Texas, 1899–1917.* College Station: Texas A&M Univ. Press, 1995.

Cohn, Carol. "Wars, Wimps, and Women: Talking Gender and Thinking War." In *Gendering War Talk,* edited by Miriam Cooke and Angela Woollacott, 227–46. Princeton, NJ: Princeton Univ. Press, 1993.

Collins, Florence M. "Interracial Group of Women Lunch in Senate Café." *Baltimore Afro-American,* Mar. 24, 1934.

Collins, Patricia Hill. *Black Feminist Thought: Knowledge, Consciousness, and the Politics of Empowerment.* Boston: Unwin Hyman Press, 1990.

———. "Producing the Mothers of the Nation: Race, Class and Contemporary US Population Politics." In *Women, Citizenship and Difference,* edited by Nira Yuval-Davis and Pnina Werbner, 118–29. London: Zed Books, 1999.

Cooper, Anna Julia. "Sketches from a Teacher's Notebook: Loss of Speech Through Isolation." In *The Voice of Anna Julia Cooper,* edited by Charles Lemert and Esme Bhan, 224–29. New York: Rowman and Littlefield, 1998.

———. *A Voice from the South: By a Black Woman of the South.* 1892; repr., New York: Oxford Univ. Press, 1988.

Cooper, Patricia. "The Limits of Persuasion: Race Reformers and the Department Store Campaign in Philadelphia, 1945–1948." *Pennsylvania Magazine of History and Biography* 127, no. 1 (Jan. 2002): 97–126.

Cott, Nancy. *The Grounding of Modern Feminism.* New Haven, CT: Yale Univ. Press, 1987.

Cross, Robert D. "How Historians Have Looked at Immigrants to the United States." *International Migration Review* 7, no. 1 (Spring 1973): 9.

Davis, Elizabeth Lindsay. *Lifting as They Climb: The National Association of Colored Women.* Washington, DC: National Association of Colored Women, 1933.

Davis, Russell H. *Black Americans in Cleveland: From George Peake to Carl B. Stokes, 1796–1969.* Washington, DC: Associated Publishers, 1972.

Desan, Suzanne. "Crowds, Community, and Ritual in the Work of E. P. Thompson and Natalie Davis." In *The New Cultural History,* edited by Lynn Hunt, 55. Berkeley: Univ. of California Press, 1989.

Detzer, Dorothy. *Appointment on the Hill.* New York: Henry Holt and Company, 1948.

Dimand, Robert W. "Economists and the Shadow of 'The Other' Before 1914." *American Journal of Economics and Sociology* 64, no. 3 (July 2005): 827–50.

Dombrowski, Nicole Ann. *Women and War in the Twentieth Century: Enlisted With or Without Consent.* New York: Garland Publishing, 1999.

Donaldson, Laura E. *Decolonizing Feminisms: Race, Gender, and Empire Building.* Chapel Hill: Univ. of North Carolina Press, 1992.

Dubois, Rachel Davis. *All This and Something More: Pioneering in Intercultural Education.* Bryn Mawr, PA: Dorrance and Company, 1984.

———. *Build Together Americans: Adventures in Intercultural Education for Secondary School.* New York: Hinds, Hayden, and Eldredge, Inc., 1945.

———. *The Contributions of Racial Elements to American Life.* Philadelphia: Women's International League for Peace and Freedom, 1930.

———. *Education in World-Mindedness: A Series of Assembly Programs Given by Students at Woodbury High School, Woodbury, New Jersey, 1927–1928.* Philadelphia: American Friends Service Committee, 1928.

———. *A School and Community Project in Developing Sympathetic Attitudes Toward Other Races and Nations.* New York: The Service Bureau for Education in Human Relations, 1934.

Dubois, Rachel Davis, and Emma Schweppe, eds. *The Jews in American Life.* New York: Thomas Nelson and Sons, 1935.

Du Bois, W. E. B. "Close Ranks." *Crisis* 16 (July 1918): 111.

———. *Darkwater: Voices from Within the Veil.* New York: AMS Press, 1920.

———. "The Essay Toward a History of the Black Man in the Great War." *Crisis* 18 (June 1919): 63–87.

———. "Liberia, the League and the United States." *Foreign Affairs* 11, no. 4 (July 1933): 682–95.

———. "Pan-Africa and New Racial Philosophy." *Crisis* 40 (Nov. 1933): 247, 262.

———. *The Philadelphia Negro.* 1902; repr., Millwood, NY: Krause-Thompson, 1973.

———. "Postscript." *Crisis* 41 (Mar. 1932): 93.

———. "Returning Soldiers." *Crisis* 18 (May 1919): 13–14.

duCille, Ann. *The Coupling Convention: Sex, Text and Tradition in Black Women's Fiction.* New York: Oxford Univ. Press, 1994.

Dunbar-Nelson, Alice. *The Goodness of St. Rocque and Other Tales.* New York: Dodd, Mead, and Company, 1899.

———. "Harlem John Henry Views the Airmada." *Crisis* 39 (Jan. 1932): 458, 473.

———. "Mine Eyes Have Seen." *Crisis* 15 (Apr. 1918): 271–75.

———. "Negro Women in War Work." In *Scott's Official History of the American Negro in the World War,* edited by Emmett J. Scott, 374–97. Chicago: Homewood Press, 1919.

Eagan, Eileen. *Class, Culture, and the Classroom: The Student Peace Movement of the 1930s.* Philadelphia: Temple Univ. Press, 1981.

Early, Frances. "New Historical Perspectives on Gendered Peace Studies." *Women's Studies Quarterly* 3, no. 4 (1995): 22–31.

———. *A World Without War: How US Feminists and Pacifists Resisted World War I.* Syracuse: Syracuse Univ. Press, 1997.

Edwards, Brent. *The Practice of Diaspora: Literature, Translation, and the Rise of Black Internationalism.* Cambridge, MA: Harvard Univ. Press, 2003.

Ellis, Mark. "W. E. B. Du Bois and the Formation of Black Opinion in World War I: A Commentary on 'The Damnable Dilemma.'" *Journal of American History* 81, no. 4 (Mar. 1995): 1584–90.

Elshtain, Jean Bethke. *Women and War.* New York: Basic Books, 1987.

Farrar, Hayward. *Baltimore Afro-Americans, 1892–1950.* London: Greenwood Press, 1998.

Fauset, Jessie. *The Chinaberry Tree: A Novel of American Life.* New York: Stokes, 1931.

———. *The Chinaberry Tree and Selected Writings.* Boston: Northeastern Univ. Press, 1995.

———. *Comedy American Style.* New York: Stokes, 1933.

———. "Dark Algiers, the White." *Crisis* 29 (Apr. 1925): 255–57.

———. "Impressions of the Second Pan-African Congress." *Crisis* 23 (Nov. 1921): 12–18.

———. "My House and a Glimpse of My Life Therein." *Crisis* 8 (July 1914): 143–45.

———. "Nationalism and Egypt." *Crisis* 19, no. 6 (Apr. 1920): 310–16.

———. "Nostalgia." *Crisis* 22 (Aug. 1921): 154–58.

———. *Plum Bun.* New York: Stokes, 1929.

———. *There Is Confusion.* New York: Boni and Liveright, 1924.

———. "Tracing Shadows." *Crisis* 10 (Sept. 1915): 247–55.

———. "What Europe Thought of the Pan-African Congress." *Crisis* 23 (Dec. 1921): 60–69.

Faver, Catherine A. "Feminist Spirituality and Social Reform: Examples from the Early Twentieth Century." *Women's Studies Quarterly* 21, no. 1–2 (1993): 90–105.

Fine, Elsa Honig. *The African American Artist: A Search for Identity.* New York: Holt, Rinehart, and Winston, 1973.

Fischer, Marilyn, Carol Nackenoff, and Wendy Chmielewski, eds. *Jane Addams and the Practice of Democracy.* Chicago: Univ. of Illinois Press, 2009.

Foley, Barbara. *Spectres of 1919: Class and Nation in the Making of the New Negro.* Chicago: Univ. of Illinois Press, 2003.

Foster, Carrie A. *The Women and the Warriors, the United States Section of the Women's International League for Peace and Freedom, 1915–1946.* Syracuse: Syracuse Univ. Press, 1995.

Foster, Catherine. *Women for All Seasons: The Story of the Women's International League for Peace and Freedom.* Athens: Univ. of Georgia Press, 1989.

Frankel, Noralee, and Nancy S. Dye, eds. *Gender, Class, Race and Reform in the Progressive Era.* Lexington: Univ. Press of Kentucky, 1991.

Frankenberg, Ruth. *The Social Construction of Whiteness: White Women, Race Matters.* Minneapolis: Univ. of Minnesota Press, 1993.

Franklin, Vincent. *The Education of Black Philadelphia: The Social and Educational History of A Minority Community, 1900–1950.* Philadelphia: Univ. of Pennsylvania Press, 1979.

Frazier, E. Franklin. *The Black Bourgeoisie.* New York: Free Press, 1957.

Freedman, Estelle. "Separatism as Strategy: Female Institution Building and American Feminism, 1870–1930." *Feminist Studies* 5 (Fall 1979): 512–29.

Gaines, Kevin. *Uplifting the Race: Black Leadership, Politics, and Culture in the Twentieth Century.* Chapel Hill: Univ. of North Carolina Press, 1996.

Gallicchio, Marc. *The African American Encounter with Japan and China: Black Internationalism in Asia, 1895–1945.* Chapel Hill: Univ. of North Carolina Press, 2000.

Gamble, Vanessa Northington. *Making a Place for Ourselves: The Black Hospital Movement, 1920–1945.* Oxford: Oxford Univ. Press, 1995.

Gatewood, William. *"Smoked Yankees" and the Struggle for Empire: Letters from Negro Soldiers, 1898–1902.* Urbana: Univ. of Illinois Press, 1971.

Giddings, Paula. *When and Where I Enter: The Impact of Black Women on Race and Sex in America.* New York: William Morrow, 1984.

Gilbert, Sandra, and Susan Gubar, eds. *No Man's Land: The Place of the Woman Writer in the Twentieth Century, Volume 3, Letters From the Front.* New Haven, CT: Yale Univ. Press, 1994.

Gilman, Sander. "Black Bodies, White Bodies: Toward an Iconography of Female Sexuality in Late Nineteenth Century Art, Medicine and Literature." *Critical Inquiry* 12, no. 1 (Autumn 1985): 204–42.

Gilmore, Glenda. *Gender and Jim Crow: Women and the Politics of White Supremacy in North Carolina, 1896–1920.* Chapel Hill: Univ. of North Carolina Press, 1996.

Gilroy, Paul. *Against Race: Imagining Political Culture Beyond the Color Line.* Cambridge, MA: Harvard Univ. Press, 2000.

Gossett, Thomas. *Race: The History of an Idea in America.* New York: Schocken Books, 1970.

Grant, Madison. *The Passing of the Great White Race or the Racial Bias of European History.* New York: Charles Scribner's Sons, 1916.

Graves, Anna Melissa. *Africa: The Wonder and the Glory (Benvenuto Cellini Had No Prejudice Against Bronze).* 1942; excerpted with a new title, Baltimore: Black Classics Press, 1961.

———. *Benvenuto Cellini Had No Prejudice Against Bronze: Letters From West Africa.* Baltimore: Waverly Press, 1943.

———. *Both Deeper than and above the Melee, Letters from Europeans.* Baltimore: Waverly Press, 1945.

———. *But the Twain do Meet: Letters from the Near East.* Privately Published, 1941.

———. *The Far East Is Not Very Far: Letters from Liu Yuan-Lung and Wang Shou-Ming.* Baltimore: Waverly Press, 1942.

———. *I Have Tried To Think.* New York, 1940.

Gray, Christine Rauchfuss. "Introduction." In *Plays and Pageants from the Life of the Negro,* edited by Willis Richardson, xxvii. Jackson: Univ. Press of Mississippi, 1993.

Gregg, Robert. *Sparks from the Anvil of Oppression: Philadelphia's African Methodists and Southern Migrants, 1890–1940.* Philadelphia: Temple Univ. Press, 1993.

Gyory, Andrew. *Closing the Gate: Race, Politics, and the Chinese Exclusion Act.* Chapel Hill: Univ. of North Carolina Press, 1998.

Hall, Jacquelyn Dowd. "The Long Civil Rights Movement and the Politics of the Past." *Journal of American History* 91, no. 4 (Mar. 2005): 1233–63.

———. *Revolt Against Chivalry: Jessie Daniel Ames and the Women's Campaign Against Lynching.* New York: Columbian Univ. Press, 1983.

Hamington, Maurice. "Public Pragmatism: Jane Addams and Ida B. Wells on Lynching," *Journal of Speculative Philosophy* 19, no. 2 (2005): 167–74.

Harding, Charles Ashely III. *Race and Opportunity: Black Philadelphians During the Era of the Great Migration.* Philadelphia: Temple Univ. Press, 1989.

Harley, Sharon. "Nannie Helen Burroughs: 'The Black Goddess of Liberty': Vindicating the Race: Contributions to African American Intellectual History." *Journal of Negro History* 81 (1996): 62–71.

Harris, Katherine. *African and American Values: Liberia and West Africa.* New York: Univ. Press of America, 1985.

Hatch, James V., and Leo Hamalian, eds. *Lost Plays of the Harlem Renaissance, 1920–1940.* Detroit: Wayne State Univ. Press, 1996.

Hatch, James V., and Ted Shine. *Black Theater U.S.A.: Forty-Five Plays By Black Americans, 1847–1974.* New York: Free Press, 1974.

Hendricks, Wanda A. *Gender, Race, and Politics in the Midwest: Black Club Women in Illinois.* Bloomington: Indiana Univ. Press, 1998.

Herman, Sondra. *Eleven Against the War: Studies in American Internationalist Thought, 1898–1921.* Palo Alto, CA: Stanford Univ. Press, 1969.

Hewitt, Nancy A., and Suzanne Lebsock, eds. *Visible Women: New Essays on American Activism.* Chicago: Univ. of Illinois Press, 1993.

Higginbotham, Evelyn Brooks. "African-American Women's History and the Metalanguage of Race." *Signs* 17, no. 2 (1992): 251–74.

———. "'In Politics to Stay': Black Women Leaders and Party Politics in the 1920s." In *Women, Politics, and Change,* edited by Louse A. Tilly and Patricia Gurin, 199–220. New York: Russell Sage Foundation, 1979.

———. *Righteous Discontent: The Women's Movement in the Black Baptist Church, 1880–1920.* Cambridge: Howard Univ. Press, 1993.

Higham, John. *Strangers in the Land: Patterns of American Nativism: 1860–1925.* New Brunswick, NJ: Rutgers Univ. Press, 1992.

Hine, Darlene Clark, ed. *Black Women in America: An Historical Encyclopedia.* New York: Carlson, 1993.

———. *Black Women in White: Racial Conflict and Cooperation in the Nursing Profession, 1890–1950.* Bloomington: Indiana Univ. Press, 1989.

Hine, Darlene Clark, and Kathleen Thompson. *A Shining Thread of Hope: The History of Black Women in America.* New York: Broadway Books, 1998.

Hoganson, Kristin. "'As Badly Off as the Filipinos': US Women's Suffragists and the Imperial Issue at the Turn of the Twentieth Century." *Journal of Women's History* 13 (Summer 2001): 9–33

hooks, bell. *Feminist Theory: From Margin to Center.* Boston: South End Press, 1984.

Huggins, Nathan Irvin. *Harlem Renaissance.* New York: Oxford Univ. Press, 1971.

Hughes, Langston. "The Negro Artist and the Racial Mountain." *The Nation* 122 (1926): 693.

Hull, Gloria. *Color, Sex and Poetry: Three Women Writers of the Harlem Renaissance.* Bloomington: Indiana Univ. Press, 1987.

———. *Give Us Each Day: The Diary of Alice Dunbar-Nelson.* New York: W. W. Norton, 1984.

———, ed. *The Works of Alice Dunbar-Nelson: Volume 2.* New York: Oxford Univ. Press, 1988.

Hunter, Jane Edna. *A Nickel and a Prayer.* Cleveland: Elli Kani Publishing, 1940.

Hunter, Tera. *To 'Joy My Freedom: Southern Black Women's Lives and Labors After the Civil War.* Cambridge, MA: Harvard Univ. Press, 1997.

Hunton, Addie W. "The National Association of Colored Women." *Crisis* 2 (May 1911): 17–18.

———. "Negro Womanhood Defended." *The Voice of the Negro* 7 (July 1904): 280–82.

———. *William Alphaues Hunton: A Pioneer Prophet of Young Men.* New York: Association Press, 1938.

———. "Women's Clubs Caring for the Children." *Crisis* 2 (June 1911): 78–79.

Hunton, Addie W., and Kathryn M. Johnson. *Two Colored Women and the American Expeditionary Forces.* 1920; repr., New York: G. K. Hall and Company, 1997.

Ifill, Sherrilyn A. *On the Courthouse Lawn: Confronting the Legacy of Lynching in the Twenty-first Century.* Boston: Beacon Press, 2007.

James, Joy. "The Profeminist Politics of W. E. B. Du Bois." In *W. E. B. Du Bois On Race and Culture: Philosophy, Politics, and Poetics,* edited by Bernard W. Bell, Emily Grosholz, and James Stewart, 141–60. New York: Routledge, 1996.

Jensen, Joan M. "'All Pink Sisters': The War Department and the Feminist Movement in the 1920s." In *Decades of Discontent: The Women's Movement, 1920–1940,* edited by Lois Scharf and Joan M. Jensen, 199–222. Westport, CT: Greenwood Press, 1983.

Johnson, Abby Arthur, and Ronald Mayberry Johnson. *Propaganda and Aesthetics: The Literary Politics of Afro-American Magazines in the Twentieth Century.* Amherst: Univ. of Massachusetts Press, 1979.

Johnson, Charles S. *Bitter Canaan: The Story of the Negro Republic.* 1930; repr., New Brunswick, NJ: Transaction Books, 1987.

———. *The Negro in American Civilization: A Study of Negro Life and Race Relations in the Light of Social Research.* New York: Henry Holt and Company, 1930.

Johnson, Robert David. *The Peace Progressives and American Foreign Relations.* Cambridge, MA: Harvard Univ. Press, 1995.

Jones, Adrienne Lash. *Jane Edna Hunter: A Case Study of Black Leadership, 1910–1950.* Brooklyn: Carlson Publishing, 1990.

Jones, Jacqueline. *Labor of Love: Labor of Sorrow: Black Women, Work, and the Family From Slavery to the Present.* New York: Basic Books, 1985.

Jones, Mary Hoxie. *Swords into Ploughshares: An Account of the American Friends Service Committee, 1917–1937.* New York: The Macmillan Company, 1937.

Jordan, William. "'The Damnable Dilemma': African-American Accommodation and Protest During World War I." *Journal of American History* 8 (Mar. 1995): 1562–83.

Kallen, Horace. *Culture and Democracy in the United States: Studies in Group Psychology of the American People.* New York: Boni and Liveright, 1924.

Keene, Josephine. *Directory of Negro Business and Professional Women of Philadelphia and Vicinity*. Philadelphia, 1939.

Kelley, Robin D. G. "But a Local Phase of a World Problem: Black History's Global Vision, 1883–1950." *Journal of American History: A Special Issue* 86, no. 3 (Dec. 1999): 1045–77.

———. *Hammer and Hoe: Alabama Communists During the Great Depression*. Chapel Hill: Univ. of North Carolina Press, 1990.

Kellogg, Charles Flint. *NAACP: A History of the National Association for the Advancement of Colored People*. Baltimore: The Johns Hopkins Univ. Press, 1967.

Kelsey, Carl. "Book Review." *Annals of the American Academy of Political and Social Science*, 1911, 233.

Kennedy, Elizabeth Lapovsky. "Socialist Feminism: What Difference Did it Make to the History of Women' Studies?" *Feminist Studies* 34, no. 3 (Fall 2008): 497–525.

Kennedy, Kathleen. *Disloyal Mothers and Scurrilous Citizens*. Bloomington: Indiana Univ. Press, 1992.

King, Deborah K. "Multiple Jeopardy, Multiple Consciousness: The Context of a Black Feminist Ideology." *Signs* 14 (Autumn 1988): 42–72.

Klein, Kerwin Lee. *Frontiers of Historical Imagination: Narrating the European Conquest of Native America, 1890–1990*. Berkeley: Univ. of California Press, 1997.

Kluger, Richard. *Simple Justice*. New York: Random House, 1975.

Kornweibel Jr., Theodore. *"Seeing Red": Federal Campaigns Against Black Militancy: 1919–1925*. Bloomington: Indiana Univ. Press, 1998.

Knupfer, Anne Meis. "'Toward a Tenderer Humanity and a Nobler Womanhood': African-American Women's Clubs in Chicago, 1890–1920." *Journal of Women's History* 7 (Fall 1995): 58–77.

———. *Toward A Tenderer Humanity and a Nobler Womanhood: African American Women's Clubs in Turn-of-the-Century Chicago*. New York: New York Univ. Press, 1997.

Kuhlman, Erika A. *Petticoats and White Feathers: Gender Conformity, Race, the Progressive Peace Movement, and the Debate over War, 1895–1919*. Westport, CT: Greenwood Press, 1997.

Lasch, Elisabeth Dan. *Black Neighbors: Race and the Limits of Reform in the American Settlement House Movement, 1890–1945*. Chapel Hill: Univ. of North Carolina Press, 1993.

Lasker, Bruno. *Race Attitudes in Children*. New York: Henry Holt and Company, 1929.

Lavrin, Ascuncion. *Women, Feminism and Social Change in Argentine, Chile and Uruguay, 1890–1940.* Lincoln: Univ. of Nebraska Press, 1995.

Lebsock, Suzanne. "Woman Suffrage and White Supremacy: A Virginia Case Study." In *Visible Women: New Essays on American Activism,* edited by Nancy A. Hewitt and Suzanne Lebsock, 62–100. Chicago: Univ. of Illinois Press, 1993.

Lee, Erika. *At America's Gate: Chinese Immigration During the Exclusion Era.* Chapel Hill: Univ. of North Carolina Press, 2007.

Lewis, David Levering. *W. E. B. Du Bois: Biography of a Race 1868–1919.* New York: Knopf, 1993.

———. *When Harlem Was in Vogue.* New York: Vintage Press, 1982.

Lewis, Reina. *Gendering Orientalism: Race, Femininity, and Representation.* London: Routledge, 1996.

Locke, Alain, ed. *The New Negro.* New York: Albert and Charles Boni, 1925.

Lynn, Eve. *No Alabaster Box and Other Poems.* Philadelphia: Alpress, 1936.

Lynn, Susan. *Progressive Women in Conservative Times: Racial Justice, Peace, and Feminism, 1945 to the 1960s.* New Brunswick, NJ: Rutgers Univ. Press, 1992.

MacLachlan, Gretchen E. "Addie Waits Hunton." In *Black Women in America: An Historical Encyclopedia,* edited by Darlene Clark Hine, 556–97. Brooklyn: Carlson, 1993.

Manheim, Frank J. "The United States and Ethiopia: A Study in American Imperialism." *Journal of Negro History* 17, no. 2 (Apr. 1932): 141–55.

McCluskey, Audrey Thomas. "'We Specialize in the Wholly Impossible': Black Women School Founders and Their Mission." *Signs* 22 (Winter 1997): 403–26.

Meir, August, Elliott Rudwick, and Francis L. Broderick. *Black Protest Thought in the Twentieth Century.* Indianapolis: Bobbs-Merrill Educational Publishers, 1971.

Miller, Francesca. *Latin American Women and the Search for Social Justice.* Hanover: Univ. of New England Press, 1991.

Miller, Nina. "Femininity, Publicity, and the Class Division of Cultural Labor: Jessie Redmon Fauset's 'There Is Confusion.'" *African American Review* 30 (Summer 1996): 205–21.

Montalto, Nicholas V. *A History of the Intercultural Education Movement, 1924–1941.* New York: Garland Press, 1984.

Moore, Alice Ruth. *Violets and Other Tales.* Boston: The Monthly Review Press, 1895.

Moore, Jesse Thomas, Jr. *A Search for Equality: The National Urban League: 1910–1961.* University Park: Penn State Univ. Press, 1981.

Morrison, Toni. *Playing in the Dark: Whiteness and the Literary Imagination.* Cambridge, MA: Harvard Univ. Press, 1992.

Morton, Patricia. *Disfigured Images: the Historical Assault on African-America Women.* New York: Praeger, 1991.

Nasstrom, Kathryn. "Down to Now: Memory, Narrative, and Women's Leadership in the Civil Rights Movement in Atlanta, Georgia." *Gender and History* 11, no. 1 (Apr. 1999): 113–44.

Neverdon-Morton, Cynthia. *Afro-American Women of the South and the Advancement of the Race, 1895–1925.* Knoxville: Univ. of Tennessee Press, 1989.

Newman, Louise Michele. *White Women's Rights: The Racial Origins of Feminism in the United States.* New York: Oxford Univ. Press, 1999.

Ngai, Mae M. "The Architecture of Race in American Immigration Law: A Re-Examination of the Immigration Act of 1924," *Journal of American History* 86, no. 1 (June 1999): 67–92.

Nicholas, Jesse L. "Conditions in Maryland." In *A Documentary History of the Negro People in the United States: 1910 1932,* edited by Herbert Aptheker, 565–69. Secaucus, NJ: Citadel Press, 1973.

Normandy, Elizabeth L. "African-Americans and US Policy Towards Liberia, 1929–1935." *Liberian Studies Journal* 18 (1993): 203–30.

Norton, Mary, and Ruth Alexander, eds. *Major Problems in American Women's History.* Lexington, MA: D. C. Heath and Company, 1996.

Olsen, Karen. "Old West Baltimore: Segregation, African-American Culture, and the Struggle for Equality." In *The Baltimore Book: New Views on Local History,* edited by Elizabeth Fee, Linda Shopes, and Linda Zeidman, 57–80. Philadelphia: Temple Univ. Press, 1991.

Omi, Michael, and Howard Winant. *Racial Formation in the United States: From the 1960s to the 1980s.* New York: Routledge, 1986.

Orleck, Annelise, Alexis Jetter, and Diana Taylor, eds. *The Politics of Motherhood: Activist Voices from Left to Right.* Hanover: Univ. Press of New England, 1997.

Pascoe, Peggy. "Miscegenation Law, Court Cases, and Ideologies of `Race' in Twentieth Century America." In *Sex, Love, Race: Crossing Boundaries in North American History,* edited by Martha Hodes, 466. New York: New York Univ. Press, 1999.

———. *Relations of Rescue: The Search for Female Moral Authority in the American West, 1874–1939.* New York: Oxford Univ. Press, 1990.

Patton, Gerald W. *War and Race: The Black Officer in the American Military, 1915–41.* Westport, CT: Greenwood Press, 1981.

Perkins, Kathy. *Black Female Playwrights: An Anthology of Plays Before 1950.* Bloomington: Indiana Univ. Press, 1989.

Perkins, Linda M. "Lucy Diggs Slowe: Champion of the Self-Determination of African-American Women in Higher Education." *Journal of Negro History* 81 (Winter–Autumn 1996): 89–104.

Phillips, Kimberley L. *AlabamaNorth: African-American Migrants, Community, and Working-Class Activism in Cleveland, 1915–1945.* Chicago: Univ. of Illinois Press, 1999.

Plastas, Melinda, "Bertha Clay McNeill," in *Notable American Women: A Biographical Dictionary.* Edited by Susan Ware. Cambridge, MA: Harvard Univ. Press, 2004.

———. "A Different Burden: Race and the Social Thought of Emily Greene Balch." *Peace and Change* 33, no. 4 (Oct. 2008): 469–506.

Pratt, Mary Louise. *Imperial Eyes: Travel Writing and Transculturation.* London: Routledge, 1992.

Randall, Mercedes M. *Beyond Nationalism: The Social Thought of Emily Greene Balch.* New York: Twayne Publishers, 1972.

———. *Improper Bostonian: Emily Greene Balch. Nobel Peace Laureate 1946.* New York: Twayne Publishers, 1964.

Renda, Mary. *Taking Haiti: Military Occupation and the Culture of US Imperialism, 1915–1940.* Durham: Univ. of North Carolina Press, 2001.

Robertson, Nancy Marie. *Christian Sisterhood, Race Relations, and the YWCA, 1906–46.* Chicago: Univ. of Illinois Press, 2007.

Roediger, David. *The Wages of Whiteness: Race and the Making of the American Working Class.* London: Verso, 1991.

Rosenberg, Emily. *Financial Missionaries to the World: The Politics and Culture of Dollar Diplomacy, 1900–1930.* Durham: Duke Univ. Press, 1999.

Ross, Edward Alsworth. "Racial Consequences of Immigration." *Century Magazine* 87 (Feb. 1914): 615–22.

Rouse, Jacqueline Ann. *Lugenia Burns Hope: Black Southern Reformer.* Athens: Univ. of Georgia Press, 1989.

Rudwick, Elliot M. "Oscar De Priest and the Jim Crow Restaurant in the US House of Representatives." *Journal of Negro Education* 35 (Winter 1966): 79–81.

Rupp, Leila J. *Worlds of Women: The Making of An International Women's Movement.* Princeton, NJ: Princeton Univ. Press, 1997.

Said, Edward. *Orientalism.* London: Routledge, 1978.

Salem, Dorothy. *To Better Our World: Black Women in Organized Reform, 1890–1920.* New York: Carlson Publishing, 1990.

Satter, Beryl. "Marcus Garvey, Father Divine and the Gender Politics of Race Difference and Race Neutrality." *American Quarterly* 48, no. 1 (Mar. 1996): 43–76.

Saxton, Alexander. *The Rise and Fall of the White Republic.* London: Verso, 1992.

Schott, Linda K. *Reconstructing Women's Thoughts: The Women's International League for Peace and Freedom Before World War II.* Stanford, CA: Stanford Univ. Press, 1997.

Scott, Emmett J., ed. *Scott's Official History of the American Negro in the World War.* Chicago: Arno Press, 1919.

Scott, Joan. "Rewriting History." In *Behind the Lines: Gender and the Two World Wars,* edited by Margaret Randolph Higonnet, Jane Jensen, Margaret Collins Weitz, and Sonya Michel, 19–30. New Haven, CT: Yale Univ. Press, 1987.

Seigfried, Charlene Haddock. *Pragmatism and Feminism.* Chicago: Univ. of Chicago Press, 1996.

Selig, Diana. *Americans All: The Cultural Gifts Movement.* Cambridge, MA: Harvard Univ. Press, 2008.

Shaarawi, Huda. *Harem Years: The Memoirs of an Egyptian Feminist: 1879–1924.* Edited by Margot Badran. New York: Feminist Press, 1986.

Shapiro, Herbert. *White Violence and Black Response: From Reconstruction to Montgomery.* Amherst: Univ. of Massachusetts Press, 1988.

Shaw, Flora L. *A Tropical Dependency: An Outline of the Ancient History of the Western Sudan with an Account of the Modern Settlement of Northern Nigeria.* London: James Nisbet Company, 1905.

Shaw, Stephanie. *What a Woman Ought to Be and to Do: Women Workers During Jim Crow Era.* Chicago: Univ. of Chicago Press, 1996.

Silver, Regene. "Jane Addams: Peace, Justice, Gender: 1860–1918." PhD diss., Univ. of Pennsylvania, 1990.

Sitkoff, Harvard. *A New Deal for Blacks: The Emergence of Civil Rights as a National Issue: The Depression Decade.* 30th Anniversary ed. New York: Oxford Univ. Press, 2009.

Skotnes, Andor. "Buy Where You Can Work: Boycotting for Jobs in African-American Baltimore, 1933–1934." *Journal of Social History* 27, no. 4 (Summer 1994): 736–61.

Smith, C. Fraser. *Here Lies Jim Crow: Civil Rights in Maryland.* Baltimore: The Johns Hopkins Univ. Press, 2008.

Snyder, R. Claire. *Citizen-Soldiers and Manly Warriors: Military Service and Gender in the Civic Republic Tradition.* New York: Rowman and Littlefield, 1999.

Stephens, Michelle A. "Black Transnationalism and the Politics of National Identity: West Indian Intellectuals in Harlem in the Age of War and Revolution." *American Quarterly* 50 (Sept. 1998): 592–608.

Stoddard, Lothrop. *Clashing Tides of Color.* New York: Charles Scribner's Sons, 1935.

Stowell, Shelia. *A Stage of Their Own: Feminist Playwrights of the Suffrage Era.* Ann Arbor: Univ. of Michigan Press, 1992.

Sundiata, I. K. *Black Scandal: America and the Liberian Labor Crisis: 1929–1936.* Philadelphia: Institute for the Study of Human Issues, 1980.

———. *Brothers and Strangers: Black Zion, Black Slavery, 1914–1940.* Durham: Duke Univ. Press, 2004.

Sylvander, Carolyn Wedin. *Jessie Redmon Fauset, Black American Writer.* New York: Whitson Publishing Company, 1981.

Tate, Claudia. *Domestic Allegories of Political Desire: The Black Heroine's Text at the Turn of the Century.* New York: Oxford Univ. Press, 1992.

Terborg-Penn, Rosalyn. *African American Women in the Struggle for the Vote, 1850–1920.* Bloomington: Indiana Univ. Press, 1998.

———. "African American Women's Networks in the Anti-Lynching Crusade." In *Gender, Class, Race and Reform in the Progressive Era*, edited by Noralee Frankel and Nancy S. Dye, 148–61. Lexington: Univ. Press of Kentucky, 1991.

———. "Discontented Black Feminists: Prelude and Postscript to the Passage of the Nineteenth Amendment." In *Decades of Discontent: The Women's Movement, 1920–1940*, edited by Lois Scharf and Joan M. Jensen, 261–78. Westport, CT: Greenwood Press, 1983.

Terrell, Mary Church. *A Colored Woman in a White World.* Washington, DC: Ransdell Incorporated Publishers, 1940.

Tylee, Claire M. "Womanist Propaganda, African-American Great War Experience, and Cultural Strategies of the Harlem Renaissance: Plays by Alice Dunbar-Nelson and Mary P. Burrill." *Women's Studies International Forum* 20 (1997): 153–63.

Valk, Anne M. *Radical Sisters: Second Wave Feminism and Black Liberation in Washington, D.C.* Chicago: Univ. of Illinois Press, 2008.

Wall, Cheryl. *Women of the Harlem Renaissance.* Bloomington: Indiana Univ. Press, 1995.

Walsh, Donald D. "Esther Crooks," *Hispania* 32, no. 4 (1949): 533.

Ware, Vron. *Beyond the Pale: White Women, Racism, and History.* London: Verso, 1992.

Wheeler, Marjorie Spruill. *New Women of the New South: The Leaders of the Woman Suffrage Movement in the Southern States.* New York: Oxford Univ. Press, 1993.

White, Deborah Gray. *Too Heavy a Load: Black Women in Defense of Themselves 1894–1994.* New York: W. W. Norton and Company, 1999.

Williams, Rhonda Y. *The Politics of Public Housing: Black Women's Struggles Against Urban Inequality.* New York: Oxford Univ. Press, 2004.

Williamson, Harvey M. "The Gilpin Players," *Crisis* 42 (July 1935): 206.

Wittner, Lawrence. *Rebels Against War: The American Peace Movement, 1933–1983.* Philadelphia: Temple Univ. Press, 1984.

Woodson, Carter G. "Celebration of Negro History Week." *Journal of Negro History* 12, no. 2 (Apr. 1927): 108–9.

Woodward, C. Vann. *The Strange Career of Jim Crow.* New York: Oxford Univ. Press, 1966.

Yeiser, Idabelle. "Gas." *Philadelphia Tribune,* Dec. 29, 1932.

Yuval-Davis, Nira. *Gender and Nation.* London: Sage Publications, 1997.

Yuval-Davis, Nira, and Floya Anthias. *Racialized Boundaries: Race, Nation, Gender, Color, and Class and the Anti-Racist Struggle.* New York: Routledge, 1992.

Zeiger, Susan. "Finding a Cure for War: Women's Politics and the Peace Movement in the 1920s." *Journal of Social History* 24 (Fall 1990): 69–86.

———. *In Uncle Sam's Service: Women Workers with the American Expeditionary Force, 1917–1919.* Ithaca, NY: Cornell Univ. Press, 2000.

———. "She Didn't Raise Her Boy to Be a Slacker: Motherhood, Conscription, and the Culture of the First World War." *Feminist Studies* 22 (Spring 1996): 7–39.

Ziegler, Valerie. *The Advocates of Peace in Antebellum America.* Bloomington: Indiana Univ. Press, 1992.

Zimmerman, Jonathan. "'Each "Race" Could Have Its Heroes Sung': Ethnicity and the History Wars in the 1920s." *Journal of American History* 87 (June 2000): 92–112.

Index